Involvement of Emplo
in the European Un

GW00792244

Involvement of Employees in the European Union

European Works Councils
The European Company Statute
Information and Consultation Rights

Bulletin of Comparative Labour Relations 42 – 2002

Editor: Roger Blanpain

2002
Kluwer Law International
The Hague/London/New York

Published by:
Kluwer Law International
P.O. Box 85889, 2508 CN The Hague, The Netherlands
sales@kli.wkap.nl
http://www.kluwerlaw.com

Sold and Distributed in North, Central and South America by:
Kluwer Law International
101 Philip Drive, Norwell, MA 02061, USA
kluwerlaw@wkap.com

Sold and Distributed in all other countries by:
Kluwer Law International
Distribution Centre, P.O. Box 322, 3300 AH Dordrecht, The Netherlands

Library of Congress Cataloging-in-Publication Data is available

Printed on acid-free paper

ISBN 90-411-1691-5

Printed and bound in Great Britain by Antony Rowe Limited

Table of Contents

TABLE OF CONTENTS

PART III. A GENERAL FRAMEWORK FOR INFORMING AND
           CONSULTING EMPLOYEES IN THE EUROPEAN
           COMMUNITY

List of Abbreviations

Art.	Article
COJ	Court of Justice
EC	European Communities
EEA	European Economic Area
EFTA	European Free Trade Association
ECS	Economic and Social Committee
EMU	European Monetary Union
EP	European Parliament
ETUC	European Trade Union Confederation
EWC	European Works Council
IGC	Intergovernmental Conference
ILO	International Labour Organisation
OECD	Organisation for Economic Cooperation and Development
O.J.	Official Journal
SE	Societas Europaea
TEC	Treaty on European Community
TEU	Treaty on European Union
UNICE	Union of Industrial and Employers Federations of Europe
v.	versus
WCL	World Confederation of Labour

Introductory remarks

RENEWED INTEREST

Recently there has been a renewed and vigorous interest in *the involvement of employees* in the European Union.

"Involvement of employees" means, according to the Council Directive supplementing the Statute for a European Company, approved by the Employment and Social Affairs Council of 8 October 2001, "any mechanism, including information, consultation and participation, through which employees' representatives may exercise an influence on decisions to be taken within the company" (Art. 2, h).

The reasons for this renewed interest are self-evident. Economic globalisation and the speedy advance of the market economy world-wide has in many countries resulted in a retreat by governments from the running of the economy and greater freedom for management, as well as the enhancement of managerial prerogative. Moreover, the concept of shareholder's value is on the move, particularly in continental Europe and Japan. Short-term financial forecasts and benefits prevail. Stakeholders' value becomes part of a lost European dream.

At the same time and as a consequence, traditional, especially national collective bargaining structures, are slowly eroding in many countries, while overall, trade unions are losing members and their grip on the labour markets. In our information-driven societies, characterised by outsourcing and more smaller enterprises than before, employees tend to unionise less.

Increased and often world-wide competition leads to ongoing restructuring, mergers, outsourcing and downsizing, and to the atomisation of individual employment relationships. Enterprises need to be competitive. So the best product or service at the lowest cost is imperative. Do more with less is the compelling objective.

EMPLOYEE INVOLVEMENT

So, and the question arises naturally, where are the employees in all this? Where do they stand? How should they be involved? What input should they have on the decision-making in the enterprises for which they work? What should the European Union do in this regard? In short, what about the employees' voice?

INFLUENCE ON DECISION-MAKING

According to the aforementioned definition, the purpose of "involvement" of employees is to "exercise an influence on decisions to be taken within the company". That influence is, however, as a rule limited to information and consultation, leaving the prerogative of management intact, as is clearly indicated in the Directives concerning the European Works Council and the European Company Statute. Moreover, management decisions are – self-evidently – increasingly dictated by market conditions, and are often made at headquarters situated in other countries, even on other continents, outside the EU. Experience, particularly with the European Works Councils, shows that strategic economic management decisions are, as a general rule, not fundamentally changed by the involvement of employees.

Consequently, the objective of "involvement of employees" has, to my mind, little to do with power, in the sense of employees getting a chance to influence management's decision-making regarding important issues such as restructures.

The involvement of employees has, in the first place, to do with the fact that enterprises need the support of their employees/collaborators in a competitive environment in which creativity and information-in-action are the basic ingredients for economic success. Information and consultation are a must in the information society and an essential factor for companies to be competitive and for employees to have good wages and working conditions.

EMPLOYABILITY

Moreover, employees want to know where they are heading in this rapidly changing world. What is happening, and what will happen to them? How will this affect their employability? Whether they will find a new job tomorrow will depend not only on the state of the economy, but also on their skills and competences.

Information and consultation, as well as dialogue within the enterprise, undoubtedly create a climate of mutual understanding and working together. Of course, the representatives of the employees have a role to play (indirect participation), but self-evidently management, will, beyond the legally imposed involvement structures, ensure that a well-conceived HRM strategy directly embraces all employees (direct participation) and will organise an ongoing dialogue with them.

THE THREE SISTERS

In the last 10 years, various European initiatives have seen the light of day that have aimed to ensure greater involvement of the employees at the European level as well as at the national level.

First there was the Directive on *European Works Councils*, promulgated in 1994 and operative since 1996. This Directive was quite successful, as no less than 600 works councils have already been established, and more are in the making. In total, there should be some 1,800 European Works Councils. Moreover, the European Works Council was the subject of an in-depth review by the European Commission and a thorough discussion by the European Parliament.

Second, and at long last, there was a break-through for the *European Company Statute* at the Nice Summit (December 2000), which was successfully carried through by the Employment and Social Affairs Council meeting of 8 October 2001. The Employment and Social Affairs Council adopted the proposals (Regulation and Directive) that had been on the table since 1 February 2000, without taking on board any of the amendments put forward by the European Parliament, which was not a big surprise. These new legal instruments were published in the Official Journal[1] and the transition period of 3 years then began.

Third, there is the proposed directive establishing *"a general framework for improving information and consultation rights of employees in the European Community"*. On 11 June 2001, the EU Employment and Social Policy Council of Ministers reached a political agreement on a common position on the proposed directive. Formal adoption of the common position would take place following legal and linguistic finalisation of the text. Thereafter, the draft directive was submitted to the European Parliament for a second reading in accordance with the codecision procedure.

COHERENCE

Undoubtedly, there is great need for coherence between these various European legal instruments.

First, regarding the **notions** used. Here, the *directive concerning the SE* is the most detailed. It contains the definition of "involvement of employees", as indicated above, as well as the following:

"*Information*" "means the informing of the body representative of the employees and/or employees' representatives by the competent organ of the SE on questions which concern the SE itself and any of its subsidiaries or establishments situated in another Member State or which exceed the powers of the decision-making organs in a single Member State at a time, in a manner and with a content which allows the employees' representatives to undertake an in-depth assessment of the possible impact and, where appropriate, prepare consultations with the competent organ of the SE";

"*Consultation*" "means the establishment of dialogue and exchange of views between the body representative of the employees and/or the employees' representatives and the competent organ of the SE, at a time, in a manner and with a content which allows the employees' representatives, on the basis of information provided, to express an opinion on measures envisaged by the

---

1.   *O.J.*, 10 November 2001 L294..

competent organ which may be taken into account in the decision-making process within the SE";

"*Participation*" means the influence of the body representative of the employees and/or the employees' representatives in the affairs of a company by way of:

- the right to elect or appoint some of the members of the company's supervisory or administrative organ; or
- the right to recommend and/or oppose the appointment of some or all of the members of the company's supervisory or administrative organ.

The EWC Directive and the general information and consultation Directive contain the notions of information and consultation, which are defined as follows:

Information means: "transmission of details by the employer to the employees' representatives so that they can take note of and consider the question" (General Directive), while

Consultation means: "the exchange of views and establishing of a dialogue between the employees' representatives and the employer" (General Directive) and: "... and central management or any other more appropriate level of management" (EWC Directive).

"*Employees' representatives*" means in the various instruments, the employees' representatives provided for by national law and/or practice; the same goes for "*employees*".

The *special negotiating body* is an institution that operates within the framework of both the SE and the EWC.

By and large, the various notions used are more or less "coherent", in the sense that they have the same meaning or point in the same direction, namely that the "involvement" exercise by the employees does not affect managerial prerogative. *It is, however, indicated that exactly identical notions should be used in the various European instruments regarding the involvement of employees.*

Similarly, the various European instruments provide for rules concerning confidential information, protection of employee representatives, protection of rights and links with other directives that provide information and consultation rights for employees, such as the directives on collective dismissals and the acquired rights in case of transfer of an enterprise. It should, however, be noted that the collective redundancies Directive provides for "consultations ... with a view of reaching agreement" (Art. 2, 1) and this is retained in the amended proposal for a general information and consultation Directive (Art. 4, 4).

SPIRIT OF COOPERATION

At the same the three aforementioned EU Directives leave enough room for Member States, when implementing the Directives, to take account of the requirements and characteristics of their own systems. In doing so, the

Directives rightfully respect the proper fabric of the national industrial relations system in each of the various EU Member States.

It is, however, remarkable that the three European involvement instruments retain the *spirit of cooperation* which should animate the relations between the involved parties – employers and employees. Indeed, quite a number of national systems do not endorse that notion, e.g. the French and the Italian ones. One wonders what meaning and significance "the spirit of cooperation" has within those national systems.

WHEN?

One point on which the various European involvement instruments lack clarity is regarding the timing of the information and consultation exercises. When should information be given and consultation be held? The different directives are extremely vague on this point. The general information and consultation Directive (Art. 4, 4) states "at an appropriate time"; the EWC Directive (annex, 3) has "as soon as possible"; while there is no answer to the question of timing in the SE Directive. This vagueness undoubtedly reflects the complexity of management decision-making, especially when decision are taken at higher levels, for example in a multinational enterprise. But at the same time it gives an indication that the real purpose of the "involvement" of the employees is not so much to have an impact on strategic management decisions but *inter alia* to help alleviate the social consequences of managerial decisions, and, as mentioned above, to gain the support of employees, particularly in view of their employability.

SUMMARY

To summarise, one can say that there is a great degree of *coherence* in the various European instruments, though improvements could still be made, especially as far as the identical meaning of the various *notions* is concerned.

Moreover, the various expressions concerning the timing of the information and consultation are unsatisfactory. It would be preferable to use the language of the OECD in its Guidelines for Multinational Enterprises (June 2000). The OECD in its employment and industrial relations guideline 6 provides that "reasonable notice of such changes should be given.... In the light of the specific circumstances of each case, it would be appropriate if management were to give such notice prior to the final decision to be taken". In other words, this means that if management cannot provide prior information it should explain to the employees why this is the case.

A final question relates to the SE. Owing to differences between the various Member States concerning the method and degree of involvement of workers, it has taken more than 30 years for the statute of SE to be adopted. The SE Directive, however, resembles in a significant way the provisions foreseen in the EWC Directive. Would it not have been easier to say that all SEs which employ 1000 employees in the EU should have a European works council? But perhaps this was too easy.

ABOUT THIS BOOK

The questions we address in this book are simple and straightforward: where are we in the EU as far as involvement of employees is concerned, and where are we going? Now is the time to give answers to these questions. As was indicated above, the EWC Directive of 1994 has been reviewed by the European Commission (2000) and debated in the European Parliament (2001); the Regulation and the Directive on the SE were adopted by the Employment and Social Affairs Council on 8 October 2001, while on 11 June 2001, the EU Employment and Social Policy Council of Ministers reached a political agreement on a common position on the proposed general information and consultation Directive.

In order to find the appropriate answers to our questions we provide for each of the three European instruments an analysis of its content (I)[2] followed by the relevant legal texts (II) and, where appropriate, the relevant documents emanating from the European Commission and the European Parliament (III).

Finally, a word of thanks must go to Joeri Lauwers for his excellent help in the preparation of this manuscript.

R.B.
Leuven
31 November 2001

---

2.   Hereby we rely on our book *European Labour Law*, 8th and revised edition, Kluwer Law International, 2002, 642 p (forthcoming).

PART I

EUROPEAN WORKS COUNCILS

1. Analysis

I. THE GENESIS OF THE DIRECTIVE – A SPIRIT OF COOPERATION

A. Genesis

Information and consultation of employees has always been part of the European social agenda, practically since the beginning of the 1960s. However, few issues have aroused such a heated debate. Now, after so many years, the adoption on 22 September 1994 of a European Directive on the establishment of an EWC or a procedure in Community-scale undertakings and Community-scale groups of undertakings[1] for the purposes of informing and consulting employees is a reality.

The Directive applies to enterprises that employ at least 1000 employees and have at least two subsidiaries in two Member States of the European Union and/or of the EEA-EFTA countries, each with at least 150 employees. It is estimated that some 1800 companies will have to comply.

Since 15 December 1999 the Directive applies to the UK.[2]

The mandatory character of the Directive has been widely criticised, especially by the employers' side. With this criticism in mind, the European Union wanted to promote "voluntarism" as much as possible, and to encouraged the voluntary conclusion of agreements on information and consultation between the central management of the companies and the representatives of the employees even before the Directive entered into force on 23 September 1996. Agreement prior to that date continues to be valid even after 1997 and can be prolonged by the parties.

Thus, Community-scale undertakings and the representatives of the employees had a choice to make: whether they wanted to wait until the Directive entered into force or whether they wanted to conclude a so-called pre-existing agreement – in force – (Article 13). Such an agreement leaves some degree of flexibility to the parties, although a number of minimum requirements have to be fulfilled.

On 5 December 1990, the Commission adopted a "Proposal for a Council Directive on the Establishment of an EWC in Community-scale

---

1.   (94/95 EC) *O.J.*, 30 September 1994, No. L 254/65.
2.   Council Directive 97/74 of 15 December 1997 extending to the UK Directive 94/45 (*O.J.*, 16 January 1998, L 10/22).

R. Blanpain (ed.), Involvement of Employees in the European Union, 1–34.
© 2002 *Kluwer Law International. Printed in Great Britain.*

Undertakings or Groups of Undertakings for the Purposes of Informing and Consulting Employees".

At none of its meetings did the Council reach unanimous agreement on the Commission's proposal, as required by the legal basis for the proposal (Article 94 of the EC Treaty). The Council did, however, establish, at its meeting on 12 October 1993, a broad consensus among the great majority of delegations on a text submitted by the Belgian Presidency. The Commission informed the Council of its intention to initiate, on entry into force of the Treaty on the European Union on 1 November 1993, the procedures provided for in the Agreement on Social Policy annexed to the Protocol on Social Policy on the basis of the text submitted by the Belgian Presidency and the views expressed in the course of the Council's discussions.

The Commission decided to set these procedures in motion. On 18 November 1993 a six-week period of consultation between the social partners at European level commenced, in accordance with Article 3(2) of the Agreement on Social Policy, with the dispatch of a first consultative document on the possible direction of Commission's action in the field of information and consultation of workers in Community-scale undertakings or groups of undertakings. The employers' associations, federations and confederations and the trade unions submitted a general opinion to the Commission on the questions put to them.

On 8 February 1994, in accordance with Article 3(3) of the Agreement on Social Policy, the Commission decided to consult the social partners at Community level on the content of the proposal, including the possible legal basis for such a proposal.

Furthermore, on 8 February 1994 the Commission introduced a new proposal relating to consultation with management and labour at European level on the content of the proposal envisaged by the Commission.

The proposal was addressed only to the 11 Member States that were signatories of the Agreement on Social Policy. The UK was therefore excluded. The main body of the Flynn proposal was intended to provide for a legal framework within which an agreement could be concluded between central management and representatives of employees. The parties are free to set up the information and consultation mechanism most suited to their needs.

By the deadline for this second phase of consultation (30 March 1994), the social partners had sent their views on the consultation document to the Commission.

Despite all the efforts made, the social partners failed to reach agreement on setting in motion the procedure provided for in Article 4 of the Agreement on Social Policy.

On 13 April 1994 the Commission, taking the view that a Community initiative on the information and consultation of workers in Community-scale undertakings and groups of undertakings was still warranted, decided to adopt the present proposal, with a view to presenting it to the Council on the basis of Article 2(2) of the Agreement on Social Policy.

This proposal preserved most of the elements of the Belgian compromise, whilst reintroducing some of the elements of greater flexibility contained in the Flynn proposal. The opt-out of the UK from the Social Agreement was completely respected. The Directive was adopted in first reading by the Council of Ministers on 22 June 1994.

The Directive was adopted in second reading on 22 September 1994, giving companies almost until the year 2000 to try to negotiate an information and consultation agreement with their employees.

In accordance with the Amsterdam European Council of 16–17 June 1997, whereby the agreement of the IGC to incorporate the Agreement of Social Policy into the Treaty was noted, Directive 94/45EC was extended to the United Kingdom. This was achieved by Council Directive 97/74 of 15 December 1997.[3] The Directive applied from 15 December 1999 onwards.

B.   A spirit of cooperation

Article 9 of the Directive, concerning the operation of EWCs and information and consultation procedures for workers, requires parties, namely central management and the EWC "to work in a spirit of cooperation with due regard to their reciprocal rights and obligations". The same applies "to cooperation between central management and employees' representatives in the framework of an information and consultation procedure for workers'. A similar obligation is also retained in Article 6(1) of the Directive in relation to the negotiation of an agreement, which should take place "in a spirit of cooperation with a view to reaching an agreement".

The deliberate choice of "cooperation" has many important consequences.

It clearly:
1. aims at integrating the employees and their representatives into the undertaking as a going concern, at promoting their understanding and involvement while respecting fully managerial prerogatives, thus backing the free market economy, but in a constructive, socially corrected way; and consequently
2. contains a rejection of the class-conflict model of IR, while at the same time furthering the model of harmony between management and labour.

Another extremely important consequence is the fact that the Directive in no way whatsoever contains a European mandate to engage in industrial warfare in whatever form. The Directive gives no right to bargain on wages and conditions, nor to call for industrial action at European level. Neither the EWC nor the procedure can, legally speaking, be vehicles for international solidarity action between the various undertakings/establishments in the European enterprises.

---

3.   *O.J.*, L 10/22, 16.1. 1998.

The fact is that Article 137(6) TEC expressly excludes matters such as the right to strike or the right to impose lock-outs, with the consequence that there is no legal basis for the establishment of such rights under Article 137(6) TEC.

II. OBJECTIVE AND SCOPE OF THE DIRECTIVE

A. Objective

The purpose of the Directive is to improve the right to information and to consultation of employees in Community-scale undertakings and groups of undertakings. To this end, appropriate mechanisms for transnational information and consultation (i.e. one or more EWCs or one or more procedures with the purpose of informing and consulting employees) have to be established in every Community-scale undertaking and every Community-scale group of undertakings, where this is requested (Article 1(1)).

B. Scope

1. Territorial

a. The 15 EU Member States
The Directive applies to the 15 Member States.

In accordance with the Amsterdam European Council of 16–17 June 1997, whereby the agreement of the IGC to incorporate the Agreement of Social Policy in the Treaty was noted, Directive 94/45 EC was extended to the United Kingdom. This was achieved by Council Directive 97/74 of 15 December 1997.[4] The Directive applied from 15 December 1999 onwards.

b. The European Economic Area (15+2)
The EEA-EFTA countries are involved in the decision-making process leading to European legislation, but have no voting rights. After a Community instrument is adopted by the Council of Ministers it then goes to the Joint Committee of the EEA which will decide whether the instrument should be translated into the national laws of the EEA-EFTA countries. Every EFTA country must agree. So formally there is a kind of opting-in to EU legislation by those Member States. If they opt in, the annexes to the EEA Treaty, which contains the list of applicable Community texts, is amended. The annexes contain a list of the applicable Community legislation. Whenever a new instrument is adopted, a corresponding amendment will be made to the annexes of the EEA Agreement.

---

4. *O.J.*, L 10/22, 16.1. 1998.

c. Companies with headquarters outside the EEA

The Directive also covers cases where undertakings or groups of undertakings have their headquarters outside the territory of the Member States. Where this is the case, such businesses should be treated in a similar way to Community-scale undertakings based on either a representative of the undertaking or group of undertakings or the undertaking with the highest number of employees in the territory of one of the Member States.

2. Personal: which companies?

The Directive applies to private as well as to public undertakings, irrespective of whether they belong to the private or to the public (economic) sphere. "Undertaking" covers any legal form of undertaking. This notion, not explicitly defined in the Directive, may be a parent company, a subsidiary, an establishment, a branch or any other form of economic entity.

An "undertaking" may also consist of a group of subsidiaries, establishments and the like.

a. Numbers

According to the Directive an EWC or a procedure for informing and consulting employees must be established in every Community-scale under-taking and in every Community-scale group of undertakings (Article 1(2)).

(1) Community-scale undertaking

A "Community-scale undertaking" means an undertaking with at least 1,000 employees within the Member States and at least 150 employees in each of at least two of the addressed Member States.

Unless a broader scope is provided for by the agreement, the powers and competence of EWC(s) and the scope of information and consultation procedures cover, in the case of a Community-scale undertaking, all the establishments located within the Member States (Article 1(4)).

The prescribed workforce size thresholds are to be based on the average number of employees, including part-time employees, employed during the previous two years, calculated (*pro rata*) according to national legislation and/or practice (Article 2(2)).

The Directive does not contain an express definition of the term "employee".

Considering that the Directive intends to achieve only partial harmonisation of information and consultation processes in the EU, the term "employee" should be interpreted as covering any person who, in the Member State concerned, is considered to be an employee under national employment law. The same goes for the notion of part-time worker, as is clearly indicated in Article 2(2).

The employees concerned must be employed by a Community-scale undertaking or establishment thereof. This means that temporary workers working for the benefit of a Community-scale undertaking user and subcontracted or posted workers will not count as employees of that undertaking, unless national law and/or practice would indicate otherwise.

It seems that it is of no interest whether the employee is engaged as a blue-collar worker, a white-collar worker, a manager or an official (*fonctionnaire*), or even whether the terms on which he is employed come under public or private law.

The Directive applies equally to employees engaged for an indefinite period and those engaged on fixed-term contracts, contracts for replacement and the like. The same normally goes for employees whose contract of employment is suspended for reasons such as sickness leave and military service, again, unless national law or practice would say otherwise.

Member States must ensure that information on the average number of employees is made available at the request of the parties concerned by the application of the Directive (Article 11(2)).

(2) Group of undertakings

A "group of undertakings" comprises, according to Article 2(b)(1) of the Directive, a controlling undertaking and its controlled undertakings.

The terms "controlled undertaking" and "controlling undertaking" are based on Council Directive 89/440/EEC of 18 July 1989, amending Directive 71/305 EEC concerning the coordination of procedures for the award of public works contracts.

For the purposes of the Directive, a "controlling undertaking" means an undertaking which can exercise a dominant influence over another undertaking ("the controlled undertaking") by virtue of, for example, ownership, financial participation or the rules which govern it (Article 3(1)). Article 3(1) aims to cover all possible "controlling undertakings".

All undertakings that may exercise a dominant influence can be deemed to fulfil the duties under the Directive (Article 4), and they themselves will have to decide which of them will be the "controlling undertaking". Equally, this can occur if employee representatives differ on which company should be looked upon as the "controlling undertaking".

The ability to exercise a dominant influence shall be presumed, without prejudice to proof to the contrary, when, in relation to another undertaking, an undertaking directly or indirectly:
(a) holds a majority of the undertaking's subscribed capital, or
(b) controls a majority of the votes attached to that undertaking's issued share capital, or
(c) can appoint more than half the members of the undertaking's administrative, managerial or supervisory body (Article 3(2)).

The controlling undertaking's rights as regards voting and appointment shall include the rights of any other controlled undertaking and those of any person or body acting in his or its own name but on behalf of the controlling undertaking or of any other controlled undertaking (Article 3(3)).

A dominant influence shall not be presumed to be exercised solely by virtue of the fact that an office holder is exercising his functions, according to the law of a Member State relating to liquidation, winding up, insolvency, cessation of payments, compositions or analogous proceedings (Article 3(5)).

The law applicable for determining whether an undertaking is a "controlling undertaking" shall be the law of the Member State governing that undertaking (Article 3(6), para. 1).

As the possibility of exercising a dominant influence can be indicated by the central management, who can equally reverse the presumption of Article 3(2), central management seems to have a certain flexibility to choose the applicable law. The same applies in the case of conflict of laws. Where the law governing that undertaking is not that of a Member State, the law applicable shall be the law of the Member State within whose territory the representative of the undertaking or, in the absence of such a representative, the central management of the group undertaking which employs the highest number of employees in any one Member State is situated (Article 3(6), para. 2).

In this case, central management can freely, without possible intervention of the employees, indicate which undertaking or person shall act as "representative", thereby choosing at the same time the law it wants to apply.

A "Community-scale group of undertakings" means a group of undertakings with the following characteristics:
- at least 1,000 employees within the Member States; at least two group undertakings in different Member States; and
- at least one group undertaking having at least 150 employees in one Member State and at least one other group undertaking with at least 150 employees in another Member State (Article 3(1)(c)).

Where a Community-scale group of undertakings comprises one or more undertakings which are Community-scale undertakings, the EWC will be established at the level of the group, unless the agreement(s) provide(s) otherwise (Article 1(3)).

Unless a wider scope is provided for by the agreements, the powers and competence of EWCs and the scope of information and consultation procedures cover, in the case of a Community-scale undertaking, all the establishments located within the Member State, and in the case of a Community-scale group of undertakings, all group undertakings located within the Member States (Article 1(4)).

b. Central management

"Central management" means the central management of a Community-scale undertaking or, in the case of a Community-scale group of undertakings, of the controlling undertaking (Article 2(1)(e)).

c. Merchant navy crews

Member States may provide that this Directive shall not apply to merchant navy crews (Article 1(5)).

III. DEFINITIONS AND NOTIONS

A. Information and consultation

The Directive does not contain a definition of the word "information". So we must refer to the ordinary meaning attributed to that term in its context and obtain such guidance as may be derived from Community texts and from concepts common to the legal systems of the Member States.

The meaning of the word "information" seems rather simple: it is the communication of knowledge. Disclosure of information to the representatives of employees means that the employer provides information regarding which explanation may be sought and questions can be raised.

"Consultation" has been defined by the Directive on EWCs or procedures as "the exchange of views and establishment of dialogue between employees' representatives and central management or any other more appropriate level of management" (Article 2(1)(f)).

Article 2(1)(f) of the Directive on the establishment of an EWC or a procedure addresses these questions only in very broad terms when it states that exchange of views and dialogue will take place between the representatives of the employees and central management or any other appropriate level of management.

First, this leaves the parties to the agreement free to decide which level of management would be more appropriate. Moreover, other questions will have to be worked out between the parties themselves, within the guidelines laid down in the Directive, unless the parties conclude a pre-existing agreement.

B. Representation of employees

The concept of "employees' representatives" has to be seen in the light of Council Directives 98/59 EC on collective redundancies and 2001/23/EC on transfer of undertakings. According to Article 2(1)(d) of the Directive on EWCs or procedures, "employees' representatives" means the representatives of the employees as provided by national law and/or practice of the Member States. In contrast to the Directive on transfer of undertakings, this Directive does not exclude members of administrative, governing or supervisory bodies of companies who represent employees on such bodies in certain Member States.

Unlike the above-mentioned Directives on collective redundancies and transfer of undertakings, this Directive on EWCs or procedures contains the very important provision that Member States must provide that employees in undertakings and/or establishments in which there are no employees' representatives through no fault of their own, have the right to elect or appoint members of the special negotiating body (Article 5(2)(a), para. 2). This is without prejudice to national legislation and/or practice laying down thresholds for the establishment of employee representation bodies (Article

5(2)(a), para. 3). This means among other things that Member States may provide that only establishments with, for example, at least 50 employees will participate in the election or appointment of members of the special negotiating body.

As the term "employees' representatives" refers to the laws or practice of the Member States, this implies that it might be possible for "non-employees" (e.g. permanent trade union business agents) to be elected or appointed, provided that national law and/or practice would allow this possibility.

IV.   ESTABLISHMENT OF AN EWC OR A PROCEDURE

The establishment of an EWC or procedure by way of agreement between the parties requires different steps which have to be accomplished within a given period of time, at the latest within a period of three years after the initial request by the employees to initiate negotiations has been launched. So, if neither party moves, nothing will happen; the process can also be terminated by the special negotiating body, which may decide not to open negotiations, or to cancel negotiations already opened, by a two-thirds majority of the members of the special negotiating body.

The steps are:
- the request to initiate negotiations, on the initiative of either the employees' representatives or the central management;
- the establishment of the negotiating body;
- the convening of a negotiating meeting;
- the conclusion of an agreement.

All this has to be accomplished within three years of the request to initiate negotiations. If not, the subsidiary requirements will apply. These rules do not apply if the parties conclude an agreement before the date of entry into force of the Directive.

The same applies *ceteris paribus* in the case of renegotiation of the agreement on the understanding that the existing EWC (or its members' employees) will constitute the negotiating body (*see* Annex – subsidiary requirements 1(f), 2nd para.).

If the subsidiary requirements apply and an EWC has been established, that EWC shall examine, four years after its establishment, the question of whether to open negotiations for the conclusion of the agreement referred to in Article 6 or to continue to apply the subsidiary requirements adopted in accordance with the annex (Annex 1(f), para. 1). This takes us to somewhere near the year 2004.

A.   The obligation to negotiate in a spirit of cooperation

The Directive contains a mandatory duty for the parties to negotiate, specifically "in a spirit of cooperation with a view to reaching an agreement on the detailed arrangements for implementing the information and consultation of employees" (Article 6(1)). This mandatory requirement is self-evidently important and has many implications.

The obligation to negotiate in a spirit of cooperation, and thus certainly not in a spirit of confrontation, is *de facto* little more than a mere policy guideline, an expectation on the part of the European authorities and hardly a legally enforceable rule. Obviously, in the case of obstinate refusal to negotiate, or obstructions to the process, measures and procedures should be available (Article 11(3)) and the subsidiary requirements (Article 7(1)) will apply. But one cannot dictate love, especially to those who still believe in class war.

However, the point is important. It underlines the need for a spirit of trust and good faith on which employee relations should be founded. But such a state of mind and soul is not necessarily present and depends to a large extent on the ideology of those involved. The truth of the matter is that trust can be built even between parties who have opposing interests. Building trust and fostering a spirit of cooperation is not a spontaneous process: it requires continuous and conscientious efforts from all sides.

B.   Responsibility and initiation of negotiations

1.   *Responsibility of central management*

The central management of the Community-scale undertaking or group of undertakings is responsible for creating the conditions and the means necessary for the setting up of an EWC or procedure for transnational information and consultation upon the terms and in the manner laid down by this Directive (Article 4(1)).

Where the central management is not situated in a Member State, a central management's representative in a Member State, to be designated if necessary, shall take on the responsibility for the setting up of an EWC or a procedure. In the absence of such a representative, the above-mentioned responsibility will lie with the management of the establishment or the central management of the group undertaking employing the highest number of employees in any one Member State (Article 4(2)). The term "employee" should be interpreted as covering any person who, in the Member State concerned, is considered to be an employee; the calculation will take place according to national legislation and/or practice. Our earlier comments concerning the term "employee" in relation to the Community-scale undertaking or group of undertakings apply accordingly.

For the purposes of the Directive, the representative of management, as provided for in Article 4(2) shall be regarded as central management (Article 4(3)).

2. Initiation of the negotiation

The procedure designed to ensure the right to transnational information and consultation of employees shall be instigated either on the initiative of the central management, or at the written request of at least 100 employees in total or their representatives in at least two undertakings or establishments in at least two different Member States (Article 5(1)). One hundred employees in total are sufficient. There is no need to have 100 employees or their representatives in each of the two undertakings or establishments in the different Member States.

3. One or more EWC or procedures

The Directive requires the setting up of only one (negotiated or standard) EWC or one alternative procedure, even if a Community-scale undertaking or group of undertakings is be composed of Community-scale undertakings or groups which on their own would also qualify for the establishment of an EWC or an alternative procedure (Article 1(2) and (3)). In this case, the Directive requires the establishment of an EWC or an alternative procedure at the "highest" level only.

C.   The negotiation of the agreement

The negotiation for the establishment of an EWC or a procedure will take place between central management and a special negotiation body, composed of representatives of the employees (Article 5(2)). With a view to the conclusion of such an agreement the central management must convene a meeting with the special negotiating body. It is required to inform the local management accordingly (Article 5(4)).

1. Parties to the agreement and the special negotiating body

Parties to the agreement are thus on the one hand the Community-scale undertaking or group of undertakings, represented by the central management, and on the other the representatives of the employees (as defined in every Member State); these parties will constitute a special negotiating body, according to Article 5 of the Directive. The special negotiating body has in a sense a specific legal personality, with the necessary competence to conclude and eventually to terminate an agreement establishing an EWC or a procedure. By the same token the special negotiation body should have the legal competence to introduce actions before the courts in the case of a dispute relating to the matters covered by the Directive. For the purposes of concluding an agreement, the special negotiating body acts by a majority of its members (Article 6(5)).

a. Composition of the negotiating body
The special negotiating body shall be established in accordance with the following guidelines:
(a) The Member States shall determine the method to be used for the election or appointment of the members of the special negotiating body who are to be elected or appointed in their territories (Article 5(2)(a), para. 1).
   The election or appointment of the members within each Member State shall be organised according to the legislation of those Member States (*see* Declaration No. 2 of Council and Commission). The Member States must pay special attention to whom can elect and be elected. Managers, for instance – at local as well as at central levels – although they may legally be considered to be employees, would qualify neither as candidates for election nor as electors. However, it seems reasonable to limit that group of managers to those who actually run the local or central undertaking (senior management) and thus to interpret this notion restrictively. This means that blue-collars, white-collars and "cadres" (middle and higher management) would qualify as electors and as elected or appointed members of the special negotiating body. To become a member, employees self-evidently need to agree to be a candidate to that end.
   This also means that, for example, trade unions could represent the employees, according to national law/practice. As indicated, Member States shall "provide that employees in undertakings and/or establishments in which there are no employees' representatives through no fault of their own, have the right to elect or appoint members of the special negotiating body" (Article 5(2)(a), para. 2). Member States have the right to lay down thresholds for the establishment of employee representation bodies (Article 5(2)(a), para. 3). As mentioned above, this means that Member States may provide that only employees of establishments/undertakings with, for example, at least 50 employees will be qualified to participate in the election or appointment of the members of the special negotiating body.
(b) The special negotiating body shall have a minimum of three members and a maximum of eighteen members (Article 5(2)(b)).
   According to Declaration No. 2 of the Commission and the Council, the maximum number of eighteen members should not necessarily be reached.
(c) In these elections or appointments it must be ensured firstly, that "each Member State in which the Community-scale undertaking has one or more establishments or in which the Community-scale group of undertakings has the controlling undertaking or one or more controlled undertakings is represented by one member" (Article 5(2)(c) indent 1). It also stands to reason that the Member States and the contracting parties should, as much as possible and where appropriate, look for ways and

means of ensuring that the different groups of employees are adequately represented in the negotiating body, namely younger and senior employees, men and women, blue- and white-collar workers and (junior) managers.

Secondly, it must be ensured that there are supplementary members in proportion to the number of employees working in the establishments, the controlling undertaking or the controlled undertakings, as laid down in the legislation of the Member State within the territory of which the central management is situated (Article 5(2)(c) indent 2).

(d)   The central management and local managements shall be informed of the composition of the special negotiating body (Article 5(2), para. (d)) by local managements and/or the representatives themselves on an individual or a collective basis. This latter way seems the most appropriate, and might be combined with a written request from the employee representatives to initiate negotiations, according to Article 5(1) of the Directive.

b.   Task of the negotiating parties

The special negotiating body and the central management of the Community-scale undertaking or group of undertakings have the task, without prejudice to the autonomy of the parties, of determining, by means of a written agreement on the detailed arrangements for implementing the transnational information and consultation of employees:

- the scope (undertakings or establishments) of the EWC;
- the composition of the EWC, the number of members, the allocation of seats and the term of office;
- the functions and the procedure for information and consultation of the EWC; the venue, frequency and duration of meetings of the EWC;
- the financial and material resources to be allocated to the EWC; the duration of the agreement and the procedure for its renegotiation or for establishing one or more information and consultation procedures instead of an EWC (Article 6(3)).

2.   Refusal or cancellation of the negotiations

The special negotiating body may decide, by at least two-thirds of the votes, not to open negotiations, or to terminate the negotiations already opened. Such a decision stops the procedure to conclude an agreement. Where such a decision has been taken, the provisions (subsidiary requirements) in the Annex do not apply. A new request to convene the special negotiating body may be made at the earliest two years after the abovementioned decision, unless the parties concerned lay down a shorter period (Article 5(5)).

3.　Experts and costs

For the purpose of the negotiation, the special negotiating body may be assisted by experts of its choice (Article 5(4), para. 2). These experts can be employees or non-employees, for example, trade union representatives. There is no doubt that the trade unions consider this to be their role, and want to assist the representatives of the employees to that end. This point is, however, also negotiable.

Any expenses relating to the negotiations must be borne by the central management so as to enable the special negotiating body to carry out its tasks in an appropriate manner (Article 5(6), para. 1). In compliance with this principle, Member States may lay down budgetary rules regarding the operation of the special negotiating body. They may in particular limit the funding to cover one expert only (Article 5(6), para. 2).

4.　Role of the trade unions and of the employers' associations

Although trade unions and employers' associations are, according to the Directive, not directly involved as parties to the agreement to be concluded concerning information and consultation, they may in practice play an active role. Undoubtedly, the European trade union secretariats (European sectoral level) and the ETUC (European inter-industry-wide level) are strongly behind the moves for a European social dialogue, but the choice by the European Union that the agreements should be concluded by the representatives of the employees and not necessarily by the trade unions has been a deliberate one. This leaves in a sense all options open. Trade unions can, however, play a role, for example in the training of members of the EWCs, by acting as experts, even as contracting parties and the like. The same goes for UNICE and the (national) employer's associations, which can help to monitor and guide member undertakings. National trade unions may play a role in the election or appointment of the (national) representatives in the special negotiating body if national law or practice provides them with such a role, as, for example, might be the case in Belgium or France.

D.　Nature, binding effect, form and language of the agreement

1.　Nature and binding effect of the agreement

The agreement can be looked upon as a special kind of collective labour agreement concluded between representatives of European management on the one hand and the European representatives of the employees under the form of a negotiating body establishing an EWC or an information or consultation procedure on the other hand. One can describe the agreement as, like the French say, a "contractinstitution", namely a contract which creates an institution, a framework for information and consultation between management and labour that will lead its own life once it has been created. The agreement has, like any other collective labour agreement, an obligatory part and a normative part. The obligatory part relates to the rights and obligations of the contracting parties, while the normative part is the information and consultation institution-procedure that has been set up, with its scope, composition, competence and the like. The contracting parties not only create but also control the very existence of the EWC or the procedure, since they will always have the right, subject to agreed formalities and/or terms of notice, to denounce the agreement.

The binding effect of both (obligatory and normative) parts of the agreement thus will depend on the law applicable to the contract. If this is Belgian, because, for example, the agreement was concluded in Brussels or because the venue of the meeting of the European committee or in the framework of a procedure as well as the central management's location are in Brussels, and parties did not choose another legal system, the relations between the contracting parties might be governed by Belgian law. This would be the general principles of Belgian contractual law, since the Belgian Act of 5 December 1968 on joint committees and collective labour agreements would not apply, because in order to qualify for a binding legal collective agreement (in the sense of the 1968 Act), parties need to be, from the employee's side, representative (Belgian) trade unions, which is not the case for the special negotiating body operating in the framework of the Directive.

2. Form and language of the agreement

It stands to reason that the agreement establishing an EWC or a procedure must be drawn up in writing, and that it must be signed by the representatives of management and by the majority of the individual representatives of the employees, assembled in the negotiating body. The negotiating body is, as already mentioned, a fully fledged legal party, and not simply a forum, an instrument, or a vehicle of communication between the actors involved. More formal aspects of the agreement regarding its legality, the number of copies to be signed and so on will be governed by the requirements of the applicable law.

The agreement could be drafted in various official languages of the Member States, depending on the (national) composition of the negotiating parties. One language is also possible, either accompanied by translations or not, provided the signing parties understand what they are signing. Special attention will have to be paid to the national legislation which is applicable to the agreement, especially if this legislation contains specific linguistic requirements as is the case in, for example, Belgium and France.

E. Content of the agreement

The content of the agreement is self-evidently the business of the contracting parties: they decide autonomously what they want to put in the agreement and what they do not. Article 6 of the Directive, however, contains a list relating to the establishment of an EWC. That list is a mandatory list of subjects, but parties are autonomous in deciding upon the concrete content to be given to the listed points.

According to the Directive, a distinction must be made between the setting up of an EWC and the elaboration of a procedure. It is not easy to see the difference between an EWC and a procedure, especially since Article 6(3), para. 2 provides, in the case of a procedure, that the employee representatives have a right to meet to discuss the information conveyed to them. Indeed "the agreement must stipulate by what method the employees' representatives shall have the right to meet to discuss the information conveyed to them. This information shall in particular relate to transnational questions which significantly affect workers' interests."

It would therefore seem logical that an EWC is a more institutionalised form of communication and dialogue, while the procedure is a much looser one. But, as stated above, it is far from clear where the procedure ends and the EWC begins, and *vice versa*.

One might say that an agreement that does not lay out in detail all the points covered by Article 6(2) may preferably qualify for a procedure instead of for an EWC. Parties could, however, make their intentions clear and indicate in the agreement whether they opt for an EWC or for a procedure.

For a procedure one could imagine *inter alia* written reports forwarded by management, and information and consultation at local level by various means. This may be within or outside existing proceedings at national level, an example being a visit of a European or national human resources manager to the employee representatives at plant or national level, provided the information and consultation relates to transnational issues. This procedure must not necessarily be the same in all undertakings, but may differ from one Member State to another, between different businesses of the group, and so on.

In any case, parties are free to decide on these matters and can qualify their arrangement as they see fit, taking into account the right of the employees' representatives to discuss the information conveyed to them and engage in a dialogue.

The agreement is not, unless it provides otherwise, subject to the subsidiary requirements referred to in the Annex (Article 6(4), para. 1).

1. Scope

The agreement has to indicate "the member undertakings of the Community-scale undertakings or the establishments of the Community-scale undertaking which are covered by the agreement" (Article 6(2)(a)).

The agreement will have to indicate the territorial and personal scope (establishments/undertakings) covered by the agreement, possibly addressed by various EWCs in the case of a group. The scope may also contain undertakings outside the EU and the EEA-EFTA countries.

2.   The setting up of an EWC

Article 6(2)(b) concerns the composition of the EWC and the number of members, the allocation of seats and the term of office.

The agreement can provide that the EWC may be composed of representatives of employees only, or that it may also include representatives of management, whilst parties could also agree that the EWC is (consecutively) chaired by a representative of either group (management, employees). Parties should reflect, as we indicated earlier, on an appropriate representation of the different groups of employees, such as blue-white collars, managerial employees, female workers and so on. Parties can also agree on other members, for instance, trade union business agents, who may also participate either as fully fledged members, as pure observer members or advisers, or as experts. Complete freedom exists for the parties to the agreement regarding these matters. Parties may also agree whether there will be a select committee for the workers' group or of the EWC itself, if the EWC is to be composed of employees only.

Major problems could arise in the case of mergers or other restructures of undertakings/establishments which might affect the composition of the EWC (especially, for example, in the event of a merger of two groups which each have their own EWC). As the Directive is silent on this issue, the matter should be addressed according to the law applicable. If the applicable law does not regulate the problem, parties will have to renegotiate their agreement. So long as a new agreement is not reached, the existing agreement(s) continue(s) to be in effect. If no new agreement is reached within the terms foreseen in Article 7, subsidiary requirements will apply.

Allocation of seats in the EWC will usually take into account the numerical strength of the employees in the undertaking(s) and establishments. Regarding elections or appointments, parties would be well advised to stick as closely as possible to the national law and/or practice, and to follow, for example, the same method as for the election of the representatives to the special negotiating body. Candidates should ideally have a minimum length of service (for example, of one year) in the establishment undertaking as an employee in order to be able to represent their colleagues with a certain degree of insight and competence. The term of office should cover a number of years, not too long and not too short. Two to three years could be the minimum, and five years the maximum.

Article 6(2)(c) concerns the functions and the procedure for information and consultation of the EWC. The agreement might specify the competencies of the EWC more precisely as far as the nature of the consultation is concerned, and among other things, indicate that the prerogatives of management shall not be affected. The agreement should also clearly indicate the subject matter of the information and consultation exercise; the subjects enumerated in the subsidiary requirements may be a source of inspiration for this.

In enumerating the subject matters one should take into account that the employees are entitled to information and consultation especially regarding transnational questions which significantly affect their interests, such as jobs, working conditions in the broad sense of the word, and so on. Employees are particularly interested in the mitigation of social consequences of some managerial decisions.

An obvious example is information about future developments and prospects: employees are more interested in the future of the business than in the socio-economic history of the company.

The agreement should also contain something on the "when" (yearly and/or *ad hoc*?) of the information and consultation (before decisions are taken or as soon as possible in case of *ad hoc* cases?), on the organisation of the exchange of views and/or the dialogue and of possible feedback, on confidential and/or prejudicial information, on the role of experts, on accountants to check the exactitude of the information, and so on. Other points may concern, for instance, voting majorities, the drafting of the agenda, the drafting of reports, the organisation of working parties, eventual training of the delegates, communication of information and consultation results to the rank and file and to the trade unions, and contacts with the press.

Other details to be specified include whether the procedure is to be written and/or oral, and the timing. Regarding information, will documents be sent beforehand, and if so, how long before the meeting takes place? One might equally specify the timing between information and consultation, the tabling of motions and voting, interpretation and translation (languages) and the role of experts, to name but a few.

Article 6(2)(d) concerns the venue, frequency and duration of meetings. The agreement may say something about invitations to the meetings and the place they are held, and draw a distinction between general, let us say yearly information, and *ad hoc* information meetings for special circumstances, such as closures and collective dismissals. The agreement may also provide for preliminary meetings and for meetings of working parties and the select committee of the workers' group, and may specify the length of such meetings.

Article 6(2)(e) concerns the financial and material resources to be allocated to the EWC. Central management must provide the necessary financial resources to pay for the functioning of the EWC (including such facilities as secretariat, catering and accommodation). The agreement has to cover payment of travel expenses, loss of wages of the employees' representatives and the like. Experts will normally be paid by the party they assist, or by the organisation they represent, which may be subsidised to this end by the EU, but the agreement could provide otherwise and may eventually indicate that the costs of the experts will be borne by central management.

Article 6(2)(f) concerns the duration of the agreement and the procedure for its renegotiation. The agreement may be open-ended, with a term of notice, and contain certain forms (e.g. a registered letter) and also proposals for renegotiation, to be respected in the case of denouncement of the agreement and the like. The agreement could be denounced, totally or partially, by either central management or the (majority of the members of) the negotiating body. Both parties may also agree to terminate the agreement.

The agreement can also be concluded for a fixed period, after which it comes automatically to an end. Parties can also foresee a fixed period with an extension (for a similar period) unless one of the parties decides to terminate the agreement before a certain date (e.g. one year before the term ends).

In any case, there must be a procedure for the renegotiation of the agreement. The renegotiation would normally take place between the central management and a negotiating body. However, according to the Annex 1(f), para. 2 this body is the (employee representatives of) EWC. If no new agreement is reached before the old one expires, the subsidiary requirements will apply.

The agreement could also expand on the law applicable to the agreement, on the settlement of interpretation or application difficulties, by way of either conciliation or arbitration, on the relevant competent court.

For the purposes of concluding the agreement the special negotiating body shall act by a majority of its members (Article 6(5)).

3.   The setting up of a procedure

Article 6(3) of the Directive states

> "that the central management and the special negotiating body may decide, in writing, to establish one or more information and consultation procedures instead of an EWC. The agreement must stipulate by what method the employees' representatives have the right to meet to discuss the information conveyed to them. This information shall relate in particular to transnational questions which significantly affect the interests of the employees."

Parties should focus on, amongst other matters,
(a)   the scope of the procedure;
(b)   the mode of operation, including "the right to meet to discuss the information";
(c)   the matters subject to information and consultation;
(d)   the financial and material resources to be allocated for the functioning of the procedure;
(e)   the duration of the agreement and the procedure for its renegotiation;
(f)   the law applicable to the agreement.

V. PREJUDICIAL AND CONFIDENTIAL INFORMATION. IDEOLOGICAL GUIDANCE

According to Article 8(2) (para. 1) of the Directive, a Member State may, in specific cases under the conditions and limits laid down by national legislation, provide that the central management situated in its territory is not obliged to transmit information when its nature is such that it would seriously harm the functioning of the undertakings concerned or would be prejudicial to them. A Member State may make such dispensation subject to prior administrative or judicial authorisation (Article 8(2), para. 2).

Member States shall, according to Article 8(1) of the Directive, also provide that members of special negotiating bodies or of EWCs and any experts who assist them are not authorised to reveal any information which has expressly been provided to them in confidence. The same applies to the employees' representatives in the framework of an information and consultation procedure. This obligation continues to apply wherever these persons are, even after the expiry of their terms of office.

One has to add that Article 8(3) of the Directive contains the facility for a Member State to lay down particular provisions for the central management of undertakings and establishments in its territory which pursue directly and essentially the aim of ideological guidance with respect to information and the expression of opinions, on condition that, at the date of adoption of the Directive, such particular provisions already existed in the national legislation. In this regard the Council and the Commission stated: "this means undertakings and establishments which directly and essentially pursue: political, professional organisation, religious, charitable, educational, scientific or artistic aims, aims involving information and the expression of opinions".

Where Member States apply Article 8 of the Directive concerning confidential (and prejudicial) information, they must provide for administrative or judicial appeal procedures which the employees' representatives may initiate if central management requires confidentiality or does not give information in accordance with Article 8 (Article 11(4)). "Such procedures may include procedures designed to protect the confidentiality of the information in question" (Article 11(4), para. 2).

VI. PROTECTION OF EMPLOYEES' REPRESENTATIVES

The employee representatives have the same protection as their national colleagues. Indeed, Article 10 of the Directive provides that members of special negotiating bodies, members of EWCs and employees' representatives exercising their functions within an information and consultation procedure enjoy in the exercise of their functions the same protection and guarantees provided for employees' representatives by the national legislation and/or practice in force in the country of employment, especially as regards attendance at meetings of special negotiation bodies or EWCs or any other meetings within the framework of the agreement establishing a procedure. This also relates to payment of wages of members who are on the staff of the Community-scale undertaking or group of Community-scale undertakings for the period of absence necessary for the performance of their duties.

Additionally, one may have to resort to international private labour law rules in order to determine which national system is applicable in the case of an employee representative who is employed in more than one country, for example in the capacity of commercial traveller.

VII. COMPLIANCE WITH THE DIRECTIVE – LINKS – FINAL PROVISIONS

A. Compliance with the directive

Each Member State must ensure that the management of establishments that form part of a Community-scale group of undertakings situated within its territory and their employees' representatives or, as the case may be, employees, abide by the obligations laid down by the Directive, regardless of whether or not the central management is situated in its territory (Article 11(1)).

Member States must ensure that the information on the average number of employees is made available by undertakings at the request of the parties concerned by the application of the Directive (Article 11(2)).

The *Bofrost* case[5] concerns the extent of the employers' obligation – set out in Article 11(2) – to respond to requests by employee representatives for information about the number and distribution of employees and corporate structure in order to prepare for the possible setting up of an EWC. The German works council at Bofrost made several requests to the company for information on employee numbers and company structure within the Bofrost group, with a view to seeking the establishment of an EWC. The company "definitively refused" to provide such information. The Court was asked to answer following questions:

> "Does the right to information under Article 11(1) and (2) of the Directive exist even where it is not (yet) established whether or not there is a controlling undertaking within the meaning of Article 3 of the Directive in a group of undertakings as defined by Article 2(1)(b) of the Directive?
>
> If so, does the right to information under Article 11(1) and (2) also include the right to request from the undertaking concerned information which gives rise to the presumption of dominant influence referred to in Article 3(2)?
>
> And

---

5. C.O.J., 29.3.2001, *Betriebsrat der bofrost* * *Josef H. Boquoi Deutschland West GmbH & Co. KG and Bofrost* * *Josef H. Boquoi Deutschland West GmbH & Co. KG*, Case C-62/99, not yet published.

Does Article 11(1) and (2) on the right to information also include the right to request documents from an undertaking to clarify and explain such information?"

The Court answered as follows:

"On a proper construction of Article 11(1) and (2) of Council Directive 94/45/EC an undertaking, which is part of a group of undertakings is required to supply information to the internal workers' representative bodies, even where it has not yet been established that the management to which the workers' request is addressed is the management of a controlling undertaking within a group of undertakings.

Where information relating to the structure or organisation of a group of undertakings forms part of the information which is essential to the opening of negotiations for the setting-up of a European Works Council or for the transnational information and consultation of employees, an undertaking within the group is required to supply the information which it possesses or is able to obtain to the internal workers' representative bodies requesting it. Communication of documents clarifying and explaining the information which is indispensable for that purpose may also be required, in so far as that communication is necessary in order that the employees concerned or their representatives may gain access to information enabling them to determine whether or not they are entitled to request the opening of negotiations."

Member States must provide for appropriate measures in the event of failure to comply with this Directive. In particular, they shall ensure that administrative or judicial procedures are available to enable the obligations deriving from this Directive to be enforced (Article 11(3)). As already indicated, Member States provide for administrative or judicial procedures that the employees' representatives may initiate when the management requires confidentiality or refuses to give information for reasons of confidentiality. Such procedures may include procedures designed to protect the confidentiality of the information in question (Article 11(4)).

Member States are thus entitled to maintain or introduce more stringent protective measures compatible with the Treaty, limited, however, to their own territory. It seems to us less likely that Member States would impose more stringent measures, since they will, for obvious reasons, look carefully at what kind of protective measures are provided for in other Member States.

B. Links

Article 12 of the Directive concerns the links between this Directive and other provisions, both European and national. It states that this Directive shall apply without prejudice to measures taken pursuant to the Directives on collective redundancies (1975) as amended and on the transfer of undertakings (1977). Regarding national provisions it indicates that "this Directive shall be without prejudice to existing rights to information and consultation of employees under national law".

C. Final provisions

"Member States shall bring into force the laws, regulations and administrative provisions necessary to comply with this Directive not later than two years after the adoption of this Directive, or shall ensure by that date at the latest that management and labour introduce the required provisions by way of agreement, the Member States being obliged to take necessary steps enabling them at all times to guarantee the results imposed by this Directive. They shall forthwith inform the Commission thereof."

This means that Article 14(1) of the Directive gives Member States the option of giving the national social partners (in conjunction with national legislation if necessary) the opportunity to conclude collective agreements implementing the Directive.

These collective agreements must be binding in law and cover all undertakings and employees concerned. This is particularly relevant where national provisions contain extension procedures which may make collective agreements binding *erga omnes*. This is the case in, for example, Belgium, France, Germany and The Netherlands, though not (necessarily) in such States as the Scandinavian countries, where this presents a special problem.

The question arises whether a collective agreement, even when extended by governmental decree and thus generally binding, is an appropriate vehicle for implementing the Directive into national law. The answer is simple, and will (partly) depend on the national law applicable to the agreement. Indeed, contrary to other labour law directives, the EWC Directive fundamentally transcends national borders; this applies to the EWC as the information/ consultation procedure. The national collective agreement transposing the Directive, must necessarily partially or totally regulate labour relations under which the participants (enterprises, establishments, representatives of employees and the like) operate in other countries. A (national) collective agreement will thus, for example, have to indicate under what conditions an Article 13 agreement is valid and indicate the number of supplementary members for the EWC to represent employees of certain addressed Member States, who are out of necessity situated in other Member States. One could give many more examples of extraterritorial realities, which have to be regulated by the national collective agreement implementing the Directive. Normally a collective agreement is legally only equipped to regulate labour relations and conditions that fall within national borders, except when national law provides otherwise, and even this issue is debatable. So, it will depend on national law whether collective agreements are the appropriate base for implementing a Directive which transcends, so to speak, national boundaries. One thing is for sure: the Belgian legislation on collective bargaining does not provide for such a legal base. Consequently, the Belgian collective agreement No. 62 of 6 February 1996 cannot be seen as an appropriate way of implementing the EWC Directive. The EWC Directive itself cannot change Belgian law concerning collective agreements. Belgian law allows for legally binding agreements in respect of Belgian labour relations, but not those relations that transcend Belgian boundaries.

"When Member States adopt these measures, they shall contain a reference to this Directive or shall be accompanied by such reference on the occasion of their official publication. The methods of making such reference shall be laid down by Member States" (Article 14(2)).

VIII. SUBSIDIARY REQUIREMENTS: A MANDATORY EWC

If the central management and the special negotiating body so decide, or if the central management refuses to commence negotiations within six months of the request by the representatives of the employees to initiate negotiations, or if, after three years from the date of this request, they are unable to conclude an agreement providing for an EWC or a procedure for informing and consulting employees, the subsidiary requirements, laid down by the legislation of the Member State in which the central management is situated, apply (Article 7(1)).

The subsidiary requirements as adopted in the legislation of the Member State must satisfy the provisions set out in the Annex to the Directive (Article 7(2)). The subsidiary requirements thus in a sense constitute the mandatory core regarding information and consultation rights, which the European legislator wants European undertakings to live up to, if the parties do not follow the voluntary road by concluding an agreement setting up an EWC or by establishing an information and consultation procedure. Indeed, the subsidiary requirements provide, as indicated, for the mandatory establishment of an EWC.

A. Composition of the EWC

The EWC is to be composed of employees of the Community-scale undertaking or Community-scale group of undertakings, elected or appointed from their midst by the employees' representatives or, in the absence thereof, by the entire body of employees (Annex 1(b), para. 1). The election or appointment of members of an EWC shall be carried out in accordance with national legislation and/or practice (Annex 1(b), para. 2).

The EWC has a minimum of 3 members and a maximum of 30. Where its size so warrants, it shall elect a select committee from among its members comprising at the most three members. It shall adopt its own rules of procedure. The maximum of 30 need not necessarily be reached. A lower number may be provided by the applicable law (the national law of the Member State in which the central management is situated) (Council and Commission Declaration No. 2).

> "In the election or appointment of members of the EWC, it must be ensured: firstly, that each Member State in which the Community-scale undertaking has one or more establishments or in which the Community-scale group of undertakings has the controlling undertaking or one or more controlled undertakings, is represented by one Member; secondly, that there are supplementary members in proportion to number of employees working in the establishments, the controlling undertakings or the controlled undertakings as laid down by the legislation of the Member State within the territory of which the central management is situated" (Annex 1(d).

> "The central management and any other more appropriate level of management shall be informed of the composition of the EWC" (Annex 1(e)).

B. Competence

The competence of the EWC is limited to information and consultation on the matters that concern the Community-scale undertaking or Community-scale group of undertakings as a whole, or at least two of its establishments or group undertakings situated in different Member States (Annex 1(a), para. 1).

In the case of undertakings or groups of undertakings, the competence of the EWC shall be limited to those matters concerning all their establishments or group undertakings situated within the Member States, or concerning at least two of their establishments or group undertakings situated in different Member States (Annex 1(a), para. 2).

1. General information (annual)

The EWC has the right to meet with the central management once a year, to be informed and consulted, on the basis of a report drawn up by the central management, on the progress of the business of the Community-scale undertaking or Community-scale group of undertakings and its prospects. The local management shall be informed accordingly (Annex 2, para. 1).

The meeting must relate in particular to the structure, the economic and financial situation, the probable development of the business and of production and sales, the situation and probable trends of employment, investments, and substantial changes concerning organisation, introduction of new working methods or production processes, transfers of production, mergers, cutbacks or closures of undertakings, establishments or important parts thereof, or collective redundancies (Annex 2, para. 2).

2. Ad hoc information

Where there are exceptional circumstances affecting the employees' interests to a considerable extent, particularly in the event of relocations, the closure of establishments or undertakings or collective redundancies, the select committee or, where no such committee exists, the EWC, shall have the right to be informed. It shall have the right to meet, at its request, the central management, or any other more appropriate level of management within the Community-scale undertaking or group of undertakings having its own powers of decision, so as to be informed and consulted on measures significantly affecting employees' interests.

Those members of the EWC who have been elected or appointed by the establishments and/or undertakings that are directly affected by the measures in question shall also have the right to participate in the meeting organised with the select committee (Annex 3, para. 2).

C. Procedure

The EWC shall have the right to meet with the central management once a year, and in the event of exceptional circumstances significantly affecting the employees' interests, as indicated above. The yearly meeting will take place on the basis of written report. The special *ad hoc* information and consultation meeting must take place as soon as possible on the basis of a report drawn up by the central management or any other appropriate level of the management of the Community-scale group of undertakings, on which an opinion may be delivered at the end of the meeting or within a reasonable time. One may assume that this report should also be in writing, unless great urgency prevents this, in which case an oral report would have to be made. This meeting shall not affect the prerogatives of the central management (Annex 3, para. 4).

Member States may provide for rules concerning the chairing of the information and consultation meetings (Annex 4, para. 1). This means that the applicable law may, for example, provide for management to preside the meeting, as this is a common practice in most Member States.

Before any meeting with the central management, the EWC or the select committee, where necessary enlarged in accordance with the second paragraph of point 3 of the Annex (*see* previous para.), shall be entitled to meet without the management concerned being present (Annex 4, para. 2).

The members of the EWC shall inform the representatives of the employees of the establishments or of the undertakings of Community-scale group of undertakings or, in the absence of representatives, the workforce as a whole, of the content and outcome of the information and consultation procedure, carried out in accordance with this Annex, without prejudice to Article 8 of the Directive, relating to confidential information (Annex 5).

The EWC shall adopt its own rules of procedure (Annex 1).

D. Role of experts

The EWC or the select committee may be assisted by experts of its choice in so far as this is necessary for it to carry out its tasks (Annex 6). These experts can be employees as well as non-employees, and thus, for example, may also be trade union representatives. There is no doubt that the trade unions consider this to be a key role for them and are eager to assist the representatives of the employees towards that end.

E. Expenses

The operating expenses of the EWC are, according to Annex 7 to the Directive, borne by the central management. The central management concerned must provide the members of the EWC with such financial and material resources as to enable them to meet and perform their duties in an appropriate manner.

F. Future developments

Four years after the EWC is established it shall examine whether to open negotiations for the conclusion of the agreement referred to in Article 6 or to continue to apply the subsidiary requirements adopted in accordance with this Annex.

Articles 6 and 7 will apply, *mutatis mutandis*, if a decision has been taken to negotiate an agreement according to Article 6, and the "special negotiating body" shall be replaced by "EWC" (Annex 1(f)).

IX. PRE-EXISTING AGREEMENTS – IN FORCE

As already indicated, the EU favours voluntarism in the setting up of an EWC or of an information and consultation procedure, and encouraged the conclusion of agreements to that end even before the Directive entered into force. With this objective in mind, Article 13 of the Directive declares:

> "the obligations arising from this Directive shall not apply to Community-scale undertakings and groups of undertakings in which, on the date of the implementation of this Directive according to Article 14(1) (22 September 1996) or the date of its earlier transposition into the law of the Member State in question, there is already an agreement, providing for the transnational information and consultation, covering the entire workforce. When the agreements referred to expire, the parties to such agreements may jointly decide to renew them. Where this is not the case, the provisions of this Directive shall apply."

For undertakings or groups of undertakings that, for reason of the extension of the Directive to the UK and Northern Ireland, fall under its scope, Article 13 agreements could be concluded up to 14 December 1999 (Article 2, Directive 97/74 of 15 December 1997).

A. Timing, form, language and format of the agreement

1. Timing, form and language

The agreement must be concluded before the implementation of the Directive into national law, that is 22 September 1996, or 15 December 1999, or the date of its transposition in the Member State in question, where this is earlier than the above-mentioned date.

Although Article 13 of the Directive does not indicate that the agreement should be in writing, it seems absolutely necessary that it should be, since it will be subject to examination to determine whether it qualifies as an agreement in force and is thus able to escape the obligations under the Directive on the establishment of an EWC or a procedure for the purposes of informing and consulting employees.

The agreement could be drafted in various official languages, depending on the composition of the negotiating parties. One language is also permissible, either accompanied by translations or not, provided the signing parties understand what they are signing. Special attention must be paid to the national legislation which is applicable to the agreement, especially if this legislation contains specific linguistic requirements as is the case in, for example, Belgium and France.

2. Format: detail or permanent negotiation?

Parties will have to choose the format of the agreement, deciding whether they want it detailed, more or less as a bible, or whether they see it as containing the essential principles regarding an evolving relationship, whereby problems are solved as parties go along. It is, however, crystal clear that the Directive itself and the subsidiary requirements are a good yardstick of what parties are entitled to expect from each other and of what can be done.

B. Nature, binding effect and applicable law

These issues are addressed in 1, IV, D of this Part.

C. Scope and parties to the agreement

Special attention must be given to the (personal) scope of the agreement. Indeed, Article 13 stipulates that the agreement should cover the entire workforce. The parties to the agreement are obviously the representatives of the Community-scale undertaking or groups of undertakings, let us say central management on the one hand and the representatives of the employees on the other.

D. Content of the agreement

1. An EWC, a procedure or another mechanism

Parties must decide whether they want to establish an EWC, a procedure or another mechanism for the purposes of information and consultation. They will also have to agree on the number of members. There is also the opportunity to create a select or executive committee, representing the employee members or the EWC as a whole, that could steer the EWC and/ or be available for *ad hoc* interventions. Pre-meetings, the role of experts and the like are other issues which must be decided.

In case of a procedure instead of an EWC committee, similar questions arise: who will be involved, who will be informed and consulted and how will parties relate to each other? Again, maximum flexibility is allowed, but at a given point representatives of employees and management should meet and engage in a dialogue, and all of this must be set down in writing.

2. Competence: information and consultation

Article 7 of the Directive and the subsidiary requirements are obvious reference points for determining the content of the information and consultation obligations between the parties. Information and consultation must, in particular, relate to transnational issues, involving undertakings/establishments of at least two Member States (Article 13(1)).

3. Functioning

Parties must decide when the representatives of the (central) management and of the employees will meet (annually and/or *ad hoc* at the occasion of important events affecting the interests of the employees), on meeting(s) of the select-executive committee, on possible preliminary meetings before meeting with central management and the like. Other issues include the drafting of the agenda (for example, every party has the right to put points on the agenda), documents to be submitted, meeting rules, ways of formulation opinions, exchange of views, dialogue, reporting (minutes of the meetings) and feedback.

Employees' representatives may need the help of some form of secretariat and perhaps the benefit of some facilities, such as a room, access to modern information technology and telecommunications. These could also be subject of the agreement.

The agreement might also contain wording concerning the languages and interpretation facilities to be used for the implementation of the information and consultation exercise. It is obvious that languages must be used which employees' and management's representatives effectively understand. This will thus entirely depend on the composition of the EWC committee or of those involved in the procedure, and on their respective linguistic skills.

4. Role of experts – expenses

The role of experts is essential for the functioning of the EWC committee or the successful conduct of a procedure. Employees' representatives should be free to choose their experts. These may be other employees, trade union representatives or even outside independent persons. The agreement may lay down rules on who can be an expert, their numbers, whether they have access to which documents, whether they can assist in preliminary meetings or meetings of an EWC procedure, and so on. It is usual for the expenses of the experts to be paid by the undertaking, unless trade unions can benefit from EU subsidies towards that end. Expenses for the functioning of the EWC procedure should be borne by the undertaking.

E.   Prejudicial and confidential information

These points could be addressed in the agreement in line with the contents of the Directive: which information will and can be given, which information is prejudicial/confidential and which information can be passed on to the employees and others.

F.   Status of the employee representatives

The status of employee representatives may also be addressed in the agreement. Parties could consider adopting language indicating that employees cannot be discriminated against for reasons of defending opinions regarding their office and/or conferring upon them the same protection as under national law. We refer to what has been said above (1, IV, VI).

G. Duration of the agreement

The agreement should indicate its duration. The agreement may be open-ended, with a term of notice and certain forms (e.g. a registered letter), and also proposals for renegotiation, to be respected in case of denouncement of the agreement. The agreement could be denounced, totally or partially, by either management or the representatives of the employees, taking the requirements of the applicable provisions into account. Both parties may also agree to terminate the agreement.

Alternatively, the agreement can be for a fixed period, after which it comes automatically to an end. Parties can also foresee a fixed period with an extension for the same period unless one of the parties has terminated the agreement before a certain date (e.g. one year before the term ends).

Parties might also agree upon a procedure for renegotiation of the agreement. In the case of renewal the agreement will continue to escape the obligations which arise under the Directive. If no new agreement is reached before the old one expires, the Directive will apply.

X. THE IMPORTANCE OF EWCS FOR EUROPEAN INDUSTRIAL RELATIONS

Although it is too early even to speculate on the impact of the EWCs on European industrial relations and labour law, some new trends have already been reported.[6]

"1. A form of 'cultural change' on the part of trade unions and employee representatives. A better awareness of the internationalisation of company strategies and more information on industrial relations and working conditions and arrangements in other countries are helping to create a new 'European mentality'.

2. The creation of networks of employee representatives in different countries may support co-ordination and joint action.

3. The establishment of group-level representative bodies in some countries as a consequence of the creation of EWCs shows a tendency towards the centralisation of company-level industrial relations. This could improve the possibility for employee representatives to gather fuller information and better understand company strategies.

These changes are probably more likely to be significant in countries where works councils have not traditionally been present. However, especially where industrial relations are more developed and trade unions are stronger, an important transformation of union attitudes is needed to go beyond the national context and face the challenges of internationalisation.

---

6.   R. Pedersini, "The impact of European Works Councils", *http://www.eurofound.ie*

4. Employers' organisations are generally not in favour of extending EWCs' rights to include bargaining. They see and often value EWCs as a forum for information and participation of employees, but consider that bargaining at European level could not be useful, since world-wide competition and globalisation make reference to the European level inappropriate."

XI. REVIEW OF THE DIRECTIVE BY THE COMMISSION

"Not later than five years after the adoption of this Directive, the Commission shall, in consultation with the Member States and with management and labour at European level, review its operation and, in particular, examine whether the workforce size thresholds are appropriate with a view to proposing suitable amendments to the Council, where necessary" (Article 15). This will bring us well into the 21st century. The information and consultation Directive may then, provided it survives the review, apply to more than 20 Member States with more than 500 million inhabitants.

The reports of the Commission and European Parliament are contained in 3 of Part I.

2. Legislation

COUNCIL DIRECTIVE 94/45/EC OF 22 SEPTEMBER 1994 ON THE
ESTABLISHMENT OF A EUROPEAN WORKS COUNCIL OR A
PROCEDURE IN COMMUNITY-SCALE UNDERTAKINGS AND
COMMUNITY-SCALE GROUPS OF UNDERTAKINGS FOR THE
PURPOSES OF INFORMING AND CONSULTING EMPLOYEES[1]

THE COUNCIL OF THE EUROPEAN UNION,

Having regard to the Agreement on social policy annexed to Protocol 14
on social policy annexed to the Treaty establishing the European Community,
and in particular Article 2(2) thereof,

Having regard to the proposal from the Commission (1),

Having regard to the opinion of the Economic and Social Committee
(2),

Acting in accordance with the procedure referred to in Article 189c of
the Treaty (3),

Whereas, on the basis of the Protocol on Social Policy annexed to the
Treaty establishing the European Community, the Kingdom of Belgium, the
Kingdom of Denmark, the Federal Republic of Germany, the Hellenic
Republic, the Kingdom of Spain, the French Republic, Ireland, the Italian
Republic, the Grand Duchy of Luxembourg, the Kingdom of the Netherlands
and the Portuguese Republic (hereinafter referred to as "the Member States"),
desirous of implementing the Social Charter of 1989, have adopted an
Agreement on Social Policy;

Whereas Article 2(2) of the said Agreement authorizes the Council to
adopt minimum requirements by means of directives;

Whereas, pursuant to Article 1 of the Agreement, one particular
objective of the Community and the Member States is to promote dialogue
between management and labour;

Whereas point 17 of the Community Charter of Fundamental Social
Rights of Workers provides, inter alia, that information, consultation and
participation for workers must be developed along appropriate lines, taking
account of the practices in force in different Member States; whereas the
Charter states that "this shall apply especially in companies or groups of
companies having establishments or companies in two or more Member
States";

---

1.   *O.J.* L 254, 30.9.1994.

R. Blanpain (ed.), Involvement of Employees in the European Union, 35–50.
© 2002 *Kluwer Law International. Printed in Great Britain.*

Whereas the Council, despite the existence of a broad consensus among the majority of Member States, was unable to act on the proposal for a Council Directive on the establishment of a European Works Council in Community-scale undertakings or groups of undertakings for the purposes of informing and consulting employees (4), as amended on 3 December 1991 (5);

Whereas the Commission, pursuant to Article 3 (2) of the Agreement on Social Policy, has consulted management and labour at Community level on the possible direction of Community action on the information and consultation of workers in Community-scale undertakings and Community-scale groups of undertakings;

Whereas the Commission, considering after this consultation that Community action was advisable, has again consulted management and labour on the content of the planned proposal, pursuant to Article 3 (3) of the said Agreement, and management and labour have presented their opinions to the Commission;

Whereas, following this second phase of consultation, management and labour have not informed the Commission of their wish to initiate the process which might lead to the conclusion of an agreement, as provided for in Article 4 of the Agreement;

Whereas the functioning of the internal market involves a process of concentrations of undertakings, cross-border mergers, take-overs, joint ventures and, consequently, a transnationalization of undertakings and groups of undertakings; whereas, if economic activities are to develop in a harmonious fashion, undertakings and groups of undertakings operating in two or more Member States must inform and consult the representatives of those of their employees that are affected by their decisions;

Whereas procedures for informing and consulting employees as embodied in legislation or practice in the Member States are often not geared to the transnational structure of the entity which takes the decisions affecting those employees; whereas this may lead to the unequal treatment of employees affected by decisions within one and the same undertaking or group of undertakings;

Whereas appropriate provisions must be adopted to ensure that the employees of Community-scale undertakings are properly informed and consulted when decisions which affect them are taken in a Member State other than that in which they are employed;

Whereas, in order to guarantee that the employees of undertakings or groups of undertakings operating in two or more Member States are properly informed and consulted, it is necessary to set up European Works Councils or to create other suitable procedures for the transnational information and consultation of employees;

Whereas it is accordingly necessary to have a definition of the concept of controlling undertaking relating solely to this Directive and not prejudging definitions of the concepts of group or control which might be adopted in texts to be drafted in the future;

Whereas the mechanisms for informing and consulting employees in such undertakings or groups must encompass all of the establishments or, as the case may be, the group's undertakings located within the Member States, regardless of whether the undertaking or the group's controlling undertaking has its central management inside or outside the territory of the Member States;

Whereas, in accordance with the principle of autonomy of the parties, it is for the representatives of employees and the management of the undertaking or the group's controlling undertaking to determine by agreement the nature, composition, the function, mode of operation, procedures and financial resources of European Works Councils or other information and consultation procedures so as to suit their own particular circumstances;

Whereas, in accordance with the principle of subsidiarity, it is for the Member States to determine who the employees' representatives are and in particular to provide, if they consider appropriate, for a balanced representation of different categories of employees;

Whereas, however, provision should be made for certain subsidiary requirements to apply should the parties so decide or in the event of the central management refusing to initiate negotiations or in the absence of agreement subsequent to such negotiations;

Whereas, moreover, employees' representatives may decide not to seek the setting-up of a European Works Council or the parties concerned may decide on other procedures for the transnational information and consultation of employees;

Whereas, without prejudice to the possibility of the parties deciding otherwise, the European Works Council set up in the absence of agreement between the parties must, in order to fulfil the objective of this Directive, be kept informed and consulted on the activities of the undertaking or group of undertakings so that it may assess the possible impact on employees' interests in at least two different Member States;

Whereas, to that end, the undertaking or controlling undertaking must be required to communicate to the employees' appointed representatives general information concerning the interests of employees and information relating more specifically to those aspects of the activities of the undertaking or group of undertakings which affect employees' interests; whereas the European Works Council must be able to deliver an opinion at the end of that meeting;

Whereas certain decisions having a significant effect on the interests of employees must be the subject of information and consultation of the employees' appointed representatives as soon as possible;

Whereas provision should be made for the employees' representatives acting within the framework of the Directive to enjoy, when exercising their functions, the same protection and guarantees similar to those provided to employees' representatives by the legislation and/or practice of the country of employment; whereas they must not be subject to any discrimination as a result of the lawful exercise of their activities and must enjoy adequate protection as regards dismissal and other sanctions;

Whereas the information and consultation provisions laid down in this Directive must be implemented in the case of an undertaking or a group's controlling undertaking which has its central management outside the territory of the Member States by its representative agent, to be designated if necessary, in one of the Member States or, in the absence of such an agent, by the establishment or controlled undertaking employing the greatest number of employees in the Member States;

Whereas special treatment should be accorded to Community-scale undertakings and groups of undertakings in which there exists, at the time when this Directive is brought into effect, an agreement, covering the entire workforce, providing for the transnational information and consultation of employees;

Whereas the Member States must take appropriate measures in the event of failure to comply with the obligations laid down in this Directive,

HAS ADOPTED THIS DIRECTIVE:

SECTION I
GENERAL

Article 1
Objective

1. The purpose of this Directive is to improve the right to information and to consultation of employees in Community-scale undertakings and Community-scale groups of undertakings.
2. To that end, a European Works Council or a procedure for informing and consulting employees shall be established in every Community-scale undertaking and every Community-scale group of undertakings, where requested in the manner laid down in Article 5 (1), with the purpose of informing and consulting employees under the terms, in the manner and with the effects laid down in this Directive.
3. Notwithstanding paragraph 2, where a Community-scale group of undertakings within the meaning of Article 2 (1) (c) comprises one or more undertakings or groups of undertakings which are Community-scale undertakings or Community-scale groups of undertakings within the meaning of Article 2 (1) (a) or (c), a European Works Council shall be established at the level of the group unless the agreements referred to in Article 6 provide otherwise.
4. Unless a wider scope is provided for in the agreements referred to in Article 6, the powers and competence of European Works Councils and the scope of information and consulation procedures established to achieve the purpose specified in paragraph 1 shall, in the case of a Community-scale undertaking, cover all the establishments located within the Member States and, in the case of a Community-scale group of undertakings, all group undertakings located within the Member States.

5. Member States may provide that this Directive shall not apply to merchant navy crews.

Article 2
Definitions

1. For the purposes of this Directive:
(a) "Community-scale undertaking" means any undertaking with at least 1000 employees within the Member States and at least 150 employees in each of at least two Member States;
(b) "group of undertakings" means a controlling undertaking and its controlled undertakings;
(c) "Community-scale group of undertakings" means a group of undertakings with the following characteristics:
    – at least 1000 employees within the Member States,
    – at least two group undertakings in different Member States, and
    – at least one group undertaking with at least 150 employees in one Member State and at least one other group undertaking with at least 150 employees in another Member State;
(d) "employees' representatives" means the employees' representatives provided for by national law and/or practice;
(e) "central management" means the central management of the Community-scale undertaking or, in the case of a Community-scale group of undertakings, of the controlling undertaking;
(f) "consultation" means the exchange of views and establishment of dialogue between employees' representatives and central management or any more appropriate level of management;
(g) "European Works Council" means the council established in accordance with Article 1(2) or the provisions of the Annex, with the purpose of informing and consulting employees;
(h) "special negotiating body" means the body established in accordance with Article 5(2) to negotiate with the central management regarding the establishment of a European Works Council or a procedure for informing and consulting employees in accordance with Article 1(2).
2. For the purposes of this Directive, the prescribed thresholds for the size of the workforce shall be based on the average number of employees, including part-time employees, employed during the previous two years calculated according to national legislation and/or practice.

Article 3
Definition of "controlling undertaking"

1. For the purposes of this Directive, "controlling undertaking" means an undertaking which can exercise a dominant influence over another

undertaking ("the controlled undertaking") by virtue, for example, of ownership, financial participation or the rules which govern it.

2. The ability to exercise a dominant influence shall be presumed, without prejudice to proof to the contrary, when, in relation to another undertaking directly or indirectly:

(a) holds a majority of that undertaking's subscribed capital; or

(b) controls a majority of the votes attached to that undertaking's issued share capital; or

(c) can appoint more than half of the members of that undertaking's administrative, management or supervisory body.

3. For the purposes of paragraph 2, a controlling undertaking's rights as regards voting and appointment shall include the rights of any other controlled undertaking and those of any person or body acting in his or its own name but on behalf of the controlling undertaking or of any other controlled undertaking.

4. Notwithstanding paragraphs 1 and 2, an undertaking shall not be deemed to be a "controlling undertaking" with respect to another undertaking in which it has holdings where the former undertaking is a company referred to in Article 3 (5) (a) or (c) of Council Regulation (EEC) No 4064/89 of 21 December 1989 on the control of concentrations between undertakings.[2]

5. A dominant influence shall not be presumed to be exercised solely by virtue of the fact that an office holder is exercising his functions, according to the law of a Member State relating to liquidation, winding up, insolvency, cessation of payments, compositions or analogous proceedings.

6. The law applicable in order to determine whether an undertaking is a "controlling undertaking" shall be the law of the Member State which governs that undertaking.

Where the law governing that undertaking is not that of a Member State, the law applicable shall be the law of the Member State within whose territory the representative of the undertaking or, in the absence of such a representative, the central management of the group undertaking which employs the greatest number of employees is situated.

7. Where, in the case of a conflict of laws in the application of paragraph 2, two or more undertakings from a group satisfy one or more of the criteria laid down in that paragraph, the undertaking which satisfies the criterion laid down in point (c) thereof shall be regarded as the controlling undertaking, without prejudice to proof that another undertaking is able to exercise a dominant influence.

---

2.   *O.J.*, L 395, 30.12.1989.

SECTION II
ESTABLISHMENT OF A EUROPEAN WORKS COUNCIL OR AN
EMPLOYEE INFORMATION AND CONSULTATION PROCEDURE

Article 4
**Responsibility for the establishment of a European Works Council or an
employee information and consultation procedure**

1. The central management shall be responsible for creating the conditions
   and means necessary for the setting up of a European Works Council or an
   information and consultation procedure, as provided for in Article 1 (2), in
   a Community-scale undertaking and a Community-scale group of undertakings.
2. Where the central management is not situated in a Member State, the
   central management's representative agent in a Member State, to be
   designated if necessary, shall take on the responsibility referred to in
   paragraph 1.
   In the absence of such a representative, the management of the establishment or group undertaking employing the greatest number of employees in
   any one Member State shall take on the responsibility referred to in
   paragraph 1.
3. For the purposes of this Directive, the representative or representatives or,
   in the absence of any such representatives, the management referred to in
   the second subparagraph of paragraph 2, shall be regarded as the central
   management.

Article 5
Special negotiating body

1. In order to achieve the objective in Article 1 (1), the central management
   shall initiate negotiations for the establishment of a European Works
   Council or an information and consultation procedure on its own initiative
   or at the written request of at least 100 employees or their representatives
   in at least two undertakings or establishments in at least two different
   Member States.
2. For this purpose, a special negotiating body shall be established in
   accordance with the following guidelines:
(a) The Member States shall determine the method to be used for the election
   or appointment of the members of the special negotiating body who are to
   be elected or appointed in their territories.
   Member States shall provide that employees in undertakings and/or
   establishments in which there are no employees' representatives through
   no fault of their own, have the right to elect or appoint members of the
   special negotiating body.
   The second subparagraph shall be without prejudice to national

legislation and/or practice laying down thresholds for the establishment of employee representation bodies.

(b)   The special negotiating body shall have a minimum of three and a maximum of 18^3 members.

(c)   In these elections or appointments, it must be ensured:
   –   firstly, that each Member State in which the Community-scale undertaking has one or more establishbments (SIC! establishments) or in which the Community-scale group of undertakings has the controlling undertaking or one or more controlled undertakings is represented by one member,
   –   secondly, that there are supplementary members in proportion to the number of employees working in the establishments, the controlling undertaking or the controlled undertakings as laid down by the legislation of the Member State within the territory of which the central management is situated.

(d)   The central management and local management shall be informed of the composition of the special negotiating body.

3.   The special negotiating body shall have the task of determining, with the central management, by written agreement, the scope, composition, functions, and term of office of the European Works Council(s) or the arrangements for implementing a procedure for the information and consultation of employees.

4.   With a view to the conclusion of an agreement in accordance with Article 6, the central management shall convene a meeting with the special negotiating body. It shall inform the local managements accordingly.

   For the purpose of the negotiations, the special negotiating body may be assisted by experts of its choice.

5.   The special negotiating body may decide, by at least two-thirds of the votes, not to open negotiations in accordance with paragraph 4, or to terminate the negotiations already opened.

   Such a decision shall stop the procedure to conclude the agreement referred to in Article 6. Where such a decision has been taken, the provisions in the Annex shall not apply.

   A new request to convene the special negotiating body may be made at the earliest two years after the abovementioned decision unless the parties concerned lay down a shorter period.

6.   Any expenses relating to the negotiations referred to in paragraphs 3 and 4 shall be borne by the central management so as to enable the special negotiating body to carry out its task in an appropriate manner.

   In compliance with this principle, Member States may lay down budgetary rules regarding the operation of the special negotiating body. They may in particular limit the funding to cover one expert only.

---

3.   Directive 97/74/EC, 15 December 1997.

Article 6
Content of the agreement

1. The central management and the special negotiating body must negotiate in a spirit of cooperation with a view to reaching an agreement on the detailed arrangements for implementing the information and consultation of employees provided for in Article 1(1).
2. Without prejudice to the autonomy of the parties, the agreement referred to in paragraph 1 between the central management and the special negotiating body shall determine:
(a) the undertakings of the Community-scale group of undertakings or the establishments of the Communityscale undertaking which are covered by the agreement;
(b) the composition of the European Works Council, the number of members, the allocation of seats and the term of office;
(c) the functions and the procedure for information and consultation of the European Works Council;
(d) the venue, frequency and duration of meetings of the European Works Council;
(e) the financial and material resources to be allocated to the European Works Council;
(f) the duration of the agreement and the procedure for its renegotiation.
3. The central management and the special negotiating body may decide, in writing, to establish one or more information and consultation procedures instead of a European Works Council.
    The agreement must stipulate by what method the employees' representatives shall have the right to meet to discuss the information conveyed to them.
    This information shall relate in particular to transnational questions which significantly affect workers' interests.
4. The agreements referred to in paragraphs 2 and 3 shall not, unless provision is made otherwise therein, be subject to the subsidiary requirements of the Annex.
5. For the purposes of concluding the agreements referred to in paragraphs 2 and 3, the special negotiating body shall act by a majority of its members.

Article 7
Subsidiary requirements

1. In order to achieve the objective in Article 1 (1), the subsidiary requirements laid down by the legislation of the Member State in which the central management is situated shall apply:
    – where the central management and the special negotiating body so decide, or

- where the central management refuses to commence negotiations within six months of the request referred to in Article 5(1), or
- where, after three years from the date of this request, they are unable to conclude an agreement as laid down in Article 6 and the special negotiating body has not taken the decision provided for in Article 5(5).

2. The subsidiary requirements referred to in paragraph 1 as adopted in the legislation of the Member States must satisfy the provisions set out in the Annex.

SECTION III
MISCELLANEOUS PROVISIONS

Article 8
Confidential information

1. Member States shall provide that members of special negotiating bodies or of European Works Councils and any experts who assist them are not authorized to reveal any information which has expressly been provided to them in confidence.

   The same shall apply to employees' representatives in the framework of an information and consultation procedure.

   This obligation shall continue to apply, wherever the persons referred to in the first and second subparagraphs are, even after the expiry of their terms of office.

2. Each Member State shall provide, in specific cases and under the conditions and limits laid down by national legislation, that the central management situated in its territory is not obliged to transmit information when its nature is such that, according to objective criteria, it would seriously harm the functioning of the undertakings concerned or would be prejudicial to them.

   A Member State may make such dispensation subject to prior administrative or judicial authorization.

3. Each Member State may lay down particular provisions for the central management of undertakings in its territory which pursue directly and essentially the aim of ideological guidance with respect to information and the expression of opinions, on condition that, at the date of adoption of this Directive such particular provisions already exist in the national legislation.

Article 9
Operation of European Works Council and information and consultation procedure for workers

The central management and the European Works Council shall work in a spirit of cooperation with due regard to their reciprocal rights and obligations.

The same shall apply to cooperation between the central management and employees' representatives in the framework of an information and consultation procedure for workers.

Article 10
Protection of employees' representatives

Members of special negotiating bodies, members of European Works Councils and employees' representatives exercising their functions under the procedure referred to in Article 6 (3) shall, in the exercise of their functions, enjoy the same protection and guarantees provided for employees' representatives by the national legislation and/or practice in force in their country of employment.

This shall apply in particular to attendance at meetings of special negotiating bodies or European Works Councils or any other meetings within the framework of the agreement referred to in Article 6 (3), and the payment of wages for members who are on the staff of the Community-scale undertaking or the Community-scale group of undertakings for the period of absence necessary for the performance of their duties.

Article 11
Compliance with this Directive

1. Each Member State shall ensure that the management of establishments of a Community-scale undertaking and the management of undertakings which form part of a Community-scale group of undertakings which are situated within its territory and their employees' representatives or, as the case may be, employees abide by the obligations laid down by this Directive, regardless of whether or not the central management is situated within its territory.
2. Member States shall ensure that the information on the number of employees referred to in Article 2 (1) (a) and (c) is made available by undertakings at the request of the parties concerned by the application of this Directive.
3. Member States shall provide for appropriate measures in the event of failure to comply with this Directive; in particular, they shall ensure that adequate administrative or judicial procedures are available to enable the obligations deriving from this Directive to be enforced.

4. Where Member States apply Article 8, they shall make provision for administrative or judicial appeal procedures which the employees' representatives may initiate when the central management requires confidentiality or does not give information in accordance with that Article.

    Such procedures may include procedures designed to protect the confidentiality of the information in question.

Article 12
Link between this Directive and other provisions

1. This Directive shall apply without prejudice to measures taken pursuant to Council Directive 98/59/EC, 20 July 1998, relating to collective redundancies,[4] and to Council Directive 2001/23/EC, 12 March 2001 on the approximation of the laws of the Member States relating to the safeguarding of employees' rights in the event of transfers of undertakings, businesses or parts of businesses.[5]
2. This Directive shall be without prejudice to employees' existing rights to information and consultation under national law.

Article 13
Agreements in force

1. Without prejudice to paragraph 2, the obligations arising from this Directive shall not apply to Community-scale undertakings or Community-scale groups of undertakings in which, on the date laid down in Article 14 (1) for the implementation of this Directive or the date of its transposition in the Member State in question, where this is earlier than the abovementioned date, there is already an agreement, covering the entire workforce, providing for the transnational information and consultation of employees.
2. When the agreements referred to in paragraph 1 expire, the parties to those agreements may decide jointly to renew them.

    Where this is not the case, the provisions of this Directive shall apply.

Article 14
Final provisions

1. Member States shall bring into force the laws, regulations and administrative provisions necessary to comply with this Directive no later than 22

---

4.   *O.J.*, L 225, 12.8.1998.
5.   *O.J.*, L 82, 22.3.2001.

September 1996 or shall ensure by that date at the latest that management and labour introduce the required provisions by way of agreement, the Member States being obliged to take all necessary steps enabling them at all times to guarantee the results imposed by this Directive. They shall forthwith inform the Commission thereof.

2.   When Member States adopt these measures, they shall contain a reference to this Directive or shall be accompanied by such reference on the occasion of their official publication. The methods of making such reference shall be laid down by Member States.

Article 15
Review by the Commission

Not later than 22 September 1999, the Commission shall, in consultation with the Member States and with management and labour at European level, review its operation and, in particular examine whether the workforce size thresholds are appropriate with a view to proposing suitable amendments to the Council, where necessary.

Article 16
This Directive is addressed to the Member States.

ANNEXE
SUBSIDIARY REQUIREMENTS referred to in Article 7 of the Directive
1.   In order to achieve the objective in Article 1 (1) of the Directive and in the cases provided for in Article 7 (1) of the Directive, the establishment, composition and competence of a European Works Council shall be governed by the following rules:
(a)   The competence of the European Works Council shall be limited to information and consultation on the matters which concern the Community-scale undertaking or Community-scale group of undertakings as a whole or at least two of its establishments or group undertakings situated in different Member States.
       In the case of undertakings or groups of undertakings referred to in Article 4 (2), the competence of the European Works Council shall be limited to those matters concerning all their establishments or group undertakings situated within the Member States or concerning at least two of their establishments or group undertakings situated in different Member States.
(b)   The European Works Council shall be composed of employees of the Community-scale undertaking or Community-scale group of undertakings elected or appointed from their number by the employees' representatives or, in the absence thereof, by the entire body of employees.

The election or appointment of members of the European Works Council shall be carried out in accordance with national legislation and/or practice.

(c) The European Works Council shall have a minimum of three members and a maximum of 30.

Where its size so warrants, it shall elect a select committee from among its members, comprising at most three members.

It shall adopt its own rules of procedure.

(d) In the election or appointment of members of the European Works Council, it must be ensured:

– firstly, that each Member State in which the Community-scale undertaking has one or more establishments or in which the Community-scale group of undertakings has the controlling undertaking or one or more controlled undertakings is represented by one member,

– secondly, that there are supplementary members in proportion to the number of employees working in the establishments, the controlling undertaking or the controlled undertakings as laid down by the legislation of the Member State within the territory of which the central management is situated.

(e) The central management and any other more appropriate level of management shall be informed of the composition of the European Works Council.

(f) Four years after the European Works Council is established it shall examine whether to open negotiations for the conclusion of the agreement referred to in Article 6 of the Directive or to continue to apply the subsidiary requirements adopted in accordance with this Annex.

Articles 6 and 7 of the Directive shall apply, *mutatis mutandis*, if a decision has been taken to negotiate an agreement according to Article 6 of the Directive, in which case "special negotiating body" shall be replaced by "European Works Council".

2. The European Works Council shall have the right to meet with the central management once a year, to be informed and consulted, on the basis of a report drawn up by the central management, on the progress of the business of the Community-scale undertaking or Community-scale group of undertakings and its prospects. The local managements shall be informed accordingly.

The meeting shall relate in particular to the structure, economic and financial situation, the probable development of the business and of production and sales, the situation and probable trend of employment, investments, and substantial changes concerning organization, introduction of new working methods or production processes, transfers of production, mergers, cut-backs or closures of undertakings, establishments or important parts thereof, and collective redundancies.

3. Where there are exceptional circumstances affecting the employees' interests to a considerable extent, particularly in the event of relocations, the closure of establishments or undertakings or collective redundancies,

the select committee or, where no such committee exists, the European Works Council shall have the right to be informed. It shall have the right to meet, at its request, the central management, or any other more appropriate level of management within the Community-scale undertaking or group of undertakings having its own powers of decision, so as to be informed and consulted on measures significantly affecting employees' interests.

Those members of the European Works Council who have been elected or appointed by the establishments and/or undertakings which are directly concerned by the measures in question shall also have the right to participate in the meeting organized with the select committee.

This information and consultation meeting shall take place as soon as possible on the basis of a report drawn up by the central management or any other appropriate level of management of the Communityscale (SIC! Community-scale) undertaking or group of undertakings, on which an opinion may be delivered at the end of the meeting or within a reasonable time.

This meeting shall not affect the prerogatives of the central management.

4. The Member States may lay down rules on the chairing of information and consultation meetings.

Before any meeting with the central management, the European Works Council or the select committee, where necessary enlarged in accordance with the second paragraph of point 3, shall be entitled to meet without the management concerned being present.

5. Without prejudice to Article 8 of the Directive, the members of the European Works Council shall inform the representatives of the employees of the establishments or of the undertakings of a Communityscale (SIC! Community-scale) group of undertakings or, in the absence of representatives, the workforce as a whole, of the content and outcome of the information and consultation procedure carried out in accordance with this Annex.

6. The European Works Council or the select committee may be assisted by experts of its choice, in so far as this is necessary for it to carry out its tasks.

7. The operating expenses of the European Works Council shall be borne by the central management.

The central management concerned shall provide the members of the European Works Council with such financial and material resources as enable them to perform their duties in an appropriate manner.

In particular, the cost of organizing meetings and arranging for interpretation facilities and the accomodation and travelling expenses of members of the European Works Council and its select committee shall be met by the central management unless otherwise agreed.

In compliance with these principles, the Member States may lay down budgetary rules regarding the operation of the European Works Council. They may in particular limit funding to cover one expert only.

3.   Relevant documents

I.   REPORT FROM THE **COMMISSION** TO THE EUROPEAN
PARLIAMENT AND THE COUNCIL ON THE APPLICATION OF
THE DIRECTIVE ON THE ESTABLISHMENT OF A EUROPEAN
WORKS COUNCIL OR A PROCEDURE IN COMMUNITY-SCALE
UNDERTAKINGS AND COMMUNITY-SCALE GROUPS OF
UNDERTAKINGS FOR THE PURPOSES OF INFORMING AND
CONSULTING EMPLOYEES (COUNCIL DIRECTIVE 94/45/EC OF
22 SEPTEMBER 1994)(4 APRIL 2000 – COM/2000/00188 FINAL)

1.   Introduction

Directive 94/45/EC on the establishment of a European works council or a
procedure in Community-scale undertakings and Community-scale groups of
undertakings for the purposes of informing and consulting employees was
adopted by the Council on 22 September 1994. Its legal basis is Article 2 (2) of
the Agreement on Social Policy annexed to Protocol 14 on Social Policy
appended to the Treaty establishing the European Community. The Directive
thus applies to all the Member States of the European Community except the
United Kingdom of Great Britain and Northern Ireland.

Council Directive 97/74/EC was adopted on 15 December 1997,
extending application of Directive 94/45/EC to the United Kingdom of Great
Britain and Northern Ireland.

Directive 94/45/EC was due to be transposed by the Member States,
with the exception of the United Kingdom of Great Britain and Northern
Ireland, by 22 September 1996. Directive 97/74/EC must be transposed by the
United Kingdom of Great Britain and Northern Ireland and all Member
States, by 15 December 1999 at the latest.

Consequently, this report deals only with the status of transposition of
Directive 94/45/EC. A further report covering transposition of Directive 97/74/
EC will be presented in due course.

In its analytic part concerning the national legal implementation, the
report follows the logic and structure of the Directive itself.

R. Blanpain (ed.), Involvement of Employees in the European Union, 51–104.
© 2002 *Kluwer Law International. Printed in Great Britain.*

2. Implementation by legal measures and evaluation of the practical application

The vast majority of countries made a major effort not only to meet the deadline for implementation, i.e. 22 September 1996, but also to integrate the Directive faithfully into their national law.

Five countries met the deadline for transposition (Denmark, Finland, Sweden, Ireland and (partly) Belgium),[1] all of which adopted a transposition text which took effect on 22 September 1996.

They were closely followed by Austria (17 October 1996), Italy (partial transposition 6 November 1996), France (12 November 1996) and Germany (1 November 1996).

Transposition in the Netherlands (5 February 1997), Greece (1 March 1997) and Spain (24 April 1997) came somewhat later.

Portugal was very late in adopting a transposing act (it was published on 9 June 1999 and entered into force on 9 July 1999).

The Luxembourg text is currently being implemented.

In Italy, the Directive has only been partly transposed, through the signing of an interconfederal agreement on 6 November 1996, and this has to be supplemented by a law extending the collective agreement erga omnes and adopting, inter alia, rules on sanctions and court jurisdiction.

The interconfederal agreement represents only partial implementation of the Directive, as its content and scope are limited (not all occupational sectors are covered).

In Belgium, the collective agreement has been supplemented by two laws.

The manner in which the Directive is implemented is in keeping with each country's domestic legal order. As a rule, laws (acts) have been adopted by parliament. In Italy and Belgium, collective agreements (supplemented in Belgium by an extension procedure) have been preferred.

The social partners have often been involved in the transposition procedure, either formally or informally.

2.1. Evaluation of implementing legislation

The evaluation of the quality of implementing measures, even though it is not long since the entry into force of the Directive, is clearly very positive.

In this connection, the expert group responsible for ensuring proper implementation played a pioneering role, with the Commission providing coordination. This method of following up the transposition work should be adopted generally, in the light of the results obtained in implementing this Directive – a Directive that was particularly complex because of its

---

1.   The country abbreviations used in this report are as follows: A:Austria, B:Belgium, D:Germany, DK:Denmark, EL:Greece, E:Spain, FIN:Finland, F:France, IRL:Ireland, I:Italy, L:Luxembourg, NL:Netherlands, P:Portugal, S:Sweden.

transnational nature and the combined use of Community concepts and rules of private international law.

However, full results cannot be provided until the remaining countries have completed transposition (Luxembourg and Italy).

Infringement proceedings were started against Luxembourg and Portugal. In the latter case the Commission has suspended the proceedings following entry into force of the transposing act.

Unless Italy takes appropriate action to supplement the interconfederal agreement signed in 1996, the Commission will open infringement proceedings for incomplete transposition.

This report draws attention to a number of minor discrepancies between the Directive and the transposing acts (method of counting part-time workers, number of representatives in the SNB (Special negotiating body) higher than the limit laid down in the Directive) or aspects where there is a lack of detail (preparatory meetings). In any event, these discrepancies must be interpreted as being in the spirit of the Directive.

There were no difficulties in integrating the Directive into domestic legal orders, firstly because the Directive very often refers to internal mechanisms in each Member State, and secondly because it has enshrined the principle of collective autonomy which in many cases is at the basis of employment law in the European Union. Even in countries such as Ireland, where representation mechanisms are optional, the Directive was well received.

However, regardless of the quality of implementing measures, there is a need for further interpretation of some issues, which have already been identified and relate to:
- the concept of "controlling undertaking";
- the effects of geographical and proportional criteria;
- the conditions for renewing agreements already in force (Article 13);
- changes in the structure of the group;
- the very concept of "expert".

In a significant number of cases those issues have been solved or will be solved by the parties concerned. In other cases the specific nature of each individual problem of interpretation means that they can best resolved by the courts.

As regards legal analysis, problems arise in determining the legal personality of the EWC in many countries, the law applicable to agreements and, naturally, the legal status of these agreements, all of which has a direct impact on the rules on international jurisdiction.

2.2. Evaluation of the practical application of the directive outlook

2.2.1. General considerations
Clearly, it is very difficult to produce a genuine summary of how the Directive has been implemented in practice, as this took place very recently, and the

Annex to the Directive, which establishes subsidiary requirements, has not yet been applied.

However, a number of general observations can be made on the basis of experience to date.

As already emphasised, up to now the Directive has been smoothly integrated into the industrial relations systems of the different countries, thanks to the Member States' freedom as regards the choice of representation mechanisms.

The attempt to ensure a harmonious link between worker representation at national level and at transnational level was one of the legislators' main concerns in transposing the Directive. In a large majority of countries the trade union organisations have been recognised as key players, so that they can preserve the role they play in national relations.

There is every reason why the transnational representation body should fit in well with the existing structures of worker representation, although it is stressed that besides the positive effects the creation of a transnational body may eventually create certain problems. Naturally it is to be hoped that the EWC (European Works Council) will give a new impetus to consultation and that a fresh dialogue will begin between the elected bodies, the trade union organisations and the "European" bodies.

But there is also the possibility of conflicts with transnational repercussions, such as the closure of establishments, and possible friction between the positions of "national" and "European" workers' representatives.

Some countries have tried to strengthen the part played by the social partners. In particular, the provision in the Directive allowing for the appointment of an expert to assist the SNB and EWC has facilitated the participation of the Social Partners in the process.

Another point to note is the practical benefit, as regards cohesion and consultation, of national measures which require details of the composition of the SNB and EWC to be sent to all the group's decentralised levels, local management and national workers' representatives.

Repeatedly the importance of opening up employment relations to the transnational dimension both with regard to worker representation and in the context of collective bargaining has been stressed.

On the purely conceptual level, it should also be noted that the Member States concerned have agreed to respect the sometimes innovative concepts enunciated in the Directive. In the field of workers' representation, always a sensitive question at European level, such precision is important.

As regards common principles, the Directive and the implementing texts introduce an obligation to negotiate in good faith, based on a spirit of cooperation between the parties into European employment relations.

In the framework of construction of Europe, the pooling of knowledge, reciprocal influence and strategies, as well as the synergy of interests of workers belonging to the same group, are all positive factors.

Transnational information and transnational representation of workers constitute a new and essential response to the impact of the global economy on Europe.

In specific terms, the implementation of transnational representation is already effective in that nearly 600 groups with a Community dimension, including the largest ones, signed pre-Directive agreements before 22 September 1996 or signed agreements based on Article 6 of the Directive after that date.

Article 13 made it easier to sign pre-Directive agreements: it allowed their validation and made it possible for the social partners themselves, and transnational firms, to carry on their own negotiations. The European trade union organisations also played an essential role in this first phase of negotiating agreements. At the moment, there are very few contentious points relating to pre-Directive agreements.

2.2.2. Specific considerations

A major conference on "European works councils: practice and development" was organised in Brussels by the social partners (ETUC, UNICE and CEEP), with the support of the European Commission, on 28–30 April 1999. This event represented a unique opportunity for nearly 650 practitioners (representatives of undertakings which have set up a European works council, EWC members, representatives of employers' and workers' organisations at national and European levels, and representatives of the Member States) to take stock of all the experience acquired in implementing the Directive.

Although none of the above social partner organisations called for an immediate revision of the Directive, the debates highlighted a number of legal and practical problems relating to its application. The following list of problems should not be regarded as exhaustive:

(a)   The Directive is based on the principle of quasi-absolute priority and the freedom of the social partners to negotiate appropriate agreements. This approach has proved effective and is the reason why so many agreements have been signed. However, some of these agreements seem to guarantee only a very low level of transnational consultation and information.

(b)   A merger of undertakings or groups of undertakings might result in there being two or more European works councils in the new undertaking or group. The Directive does not currently require existing agreements to contain an adaptation clause covering changes in the make-up of the undertaking or group. However, the spirit of the Directive is that agreements must cover all workers at all times. Some Member States have in fact already made provision for adaptation clauses to existing agreements.

(c)   Between adoption of the Directive (22 September 1994) and transposition (22 September 1996), some 450 "pre-Directive agreements" were signed. After 22 September 1996, the frequency and number of agreements signed fell sharply. The success of pre-Directive agreements is explained by the extensive involvement of European trade unions in the negotiating process leading up to most of these agreements, which is not the case with agreements negotiated on the basis of Articles 5 and 6 of the Directive. Another reason for the fall in the number of negotiations and agreements might be the fact that most large undertakings already have an agreement, and it is now the turn of small and medium-sized multinationals to establish European works councils. These undertakings have specific characteristics and requirements, and often only a small proportion of their employees are members of a union.

(d)   Although the Directive on European works councils has given rise to few disputes, considering the novelty of the transnational provisions designed to set up a cross-border system of information and consultation, one case in particular has highlighted the problem of whether the present text is sufficiently clear with regard to ensuring that information is provided and consultation takes place "within a reasonable time limit" and in any event before a decision is taken.

(e)   During the debates on the practical application of the Directive, repeated reference was made to the importance of the right to training for members of the special negotiating body and the European works council. The main argument put forward is that the Directive on the European works councils is an instrument of transnational representation opening up new possibilities for the representation of interests and for transnational communication. Consequently, a certain skill level is needed by the members of the European works council.

(f)   Another problem raised during the discussions on the practical application of the Directive concerns the effectiveness of the flow of information between the different levels of worker representation. In order to exchange information and be consulted effectively at Community level, it is necessary for efficient information and consultation systems to exist at national level and for the different levels of worker representation within undertakings or groups of undertakings to be linked with each other.

Article 15 of Directive 94/45/EC on the establishment of a European works council or a procedure in Community-scale undertakings and Community-scale groups of undertakings for the purpose of informing and consulting employees states that:

"Not later than 22 September 1999, the Commission shall, in consultation with the Member States and with management and labour at European level, review its operation and, in particular, examine whether the workforce size thresholds are appropriate with a view to proposing suitable amendments to the Council, where necessary".

In order to comply with this Article, the Commission consulted the Member States and the social partners at European level.

The review process will continue taking into consideration the debates in the Council and in the European Parliament on the dossiers closely linked with the Directive (proposal for a Directive establishing a general framework for informing and consulting employees in the European Community (COM(98)612 final, 11.11.1998), Draft Directive on employee involvement within the European Company).

On the basis of the results of this review as well as on the basis of the evolution of the other dossiers the Commission will at the given moment decide on the possible revision of the Directive.

3.   Analysis of national implementating measures

3.1.   Scope

3.1.1.   Material and geographical scope
(a)   All Member States stipulate that the territorial scope is the European Union and the European Economic Area. As some of them have specifically excluded the United Kingdom, their provisions must be amended before 15 December 1999 following the extension to the United Kingdom of Directive 94/45/EC under the terms of Directive 97/74 of 15 December 1997.
(b)   In certain countries, the scope of the transposition text implicitly or explicitly includes the merchant navy (B, E, IRL, FIN, S, D, A, P), whereas other countries (EL, I) exclude this sector. In Denmark and the Netherlands, persons working in the merchant navy are not excluded from the scope of the transposition text, but they may not be elected or appointed as members of the special negotiating group or European works council.
(c)   All Member States respect the material domain of application laid down by the Directive, both as regards the number of employees which Community-scale undertakings and groups must have (1 in total, and at least 150 in two subsidiaries or establishments) and the requirement that there must be units in at least two Member States.
(d)   In calculating the size of the workforce, all countries use the definition of "employee" provided by their national law, in accordance with the lex fori qualification procedure authorised by the Directive. The essential criteria applied for defining an employment relationship are the payment of a remuneration and a subordination relationship.
In calculating workforce numbers as such, reference is made directly or indirectly to a period of two years.
There are differences in the way part-time employees are taken into account. In Belgium the calculation method used diverges slightly from the pro rata temporis rule.[2] In Ireland, if workers have worked less than eight hours a week for less than 13 weeks, they are not taken into account in calculating the workforce. In Spain, part-time workers may or may not be counted depending on the length of their employment

---

2.   If employees work three-quarter time they are counted as full-time workers, if not they are counted as half-time workers.

contract.[3] Employees are counted as full-time workers in seven countries
(A, D, EL, F, FIN, NL, P), while elsewhere the pro rata temporis rule
applies (I).

Certain categories are excluded, such as apprentices (I, IRL), home-
workers (I), seasonal/casual workers (FIN), or management personnel (A,
D, IRL).

(e) All countries except France, Finland, Denmark, the Netherlands and
Sweden make provision in their transposition text for the powers and
responsibilities of the European works councils and the scope of
procedures for information and consultation of workers to relate, in the
case of a Community-scale undertaking, to all establishments situated in
the Member States and, in the case of a Community-scale group of
undertakings, all the member undertakings situated in the Member States;
nevertheless, the agreement referred to in Article 6 of the Directive may
provide for a wider scope.

3.1.2. Concept of undertaking or group of undertakings

(a) In many countries, the concept of "undertaking" as such is not defined;
those countries refer explicitly (EL, IRL, I) or implicitly to the definition
adopted by the Court of Justice of the European Communities (CJEC).

The concept of "establishment" is spelt out in Ireland on the basis of a
criterion of geographic separation. In Belgium, an establishment is a part
of an undertaking which does not possess legal personality. The Austrian
transposition text refers to section 34 of the Work Organisation Act. Only
the Spanish and Swedish transposition texts explicitly mention the case of
public-sector undertakings. Public-sector undertakings are not covered in
Italy and Belgium, where the Directive has been transposed into national
legislation by means of collective agreements (in Belgium supplemented
by a royal extending decree which does not cover public-sector undertakings). This gap must be plugged.

(b) The concept of "controlling undertaking" is sufficiently developed in the
text of the Directive, such that the transposition texts have not sought to
amend it. The text has been incorporated as it stands by Italy, Greece,
Sweden, Ireland, Belgium, Austria, Denmark and Portugal. Sometimes
the terms used are different, although they tally with the presumptions of
the Directive and their hierarchy; this is the case in Ireland, Germany and
Spain and also, with some additional qualifications, in France.

The transposition acts also frequently refer to ordinary company law,
either in fleshing out or in supplementing the general mechanisms of the
Directive.

---

3.   Part-time workers with open-ended contracts or contracts for more than two years are
      included in their undertaking's permanent workforce. Fixed-term contracts of less than
      two years are taken into account on the basis of the number of days worked over the two
      years preceding the date on which the negotiation procedure started. One additional
      worker is counted for every 400 days or part-days worked.

In the Netherlands, for example, the Directive's presumptions, as well as their hierarchy, are respected, but the text, in determining capital and voting rights, excludes situations in which an undertaking holds rights on behalf of another (indirect participation). On the other hand, bonded shares are allocated to creditors.

In Finland the reference to company law would suggest that the Directive's presumptions are also upheld, as well as the criterion of "controlling interest" in describing control of subsidiaries.

The Irish text has the merit of addressing the difficulty created by the inclusion of joint ventures (50%/50% holdings).

3.2.   Request to open negotiations

All countries comply with the Directive's requirements as regards both the obligations incumbent on the central management and selection of the bodies entitled to initiate negotiations (100 employees or their representatives in at least two States).

Italy's provisions also stipulate that the trade union organisations which have signed the collective agreement applicable may request the creation of a special negotiating body.

The obligations incumbent on the central management are spelt out in detail in Sweden and reinforced in the Netherlands, Germany and Austria as regards the circulation of information to local management and trade union organisations. In Austria, requesting parties are entitled to ask central and local management how many persons are employed in the undertaking or establishment. These details are of interest in that information concerning the creation of an SNB is then conveyed to all interested parties in the Community-scale group.

3.3.   Special negotiating body (SNB)

3.3.1.   Geographical and proportionality criteria

All countries comply with the Directive as regards the geographical distribution of SNB members (one per country) and the proportional distribution of additional members as a function of the size of the workforce in each country. Several Member States have introduced a finer-grained breakdown (six workforce size classes), and Denmark has established thresholds for the additional members (thresholds of 2, then 5000), but the principle of proportionality seems to have been respected in all cases.

3.3.2.   Number of representatives

The number of representatives on the SNB (3–17) is often stipulated (DK, EL, FIN, I, IRL, NL) but sometimes omitted (B, D, E, S, A, P). In some cases distribution is not consistent with the maximum of 17 members stipulated in the Directive (A, D, E, F), but the group has to be established in more than 14 States for the maximum of 17 to be exceeded in these countries.

3.3.3. Modification of the structure of the group during negotiations

Most countries do not provide for changes to the composition of the SNB during negotiations (A, F, FIN, I). However, specific rules have been laid down in Spain, the Netherlands, Portugal and Greece covering changes to the structure of the Community-scale undertaking or group of undertakings.

3.3.4. Representatives of third countries

Most Member States provide for including representatives of third countries, but procedures differ from country to country. They may be included as observers without voting rights (EL, E, F, NL, P), they may be entitled to be elected or appointed as full members in accordance with national legislation (DK), or provision may be made for details concerning their appointment and status to be set out in an agreement signed by the central management and the SNB (A, D, EL). In Portugal, the central management is not obliged to cover observers' costs.

Finland, Denmark, Italy and Belgium do not have any provisions concerning third countries outside the EEA.

3.3.5. Information on the composition of the SNB

Most Member States require the central management to be informed of the composition of the SNB, but others (e.g. Finland) widen the scope of this information obligation to include all employees. The scope has been extended in Italy to include trade union organisations and local management, and in Austria it includes local management. Similarly, in Germany, the central management must inform local management, employee representatives, and trade unions present in establishments located in Germany.

3.3.6. Composition of the SNB

In each country the appointment of SNB representatives depends on and is in line with the country's existing representation arrangements.

Belgium: Election by the members of the works council if there is one, or otherwise by the health and safety committee. Failing this, the joint committee may allow the trade union delegation to select the SNB members for Belgium.

Denmark: Election by the representatives of the cooperation committee, otherwise by the shop stewards, or failing that by the employees.

Germany: Appointment by the existing structures in the following order of priority: group committee, central works council (Zentralbetriebsrat), works council (Betriebsrat), or works committee (Betriebsauschuss).

Greece: Election in the following order of priority: by the trade union organisations, in their absence by the works council, or failing that by the workers.

Spain: Appointment by joint agreement among the trade union representatives, who together form the majority of members of the works council(s), or the employee delegates where appropriate, or by agreement of the majority of the members of those councils and delegates.

France: Appointment by the trade union organisations from among the elected members of the works council or establishment council or from the trade union representatives in the group; in the absence of a trade union organisation in the group in France, election by the employees.

Ireland: Appointment or election by the employees, possibility of an agreement between central management and employees.

Italy: Appointment by the trade union organisations that have signed the collective agreement. Otherwise, agreement between the trade union organisations and the central management on the appointment of members.

Netherlands: Election by the highest-level council: group council, central council, works council; if not all the works councils are represented in these other councils, the appointment must be made jointly by the councils that are not represented and the group council; if some of the workers are not represented on the works council, they must be consulted on the choice of SNB members; in the absence of a works council, election by the employees.

Austria: Appointment by existing structures in the following order of priority: group committee, works council or works committee; trade union representatives may be appointed as SNB members even if they are not members of a committee or council.

Portugal: Appointment by joint agreement between, in order, the elected bodies and trade unions, between the elected bodies if no trade unions are represented in the undertaking or establishment, between the trade unions representing at least two thirds of the workers, or between the trade unions representing at least 5% of the workers; failing agreement, if no representatives are appointed, if there is no elected body or trade union, or if at least one third of the workers so request, the SNB members are directly elected by secret ballot, on the basis of lists presented by at least 100 or 10% of workers.

Finland: Organisation of an election by agreement; in the absence of an agreement, the election must be organised by the health and safety delegates and the most representative workforce delegates.

Sweden: Election by the trade union which has signed the collective agreement with the controlling undertaking; if there are several such unions they must negotiate an agreement to organise the election; in the absence of agreement, the most representative union makes the appointment.

Hence, in all the countries which give the works council or elected representatives a major role in the representation of workers, notably as regards information and consultation of workers (or co-decision), it is they who appoint the members of the SNB. Thus the central role is vested in the works council (or central council or group council) in Germany, Austria, Denmark, Finland, France, the Netherlands and Belgium, while workforce delegates or shop stewards play a subsidiary role in Denmark and Belgium.

The trade unions play a central role in appointing members in Italy, Greece, Portugal and Spain, jointly with the works council.

But they also have an indirect role, either because the trade union organisations draw up the lists of candidates (F, S), because they play an essential part in constituting the works council or group council, or because the members of the SNB must have been elected from the lists prepared by the trade union organisations (F) or appointed on a delegation basis (B).

The trade union organisations also play an important role in Sweden, where elections are organised amongst the representatives of the unions which have signed the collective agreement applicable.

Because of the voluntary approach to representation in Ireland, the election system there is not grounded in already existing representation. Election by all employees may thus be replaced by an agreement signed by the employees and management of each undertaking concerned by transnational representation.

In the absence of the body chiefly responsible for appointing or electing SNB members, the Member States rely on various systems: either appointments are made by the workforce delegates (B, DK) or the health and safety delegates (B, FIN), or the members are appointed by agreement between the central management and the trade union organisations (I) or employees (IRL), or they are elected by all the employees (F, NL, P). In Sweden, in the absence of a trade union bound by a collective agreement with the controlling undertaking, the local employees' organisation representing the greatest number of employees assumes responsibility for appointing the members.

Only three Member States have failed to provide for subsidiary mechanisms, namely Spain, Germany and Austria. In these countries workers have the right to establish representations, and it is their responsibility if there is no works committee. The threshold for the creation of such a committee is very low (five employees in Austria and Germany, and six in Spain).

Finally, all Member States have taken measures to ensure worker representation and establish a system for the appointment of SNB members which is in keeping with their domestic representation arrangements and the role handed down to the trade union organisations in each country.

3.4. Agreements – Article 6

Most Member States comply with the Directive's provisions concerning the content of the agreement resulting from negotiations between the central management and the SNB. However, several of them have inserted in their national texts certain rules which are not laid down in the Directive:

- rules concerning the selection of workers' representatives for the negotiations and the establishment of the European works council are provided for in Spanish, Finnish, French, Irish and Italian legislation;
- concerning the content of the agreement establishing the European works council, the Spanish and Greek legislation requires full identification of the parties to the agreement; the Italian interconfederal agreement requires the

content of information and consultation to be laid down in the agreement; the Irish act requires the agreement to specify how the information given to employees' representatives is to be passed on to employees in the Member State concerned and how employees' opinions on that information are to be recorded; Portuguese legislation allows the parties to specify the law applicable to the agreement and the subjects to be treated as confidential;

– concerning the content of the agreement establishing the information and consultation procedures, French, Irish and Netherlands legislation requires the agreement to stipulate the establishments to which the procedure is to apply, the way in which workers or their representatives are to be informed and consulted on transnational questions significantly affecting the workers, the material and financial resources allocated for the procedure, the duration of the agreement and the procedure for renegotiating it. Austrian legislation requires the agreement to specify the consequences to the EWC in the event of restructuring.

Most of the transposition texts refer to the principle of collective autonomy. The others assume it implicitly. Hence in all countries the agreement must lay down all the conditions for the creation and operation of the transnational representation body chosen.

Several texts establish the principle of negotiating in good faith or in a climate of cooperation.[4] In Spain there is an express provision that negotiations may be suspended in the case of bad faith on the part of one party, which is regarded as equivalent to refusing to start negotiations.

Belgium, in addition to the compulsory particulars required under the Directive, prescribes the preparation of a protocol laying down all the concrete rules governing the operation of the European works council. In the other countries these rules are set out in detail in the works council's rules of procedure.

With regard to the operation of the European works council and the worker information and consultation procedures in their relations with the central management, the Danish, French, Finnish and Netherlands texts do not explicitly impose an obligation to work in a spirit of cooperation in compliance with their reciprocal rights and obligations.

A two-thirds majority is required in several countries (A, D, F, I, E, P) in order to decide not to start negotiations or to suspend negotiations in progress. This point is not specifically covered in the other Member States' transposition texts.

---

4.   In their transposition texts, Finland, France, the Netherlands and Sweden omit any reference to negotiating in a spirit of cooperation. However, in some States, including the Netherlands, negotiating in a spirit of good faith is a general principle of civil law. Furthermore, given the legal scope of the preamble and national case law on the subject, the absence of this concept in certain transposition texts does not limit its legal scope.

3.5. Subsidiary requirements

All Member States respect the conditions for application of the subsidiary requirements (refusal to commence negotiations within six months of being requested to do so and failure to reach an agreement within three years). Sometimes there are variations.

Finland, Italy and Sweden make provision for the application of the subsidiary requirements where an expired agreement predating the Directive has not been renewed within six months of termination (FIN) or expiry (S).

Spain and Sweden make provision for the application of the subsidiary requirements where an agreement post-dating the Directive has not been renewed within six months of the expiry of its period of validity.

3.5.1. Composition of the European works council

All Member States have adopted rules governing appointment to the European works council which are identical to those used for the SNB.

The rules on geographical distribution are also identical to those for the SNB (one member per country). The same applies to the proportional distribution of members as a function of workforce size.

All Member States provide for the possibility of appointing a select committee of three members. In some (B, E, IRL), the select committee may be enlarged in exceptional circumstances.

Most Member States expressly prescribe a minimum of three and a maximum of thirty members (not specified in B, NL and P).

Austria and Denmark permit the presence of permanent trade union representatives if they are already members of a works council.

3.5.2. Information and consultation

All Member States provide for information and consultation of workers within the meaning of the Directive, including (in Italy, France, Spain, Greece and Portugal) the right to express an opinion in exceptional circumstances. In the Netherlands an opinion may be delivered within a reasonable time limit after a meeting.

Certain Member States (e.g. IRL) specify that the SNB must be informed and consulted in good faith. Even if texts do not spell out the need for this spirit of cooperation, it may be considered as implicit, or as resulting from the spirit of the text or from general legal principles.

Austria and Germany partially exclude ideologically oriented enterprises from the domain of information and consultation of the EWC. Sweden merely excludes them in relation to the objectives and direction of their activities.

3.5.3. Competence of the European works council

The competence of the European works council as prescribed by the Directive, as regards both the annual meeting and exceptional circumstances, have been faithfully reproduced by all Member States. As regards the transnational dimension of the subjects dealt with, the wording of national provisions sometimes differs slightly from that of the Directive.

As regards the annual meeting, besides the requirement on the prior circulation of an information report, the provisions governing general competence are taken over almost verbatim by all Member States. Italy adds equal opportunities, while the Netherlands adds the environment. As in the Directive, the list of subjects is not exhaustive.

Exceptional circumstances within the meaning of the Directive (or similar terms, as in Italy, where reference is made to a substantial impact on workers' interests) are valid grounds for extraordinary meetings in all Member States.

Finally, preparatory meetings are explicitly provided for in certain national texts (A, B, IRL, P) to enable the European works council to be convened before meeting the central management. Other Member States do not mention this possibility, even though preparatory meetings are specifically provided for in the Directive. But the lack of appropriate provisions does not entitle the central management to disallow such meetings, or any other measure, if they are necessary for the operation of the European works council.

3.5.4. Temporal organisation of information and consultation

The terms used in some transposition texts concerning the moment of consultation in the event of exceptional circumstances are different, but all are inspired by the principle of timely fulfilment of obligations enshrined by the CJEC. Consultation must take place either as soon as possible (IRL, FIN, NL, P) or soon enough to have a useful effect (E).

The absence of specific provisions does not detract from the obligation on the central management to comply with its information and consultation obligations "in good time", in line with the CJEC's interpretation of the obligation to ensure that Community legislation has a useful effect. This interpretation is also binding on national courts.

Several Member States (A, I, F, NL, P) also require negotiations to be reopened within four years of the application of the subsidiary requirements with specific provisions. In Germany and Austria, the EWC must make a decision with a view to reopening negotiations based on Article 6 of the Directive.

3.5.5. Changes to the structure of the group

Adjustments to the composition of the European works council are provided for: in Denmark, Germany and Portugal as a function of the number of employees in the different countries; in France when a new European works council is appointed (every two years); in the Netherlands when justified by changes (integration of additional members).

3.5.6. Chairing of the EWC

Specific rules have been adopted in some Member States for selecting the chairman of the European works council. He or she may be appointed on the basis of an agreement between the central management and the European works council (EL, E, IRL), the chair may alternate between the management and the European works council (NL), the rules of procedure may cover the matter (B), the members of the European works council may elect the chairman (A, D) or the head of the controlling undertaking may take the chair (F).

3.6. Agreements in force – Article 13

All Member States comply with the requirements of Article 13 of the Directive concerning the applicability of agreements already in force.

In several countries there is a gap between the date laid down in the Directive (22/09/1996) and the date of entry into force of the transposition text validating these agreements (D, F).

The Austrian legislation backdates the validity of agreements to the date stipulated in the Directive. Italy and the Netherlands make provision for the validity of agreements signed after 22 September 1996; in Italy, agreements signed by November 1996 are valid, in the Netherlands those signed by February 1997.

The Portuguese act explicitly recognises agreements entered into in third countries, provided they comply with the conditions laid down there, wherever national law is applicable.

The conditions set out in the Article are spelt out explicitly in Belgium (where all situations in which signatures validate the agreement are provided for[5]), in Germany and the Netherlands (where appropriate worker participation is required) and in Spain (where the legitimacy of signatories is checked).[6]

In addition, some Member States have introduced additional criteria to those laid down in Article 13 of the Directive for the validity of agreements in force. In Ireland, the agreement must have been accepted by the majority of the workforce to which it applies. In Austria, the protection of workers' representatives applies ex lege, also in the case of Article 13 agreements, and all bodies representing staff must be informed of the text of the agreement. In Denmark, the agreement must relate to information and consultation on matters concerning undertakings or establishments located in several Member States.

Certain Member States (A, B, D, FIN) allowed revision of agreements in force within the six months following 22 September 1996, with a view to making them compatible with the requirements of Article 13.

In Greece and Belgium, conditions governing the written form of agreements have been added to authorise their validation.

---

5. Signature by the trade unions that have signed the collective agreement and are represented in the group, by the majority of workforce delegates in the country concerned, by the majority of employees, by a European organisation acting on behalf of the undertaking's trade union organisations. This presumption of validity for certain types of signatory also exists in Germany, France and Italy.

6. Provision for checking the legitimacy of signatories is also made in Finland and the Netherlands.

Ireland, Austria, France, Germany, Belgium, Spain and the Netherlands provide for the possibility of renewing these agreements. The provisions differ, depending on whether or not agreements were concluded for a specific period.

Finally, some Member States provide for incorporating changes in the structure of the group into the system established through earlier agreements (NL after five years).

3.7. Experts

All countries have provisions authorising the SNB and the European works council to consult experts. Most countries stipulate that recourse to experts must be essential (EL, DK, FIN, S) and/or that the associated costs may be charged to the central management in respect of one expert only (A, D, B, EL, F, IRL, NL, P).

Netherlands law specifies that this means one expert per agenda item. The right to consult several experts, even if the central management must pay for only one of them, means that SNBs and EWCs can draw on the assistance of trade union representatives belonging to national or European confederations, while at the same time seeking the help of a "technical" expert.

In agreements concluded pursuant to Article 6, the consultation of experts and rules on the covering of costs are clearly matters for negotiation.

3.8. Other operating rules

3.8.1. Material and financial resources

All countries stipulate that the central management shall bear the operating expenses of the transnational representation bodies.

As regards the SNB, it is generally specified that these expenses include the material and financial resources it needs to perform its task (DK, FIN, P, A). Even if this is not spelt out, it is clear that the expenses to be borne by the central management are those essential to the functioning of the SNB.

Sometimes, these are set out in detail (I, IRL, P, A): meetings, equipment, travel, translation, accommodation, experts' costs. In Sweden and Spain, the costs of appointing the SNB members are also mentioned.

As regards EWCs set up under the subsidiary requirements, the same general formula applies: the central management has to cover essential operating expenses. These are almost always specified: travel, translation, organisation of meetings, accommodation, equipment (without details as regards fax machines, telephones or computers). In Germany, the central management has to provide premises.

All countries anticipate disputes as to whether costs incurred by the EWC are necessary and/or reasonable. The national courts carry out an assessment based on the objective utility of operating expenses in the context of transnational representation.

3.8.2. Resources given to the representatives

In all countries, representatives are entitled to paid absence to perform their duties. However, the number of hours granted varies tremendously: 20 hours a month in France, eight hours every four months in Italy, two hours a week in Greece, 60 hours a year in Spain, necessary absence in Austria, reasonable absence in Ireland, a non-specified general entitlement in the Netherlands, and absence agreed between the employer and the representative employees' organisation in Sweden.

3.9. Confidentiality

3.9.1. General confidentiality requirement

With the exception of Belgium, where the confidentiality requirement is contained only in a text accompanying the transposition act, all countries' transposition texts impose confidentiality requirements on SNB and EWC representatives and experts.

The requirement is a general and continuous one, generally of unlimited duration, but sometimes limited in time (end of all terms of office in Ireland, three years in Italy).

Naturally the confidentiality requirement covers representatives' and experts' relations with third parties, but in Sweden and Austria the it does not bind representatives inter se, so as to avoid disputes concerning the circulation of information within the EWC.

3.9.2. Right to withhold confidential information

The central management's right to withhold information it deems to be confidential (Article 8) has been enshrined in Denmark, Sweden, Italy, Greece, Ireland, Spain, the Netherlands and Portugal. France and Austria have not made use of this possibility, and Germany has not used it for the SNB.

The confidential nature of information must be assessed on the basis of objective criteria. Besides standard legal procedures, specific procedures are sometimes provided for in Greece, Belgium and Portugal, while Finland makes provision for arbitration.

3.9.3. Penalties for infringement of the confidentiality requirement

All countries provide for penalties, but their nature differs from one country to another. Sometimes civil penalties are stipulated (F, P), but as a rule sanctions are of a penal nature: Ireland ("offence"), Germany, Finland, France ("manufacturing secrets").

Spain and Greece do not make specific provision for penalties. In Denmark, penalties are set out in a separate text (not in the transposition text).

Several countries have specific (often emergency) procedures for disputes relating to infringement of manufacturing secrets (notably France, Germany and Belgium).

3.10. Protection of workers' representatives

Protection is provided in all countries for workers exercising representative functions. The principle of equal treatment is expressly reiterated in certain countries (D, EL, IRL) as a fundamental guarantee of performance of the functions in question.

In each country, protection is organised in line with the rules governing worker representation.

Sometimes, this protection results from a collective agreement (DK), but as a rule the transposition text contains a reference to the country's general rules governing representatives (shop stewards or trade union representatives) (B, E, F, I, NL, S, A, P).

Representatives may be dismissed only on serious grounds not related to the activity, or for serious misconduct (FIN, F). Grounds which the employer may not invoke are specified in Finland (illness, strike, religious opinions, etc.).

Specific procedures concerning prior authorisation of dismissal exist in France, Germany and Finland.

3.11. Penalties

All countries prescribe penalties in the event of infringement of the Directive's requirements, as regards both the obligation to set up a special negotiating body (SNB) and obligations concerning the operation of the transnational representation body.

There are various systems: penalties for infringement of collective agreements (DK, S), or general procedures under employment law.

Some countries impose penalties in the form of various types of fine ("compensatory fine" in DK, "conditional fine" in FIN) or, more broadly, penal sanctions which in some cases allow the court to impose a range of penalties: IRL ("offence"), EL, E ("administrative offence"), B ("administrative fines"), A and D ("administrative offence"), F ("obstructionism"), P ("quasi-offence").

Not all countries specify how these penalties are to be applied in the case of infringement of obligations entered into under an earlier agreement, and so it may be assumed that they also apply in this case, except in Denmark and Sweden, where agreements already in force are not covered by the system of penalties.

As a rule, penalties are imposed by the general courts. In Greece it is the prefectoral administration that is responsible, and fines are paid into a workers' welfare fund.

3.12. Remedies

Jurisdiction in all countries lies with the courts that adjudicate on disputes concerning worker representation.

These are usually (A, B, D, E, EL, F, I, S, NL, P) the employment tribunals for individual disputes and/or the general courts (DK, FIN, F for collective disputes), or courts dealing with company law (NL).

In Ireland, arbitration is the rule. This should be emphasised in the light of the transnational nature of disputes (appeals possible only if questions of law are involved).

Finally, some countries have particular rules. In Finland, the Ministry of Employment has a supervisory role, while in Italy the interconfederal agreement provides for the creation of a special committee to deal with questions connected with the transnational body.

ANNEX

References of measures transposing Directive 94/45/EC on European works councils

– Council Directive 94/45/EC of 22 September 1994 on the establishment of a European Works Council or a procedure in Community-scale undertakings and Community-scale groups of undertakings for the purposes of informing and consulting employees – Published: Official Journal of the European Communities; 30.9.1994; L 254/64

– Council Directive 97/74/EC of 15 December 1997 extending, to the United Kingdom of Great Britain and Northern Ireland, Directive 94/45/EC on the establishment of a European Works Council or a procedure in Community-scale undertakings and Community-scale groups of under-takings for the purposes of informing and consulting employees – Published: Official Journal of the European Communities; 16.1.1998; L 10/23

Belgium

– Arrêté royal du 22.03.1996 rendant obligatoire la convention collective de travail n° 62, conclue le 6 février 1996 au sein du Conseil national du Travail, concernant l'institution d'un comité d'entreprise européen ou d'une procédure dans les entreprises de dimension communautaire et les groupes d'entreprises de dimension communautaire en vue d'informer et de consulter les travailleurs. Published: Moniteur Belge, 11.04.1996, p. 8465.

- Arrêté royal du 27.11.1998 rendant obligatoire la convention collective de travail n° 62bis du 6 octobre 1998 modifiant la convention collective de travail n° 62 du 6 février 1996, conclue au sein du Conseil national du Travail, concernant l'institution d'un comité d'entreprise européen ou d'une procédure dans les entreprises de dimension communautaire et les groupes d'entreprises de dimension communautaire en vue d'informer et de consulter les travailleurs. Published: Moniteur Belge, 16.12.1998, p. 935.
- Arrêté royal portant exécution de l'article 8 de la loi du 23 avril 1998 portant des mesures d'accompagnement en ce qui concerne l'institution d'un comité d'entreprise européen ou d'une procédure dans les entreprises de dimension communautaire et les groupes d'entreprises de dimension communautaire en vue d'informer et de consulter les travailleurs. Published: Moniteur Belge, 17.10.1998, p. 1252.
— Loi du 23 avril 1998 portant des mesures d'accompagnement en ce qui concerne l'institution d'un comité d'entreprise européen ou d'une procédure dans les entreprises de dimension communautaire et les groupes d'entreprises de dimension communautaire en vue d'informer et de consulter les travailleurs – Published: Moniteur Belge, 21.05.1998, p. 2192.
— Loi du 23 avril 1998 portant des dispositions diverses en ce qui concerne l'institution d'un comité d'entreprise européen ou d'une procédure dans les entreprises de dimension communautaire et les groupes d'entreprises de dimension communautaire en vue d'informer et de consulter les travailleurs – Published: Moniteur Belge, 21.05.1998, p. 2192.

Denmark
Lov N. 371 af 22.05.1996 om europaeiske samarbejdsudvalg – Published: Ministerialtidende, j. nr. 1996-534-8

Germany
Gesetz über Europäische Betriebsräte (EBRG) vom 28.10.1996 – Published: Bundesgesetzblatt Teil I, 31.10.1996, S. 1548

Greece
Presidential Decree n° 40/97; 18.3.1997 – Published: FEK A n° 39; 20.3.1997; p. 599

Spain
Ley 10/1997, de 24 de abril, sobre derechos de información y consulta de los trabajadores en las empresas y grupos de empresas de dimensión comunitaria N 10/97; 24.4.1997 – Published: Boletín oficial del Estado N 99; 25.4.1997; p. 13258

France
Loi N. 96–985 du 12.11.1996 relative à l'information et à la consultation des salariés dans les entreprises et les groupes d'entreprises de dimension

communautaire, ainsi qu'au développement de la négociation collective – Published: Journal Officiel de la République Française; 13.11.1996; p. 16527

Intégration au Code du Travail sous les articles L 439–1 modifié, L 439–6 à L 439–24, L 483-1-2

Ireland

Transnational Information and Consultation of Employees Act of 1996; Transnational Information and Consultation of Employees Act of 1996 (Commencement) Order of 1996; 3.7.1996 – Published: Statutory Instruments n° 20 of 1996; Statutory Instruments n° 276 of 1996

Italy

Accordo Interconfederale per il Recepimento della direttiva 94/45 CE del 22.9.1994; 06.11.1996

Netherlands

Wet van 23.1.1997 op de Europese ondernemingsraden tot uitvoering van richtlijn nr. 94/45/EG – Published: Staatsblad 1997/32 pp 1–15; 4.2.1997

Portugal

Lei n° 40/99 de 9 de Junho que assegura a informação e consulta dos trabalhadores em empresas ou grupos de empresas transnacionais e regula a instituição de conselhos de empresa europeus ou de procedimentos simplificados de informação e consulta em empresas e grupos de empresas de dimensão comunitária. DR n° 133, 9.6.1999, p. 3237 et seq. Entry into force: 9.7.1999.

Austria

Bundesgesetz vom 17. Oktober 1996, mit dem das Arbeitsverfassungsgesetz, das Arbeits- und Sozialgerichtsgesetzes und das Bundesgesetz über die Post-Betriebsverfassung geändert werden – Published: Bundesgesetzblatt für die Republik Österreich Nr. 601/96, 31.10.1996

Finland

Laki yhteistoiminnasta yrityksissä annetun lain muuttamisesta 614/96; 9.8.1996

Sweden

Lag (1996:359) om europeiska företagsråd; utfärdad den 9 maj 1996

Luxembourg

Transposition delayed

II.   EUROPEAN PARLIAMENT

A.   *REPORT on the Commission report on the application of the Directive on the establishment of a European works council or a procedure in Community-scale undertakings and Community-scale groups of undertakings for the purposes of informing and consulting employees (Council Directive 94/45/EC of 22 September 1994) (17 July 2001)*

PROCEDURAL PAGE

By letter of 4 April 2000, the Commission forwarded to Parliament its report on the application of the Directive on the establishment of a European works council or a procedure in Community-scale undertakings and Community-scale groups of undertakings for the purposes of informing and consulting employees (Council Directive 94/45/EC of 22 September 1994) (COM(2000) 188 – 2000/2214(COS)).

At the sitting of 8 September 2000 the President of Parliament announced that she had referred the report to the Committee on Employment and Social Affairs as the committee responsible and the Committee on Legal Affairs and the Internal Market and the Committee on Industry, External Trade, Research and Energy and for their opinions (C5-0437/2000).

The Committee on Employment and Social Affairs had appointed Winfried Menrad rapporteur at its meeting of 12 April 2000.

The committee considered the Commission report and the draft report at its meetings of 4 December 2000, 25 April, 29 May, 21 June and 10 July 2001.

At the last meeting it adopted the motion for a resolution unanimously.

The opinions of the Committee on Legal Affairs and the Internal Market and the Committee on Industry, External Trade, Research and Energy are attached.

The report was tabled on 17 July 2001.

The deadline for tabling amendments will be indicated in the draft agenda for the relevant part-session.

MOTION FOR A RESOLUTION

European Parliament resolution on the Commission report on the application of the Directive on the establishment of a European works council or a procedure in Community-scale undertakings and Community-scale groups of undertakings for the purposes of informing and consulting employees (Council Directive 94/45/EC of 22 September 1994)

The European Parliament,

– having regard to the Commission report (COM(2000) 188 – C5-0437/ 2000),[7]
– having regard to Council Directive 94/45/EC of 22 September 1994 on European works councils,[8]
– having regard to Council Directive 98/59/EC of 20 July 1998 on collective redundancies[9] (consolidated versions of Directives 75/129/EEC and 92/56/ EEC) and Council Directive 2001/23/EC of 12 March 2001 on the approximation of the laws of the Member States relating to the safeguarding of employees' rights in the event of transfers of undertakings, businesses or parts of undertakings or businesses[10] (consolidated version of Directive 77/187/EEC as amended),
– having regard to the Davignon report of the Group of Experts on "European Systems of Worker Involvement" (C4-0455/1997) and its Resolution of 19 November 1997 thereon,[11]
– having regard to the proposal for a Council directive establishing a general framework for informing and consulting employees in the European Community (COM(1998)612 – C4-0706/1998 – 1998/0315(SYN) and its opinion of 14 April 1999 thereon,[12]
– having regard to the proposals for a Council regulation on the Statute for a European Company (C5-0092/2001)[13] and a Council directive supplementing the Statute for a European Company with regard to the involvement of employees (C5-0093/2001),[14]
– having regard to the publication of the Commission report, as a contribution to the continuing debate as to how effective Directive 94/45/ EC on the establishment of procedures for informing and consulting employees in undertakings operating in more than one Member State is, but whereas it should be noted that the Commission report, despite a brief assessment of the implementing legislation and of the application of the Directive in practice, is essentially limited to a description of the national implementing measures,
– having regard to the findings of the public hearings held by the Committee on Employment and Social Affairs on 26 January 1999 and 25 April 2001 on the subject of European works councils,
– having regard to Rule 47(1) of its Rules of Procedure,
– having regard to the report of the Committee on Employment and Social Affairs and the opinions of the Committee on Legal Affairs and the Internal Market and the Committee on Industry, External Trade, Research and Energy (A5-0282/2001),

---

7.   Not yet published.
8.   *O.J.*, L 254, 30.9.1994.
9.   *O.J.*, L 225, 12.8.1998.
10.   *O.J.*, L 82, 22.3.2001.
11.   *O.J.*, C 371, 8.12.1997.
12.   *O.J.*, C 219, 30.7.1999.
13.   Not yet published.
14.   Not yet published.

(a) whereas the main goal of the Directive is to lift obstacles to information, consultation and communication with the workforce in companies operating in more than one Member State in order to facilitate social dialogue in these companies,

(b) whereas the transposition of the Directive into national law within the time limits laid down was generally successfully achieved,

(c) whereas the immediate impact of the Directive can be seen in the sheer numbers of European works councils formed since the adoption of the Directive in 1994, amounting to some 650 under either Article 6 or Article 13 agreements,

(d) whereas, however, as many as 1800 companies across the EU meet the criteria and thresholds above which a European works council should be established according to the terms of the Directive, and whereas the level of cover is therefore unsatisfactory, which may encourage further initiatives,

(e) whereas various cases of restructuring and collective redundancy have highlighted gaps in European legislation on workers' rights to information and consultation, particularly with regard to timeliness and possible sanctions in the event of non-compliance,

(f) whereas there is a need to balance the competitive needs of companies in an ever-changing market with the rights of employees to information and consultation which can in particular be achieved through collective agreements with management, in particular at times of industrial change,

(g) whereas, therefore, it is vital to create a culture of partnership between employers and employees in all Member States where companies are based, so that the spirit of cooperation called for by the directive will also be put into practice in relations with local workers' representatives,

(h) whereas it is difficult to create such a culture if a European works council meets only once a year, as is the fact in 85% of cases,

(i) whereas the interests and concerns of employees can only be taken into account at a time of restructuring if the information and consultation is in good time and adequate; whereas there has been a number of highly-publicised cases in recent months where this was not the case, and workers learnt of major restructuring in their company through the press and/or after decisions on restructuring were already taken; whereas employees must be able to exercise their rights to information and consultation at the appropriate stage of the process,

(j) whereas there is a close link between the revision of the Directive on the establishment of a European works council, the current proposals with regard to information and consultation at national level and the extension of the Statute of the European Company with regard to workers' participation; whereas, furthermore, in the interests of clarity and legal precision these three items of legislation should, in the medium term, include appropriate rules on information and consultation,

(k)   whereas trade unions can play a vital role both in support of European works councils and in transmitting information to the workforce as a whole from management via the works council; whereas the management right to communicate directly with the workforce remains unaffected, as does its right to manage the company,

(l)   whereas research has shown that women are seriously under-represented on European works councils, given that nine out of ten works council representatives are men,

(m)   whereas the Commission's report is a means of keeping the discussion moving on how effective the Directive has been in setting up information and consultation procedures in companies based in more than one Member State,

(n)   whereas the Directive takes account of the different forms of worker participation in companies which exist in Europe, thereby safeguarding the subsidiarity principle,

(o)   whereas an evaluation of the Directive has also revealed weaknesses which must be addressed if the Directive is to be effective in achieving its aims;

1.   Emphasises that social relations based on dialogue, genuine information and consultation of employees and their representatives will benefit collective negotiations and reduce the risk of conflict, and that it may also prove to be a factor for undertakings' success;

2.   Reiterates its call on the Commission to submit a proposal for the revision of Directive 94/45/EC at an early date and to include in that proposal the following improvements:

i.   a precise definition of information and consultation of employees as being the implementation of an exchange of views and dialogue between employee representatives and the employer, pursuant to document COM(1998) 612,[15] so as to ensure that such information and consultation takes place in good time and at regular intervals before the decision by the company or group management, so as to allow the employees genuinely to influence the management's decision-making process; decisions of central management or any other management level shall be valid only if information and consultation are properly carried out, with due regard for the principles of confidentiality of the information;

ii.   an enhanced obligation to convene special meetings of the European works council in good time in order to convey information to employees on company proposals regarding restructuring and decisions having implications for the continued existence and future of the company and its various sites and subsidiaries, with a view to allowing employees and their representatives time to study the information provided by management, to present their point of view and put forward alternative proposals to those of management in the form of opinions;

---

15.   Proposal for a Council directive establishing a general framework for informing and consulting employees in the European Community.

iii. the introduction of an enhanced consultation procedure, within the meaning of Directives 75/129/EEC and 98/59/EC[16] with a view to reaching agreement on certain issues which particularly affect employees (in particular collective redundancies and transfers of companies and transfer of production);

iv. a reduction from three years to 18 months for the introduction of the minimum standards in the Annex to the Directive, should central management and the special negotiating body be unable to reach agreement;

v. a reduction in the thresholds for companies to be included within the scope of the Directive from 1000 to 500 employees for the company as a whole and from 150 to 100 employees per establishment in at least two Member States;

vi. clarification of the need for the works council to continue functioning during periods of company mergers;

vii. a new clause in the Directive allowing for adjustments in numbers of members of the European works council and the special negotiating body following major restructuring of the company so that these bodies properly reflect the proportions of employees working in the establishments after restructuring;

viii. discussions about more rights for trade unions, particularly as experts, within the remit of works councils and a more prominent role for national and/or European trade unions on European works councils and the special negotiating bodies themselves, in accordance with employees' wishes;

ix. more opportunities and proper resources for members of European works councils to be offered training, aiming in particular at awareness of accounting regulations and employment law in other countries and at improving language skills, and the provision of the necessary time off;

x. the strengthening of the provisions concerning the protection and rights of workers' representatives to enable them to have access to all establishments and firms and to fulfil their tasks and mandates without loss of pay, to inform workers and take advantage of additional training;

xi. specifying that members must have facilities at their disposal, e.g. meeting rooms with use of fax, phone and Internet between meetings so as to enable them to fulfil the tasks imposed upon them by the Directive;

xii. general extension of the matters covered by the information and consultation process with the European works council to include measures planned by the company and group management in connection with the situation as regards health, safety, job rotation, the environment, in-service training, lifelong learning, equal opportunities and financial participation by employees (e.g. share options);

xiii. adequate sanctions at national and European level for non-compliance with the Directive and the following measures to implement the law:

---

16. Council Directive of 17 February 1975 on the approximation of the laws of the Member States relating to collective redundancies.

1. The Member States shall introduce appropriate measures at national and European level for cases of failure by employers or employees' representatives to comply with this Directive; in particular, they shall ensure that there are administrative and legal procedures which can be used to bring about compliance with the obligations arising from the Directive, including procedures whereby employers or employees' representatives may seek legal remedy, either administratively or through the courts, if they consider that the other party is failing to fulfil its obligations.

2. Provision of a clause that decisions of the management will only be regarded as legitimate if an orderly information and consultation process as defined in the renewed Directive has taken place beforehand;

xiv. in cases in which the application of a decision may have major negative effects on workers, provisions to the effect that the adoption of the final decision may be suspended for an appropriate period at the request of the workers' representatives, in order to continue the negotiations to avoid or ameliorate the negative effects;

xv. greater clarification of the conditions for renewing agreements reached under Article 13 of the Directive;

xvi. the opportunity to terminate voluntary agreements (Article 13 of Directive 94/45/EC) which were concluded for an unspecified period and make no provision for cancellation of the agreements;

xvii. recommendations on the relative numbers of men and women serving on the special negotiating bodies and European works councils;

xviii. a recommendation that representatives of employees on works councils should be freely chosen by employees;

xix. a higher minimum number of preparatory and compulsory meetings per year;

xx. any revision of the Directive should result in mandatory, rather than merely optional, coverage of merchant navy crews;

xxi. as the Commission points out in the report, the Directive does not currently require agreements to contain an adjustment clause covering changes to the make-up of the undertaking; it should be revised to ensure that agreements actually do cover all the undertaking's or group's workers at all times;

3. Calls on the Commission to notify those Member States which have not yet taken steps to transpose the Directive;

4. Reminds the Commission of the need, pursuant to Article 127 of the Treaty, to ensure a coherent link between competition rules and Community social legislation; calls for clearance for mergers to be subject to proof of compliance with the obligation to inform and consult employees and European works councils;

5. Insists that no Structural Fund monies should be granted to companies which have breached major aspects of their obligations under the Directive, and/or that such companies should be required to repay these and any other Community funds or national aid given to such companies

for the promotion of regional development and employment, and that they should be excluded from public procurement and public subsidies;

6. Promotes the ideal of the creation of world-wide works councils where a company has employees in countries outside the EU and welcomes the initiatives already taken in certain companies to ensure equal access to information and consultation wherever the workforce is based;

7. Calls for the inclusion, in the context of discussions on future Treaty amendments, of the concept of worker participation (Mitwirkung) in addition to information and consultation under Article 137 of the Treaty, subject to the agreement of the social partners, and calls for only genuine codetermination to be subject to the unanimity rule;

8. Instructs its President to forward this resolution to the Council, the Commission and the social partners.

EXPLANATORY STATEMENT

1. Background to the Commission's report

Article 15 of the European works councils Directive states that: "Not later than 22 September 1999, the Commission shall ... review its operation and, in particular examine whether the workforce size thresholds are appropriate with a view to proposing suitable amendments to the Council, where necessary".

The rapporteur therefore welcomes the publication of the Commission's report as a means of keeping the discussion moving on how effective the Directive has been in setting up information and consultation procedures in companies based in more than one Member State.

That said, while the report does contain some evaluation of the implementing legislation and the practical application of the Directive, the bulk of the Commission's report is limited to a description of the national implementing measures.

In fact, discussion on the effective functioning of the Directive, and indeed on overall progress in information, consultation and participation of workers in companies, began much earlier:

- The rapporteur, who has been Parliament's rapporteur on the subject since the initial proposal for a Directive in 1994, has himself maintained contact with numerous experts and practitioners in the field;
- The Dublin Foundation for the Improvement of Working and Living Conditions has published a series of reports analysing the works councils that have been set up; the most recent study, published early in 2001, entitled "Negotiating European works councils", makes a comparison between Article 6 and Article 13 agreements;
- In April 1999, the Commission, in conjunction with the social partners, held a conference to assess the implementation of the Directive, and this formed the basis of the Commission's report;
- In January 1999, and again in April 2001, this committee held public hearings on the works councils Directive, with experts from both sides of industry as well as researchers in the field.

2. The context for this report

2.1. *Economic and social*: since the publication of the Commission's report in April 2000, the European labour market has been through a period of tremendous flux. A series of major companies operating in both new technology sectors such as telecommunications and banking, and more traditional industries such as food, steel, textiles and motor vehicles, have undergone major restructuring, often resulting in thousands of jobs being lost. In many cases, regrettably, the workforce in these companies learnt about the restructuring through the press rather than the works council, where these existed. This has made the current discussion on the effectiveness of the

European works council Directive all the more topical and of direct relevance to the daily lives of thousands of citizens working in companies based in more than one Member State.

2.2. *Legislation*: the legislative context has also shifted since the publication of the Commission's report. In December 2000, after 30 years of negotiations, agreement was reached in the Council of Ministers on proposals for the Statute for a European Company, and the involvement of workers in such a company. At the same time the rapporteur is hopeful of progress in Council on the proposal for a framework directive on information and consultation at national level.

3. The directive's successes

The rapporteur would like to underline some of the overall successes of the Directive:

3.1. The generally successful transposition of the Directive into national law, within the time limits laid down, i.e. by 22 September 1996.

3.2. The direct impact the Directive has had on the sheer numbers of works councils set up.

From fewer than 40 in 1994 at the time of the Directive's adoption, to about 650 today, some 400 of which were set up under the Directive's Article 13 (allowing the maintenance of voluntary agreements on transnational information and consultation, where these were established before 22 September 1996). However, experts at the committee's hearing in April 2001 pointed out that some 1800 companies across the Union come within the scope of the Directive.

3.3. Where European works councils are accompanied by a select committee, meeting more frequently than once or twice a year, it has been found that European works councils can contribute to the learning process of employee representatives and in particular to the development of a European consciousness among them.

Unfortunately, although this may be the case in many large companies, experts at the April 2001 hearing pointed out that as many as 85% of European works councils meet only once a year. Much work therefore remains to be done to fulfil the Directive's potential for creating a European culture of information and consultation.

3.4. In many companies the Directive has had immediate success in lifting obstacles to information, consultation and communication with the workforce. Successful case studies were brought to the attention of Members at the April 2001 hearing (in particular Daimler-Chrysler and Air France). However, this has to be seen in conjunction with some of the weaknesses of the Directive in other cases, of which more will be revealed below.

The rapporteur would, in this context, highlight the wording of paragraph 5 of the Annex to the Directive which lays down that: "Without prejudice to Article 8 of the Directive, the members of the European works council shall inform the representatives of the employees ... or, in the absence of representatives, *the workforce as a whole* (rapporteur's italics), of the content and outcome of the information and consultation procedure carried out in accordance with this Annex".

The rapporteur would wish to consider the merits of bringing the right to information for all the workforce into the body of the Directive rather than leaving it in the Annex (which only applies where there is no agreement between management and the special negotiating body). The principle of information reaching all members of the workforce is vital. Experts at the April hearing suggested, however, that some problems were being encountered in ensuring that information reaches every factory within a group of undertakings. Trade unions have been found to be vital in this process (see below).

3.5. The existence of a European works council means that the interests and concerns of employees are more likely to be taken into account at a time of restructuring of the undertaking or group concerned.

Research has shown that many companies have now recognised that early involvement of the European works council in any decision-making process can reduce the potential for conflict and increase the likelihood of employee acceptance of the decisions taken. There has been a number of examples of successes in this respect in the fields of health and safety at work, equal opportunities, and one outstanding example in the automobile industry, at Ford: when Ford moved to contract out one of its supply sections and effectively release from Ford's employment the workers concerned, the European works council reached an agreement whereby those workers would retain the protection and rights they had enjoyed under Ford's employment.

The rapporteur would also make the following specific comments on the Directive and its positive impact:

3.6. The very fact of having collective agreements between the central management and the employees' special negotiating body on setting up a works council has strengthened the negotiating autonomy of the social partners.

3.7. The wording of the Directive is sufficiently flexible to encompass the various models for workers' participation in companies which exist in Europe. Subsidiarity has therefore been respected in this Directive. As the Commission's report itself points out: "up to now the Directive has been smoothly integrated into the industrial relations systems of the different countries, thanks to the Member States' freedom as regards the choice of representation mechanisms". The Commission also observes that the national provisions brought in to implement the Directive meet the standards laid down in the Annex.

3.8. Without ignoring the many companies coming within the scope of the Directive which have not yet established a works council, there appears to have been a successful negotiation of either an Article 6 or an Article 13 agreement in every undertaking where this has been attempted, so formal recourse to the formal minimum standards in the Annex has been had only in very rare and exceptional cases.

4. The Directive's weaknesses

The Commission itself acknowledges that there is a need for "further interpretation of some issues", and lists these without entering into detail. The various hearings on the implementation of the Directive have also thrown up a number of weaknesses in the Directive, many of which would no doubt have been avoided if the Parliament's proposals on the original draft Directive had been taken on board by the Council.

4.1. The first weakness, which has recently been the focus of public interest, concerns the timing of information and consultation when there are "exceptional circumstances affecting the employees' interests to a considerable extent, particularly *in the event of relocations, the closure of establishments or undertakings or collective redundancies...* " (rapporteur's italics) (paragraph 3 of the Annex).

In 1994 Parliament had tabled an amendment at first reading providing for such information and consultation "in good time before the decision of the undertaking".

Sadly, the final text of the Directive refers only to the fact that in the case of emergency consultation a meeting with the select committee or the full works council should take place "as soon as possible" in such circumstances. This text appears only in a recital and in the Annex.

In many recent cases such meetings have not been taking place in good time, and there is a definite need to re-examine the provisions on this in the near future. The hearing in April 2001 heard of two cases (Alstom-ABB, Corus) where workers had been informed via the press or presented with a final decision by management. But these are by no means isolated cases; indeed, the most recent example from Marks & Spencer has led to court action at Member State level on the grounds that employees were not given adequate information prior to decisions being taken. In a discussion with the rapporteur the company's representatives presented the situation differently.

It is clear that adequate information is needed in good time in order that workers' representatives have the opportunity to offer alternatives to a company's restructuring plans with a view to diminishing, for example, any job losses. The rapporteur believes that a definition of "adequate information" and "consultation" might be needed in any revised Directive in order to avoid the unacceptable events we have seen in recent months. In this connection the rapporteur points to the improved definition in the framework Directive on information and consultation. Moreover, if there are special circumstances, and particularly if restructuring is envisaged, an enhanced consultation procedure should be provided for.

4.2. The second weakness concerns the period of three years laid down in Article 7(1) before the minimum standards in the Annex come into effect. In 1994, Parliament had considered that three years was too long a period to wait if central management and the special negotiating body were unable to conclude an agreement, and Parliament's amendment at the time suggested an 18-month period, after which the provisions of the Annex would come into force. The rapporteur believes that consideration should be given again to reducing the three-year period. Most experts at the April 2001 hearing concurred with this view.

4.3. Article 2 of the Directive lays down the size of undertaking to which the Directive applies, and this is precisely the area mentioned in Article 15 (see above, point 2) which should be re-examined. The rapporteur recalls that the following positions were taken up in 1994:

Parliament: Undertakings with at least 500 employees in the Member States, and at least 100 in each of at least two Member States;

Commission: Undertakings with 1000 employees, and at least 100 in two Member States;

Council: Undertakings with 1000 employees, and at least 150 in two Member States.

We all know, of course, that the Council's view prevailed, but we also know that these figures are to a large extent arbitrary. The rapporteur suggests that the most reasonable threshold to apply is that proposed by Parliament in 1994.

5.   Other areas for possible amendments to the Directive

The rapporteur would like to draw attention to the following issues, which he believes should be given consideration in any future amendment of the Directive.

5.1. It was revealed at the April 2001 hearing that nine out of ten representatives on the special negotiating bodies and on European works councils are men. The rapporteur calls for balanced representation of men and women.

5.2. Article 5(2)(c) should also provide for a more prominent role for trade unions in the establishment of European works councils, and a model for this might be Austria, where trade union representatives can be members of the special negotiating body even if they are not employees of the undertaking concerned but are members of one of its bodies representing employees. The whole relationship between European works councils and trade unions needs to be addressed. While trade union rights had not been raised in 62% of works councils, according to figures produced by the experts at the April 2001 hearing, it remains an issue for a substantial number of employee representatives.

5.3. Consideration should be given to a clause in the Directive which would allow for an adjustment in the numbers of members of both the European works council and the special negotiating body where there is a major restructuring of a company, so that the composition of both bodies properly reflects the proportion of employees working in the establishments after restructuring.

5.4. Several experts at the April 2001 hearing raised problems relating to mergers and joint ventures. A revised Directive needs to make it quite clear what is the status of a works council and its members in the case of a joint venture where there is no dominant company. Moreover, there appears to be an anomaly whereby when two merging companies are dissolved prior to merger, there is no legal entity and therefore no official status for participation of employees. This means that at the very stage of the restructuring process when worker information and consultation is most important, no works council can legally exist under the current provisions.

5.5. Investment in training of employee representatives is vital if works councils are to function effectively. Language difficulties have long been known about in terms of the practical application of the Directive. For this reason, the rapporteur would like to see specific mention of the possibility of language training for members of the works councils and the special negotiating bodies, as this will in the long term improve communication with the whole workforce of the undertaking. More importantly, however, research unveiled at the April 2001 hearing showed that training is more urgently needed in accounting regulations, employment law and industrial relations systems applied in other Member States.

5.6. Article 11 of the Directive deals with compliance. The wording is weak, however, as paragraph 3 states merely that "Member States shall provide for *appropriate measures* (rapporteur's italics) in the event of failure to comply with this Directive". The rapporteur wishes to see the introduction of appropriate sanctions for non-compliance in Article 11. He also wishes to see the introduction of an obligation on companies proposing to merge to prove that they have complied with this Directive before the merger is authorised by the Commission. He would further like to see a requirement for the repayment, in certain circumstances, of any Structural Fund monies or national aid given to companies for the promotion of regional development and/or employment, should they not have respected their obligations under the Directive.

5.7. The rapporteur believes that Article 6 is not explicit enough about what areas can be discussed in the works councils, and he would suggest that measures planned by company or group management relating to training, equal opportunities, health and safety, and possible employees' financial participation in the undertaking (e.g. share options) should also form part of the information and consultation process. It is necessary to examine in this connection whether, in addition to the binding provisions laid down in Article 6(2), directive provisions might also be incorporated into this provision or whether, if appropriate, the "general competence" pursuant to (2) of the subsidiary requirements ought to be extended accordingly.

Owing to the requirement for brevity the rapporteur is unable to address every aspect. Where other major issues are concerned, such as the numerical composition of bodies, confirmation of the agreements concluded before the Directive came into force, the extent of protection of employees' representatives and the involvement of experts, he therefore refers readers to his working document (PE 300.488/rev.).

6. Link between the different proposals on information and consultation

There is a clear link between the three sets of possible legislation at Community level:
- The possible amendment to the European works council Directive;
- The general framework Directive on information and consultation at national level (awaiting Council Common Position)
- The Directive on workers' involvement in the European Company Statute (Council agreement December 2000, and referral to Parliament March 2001).

The rapporteur believes the time is right to proceed with an immediate revision of the European works council Directive. Following consultation with the social partners, and taking into account the various evaluations of the Directive already undertaken by the Dublin Foundation and other academic sources, he wishes to see a new proposal for a revision of Directive 94/95/EC put forward as soon as possible, following consultation of the social partners in 2001.

The rapporteur recognises that all three proposals above are intrinsically linked. Indeed, in the medium term he would like to see information and consultation provisions being analogous in all documents, and, specifically, in line with the 1997 proposals from the Luxembourg Presidency and the Davignon Report (which, as we know, was supported at the time by both UNICE and the ETUC).

These proposals are also contained in the proposal for a Council Directive complementing the Statute for a European Company, with regard to the participation of employees in the European Company. Political agreement was reached on that proposal at the Nice Conference in December 2000.

The rapporteur believes in particular that the (transnational) body representing employees provided for in the case of the European Company, as a special European works council for that form of company, should be used in the medium term as the model for the amendment of the Directive on the establishment of a European works council (especially in view of Part 2 (c) of the catch-all provisions).

In the longer term, a common formulation of all the rules on information, consultation and participation might even result in the Directive on collective redundancies and the Directive on the safeguarding of employees' rights in the event of transfers of undertakings or businesses being extended beyond the national provisions to cover the transnational aspects of the Directive on a European works council.

The rapporteur believes that if appropriate the post-Nice discussions should examine whether the rules laid down in Article 137 of the Treaty of Amsterdam ought perhaps to be amended as follows: information, consultation and participation (*coopération; Mitwirkung*) should be subject to the principle of majority voting in the Council of Ministers and to Parliament's right of assent. Only real economic codetermination within the board of directors or supervisory board of a company limited by shares should still be subject to the unanimity rule, in other words parity codetermination such as exists in the German coal, iron and steel industry could only be decided unanimously within the Council, as before.

The rapporteur takes the view that it would be appropriate to seek such an amendment of the EU Treaty (information, consultation, participation – codetermination) only in agreement with the social partners.

7. The future is global

With the increasing globalisation of the economy, and the presence of major European-based companies in many countries outside the Union, thought must be given in the long term to the provision of information and consultation with workers at all levels of companies throughout the world. The expert from Daimler-Chrysler at the April 2001 hearing suggested that this process had already begun in his company and this is bound to be an issue in other companies as the trend towards globalisation continues.

B. OPINION OF THE COMMITTEE ON LEGAL AFFAIRS AND THE INTERNAL MARKET FOR THE COMMITTEE ON EMPLOYMENT AND SOCIAL AFFAIRS

on the Report from the Commission to the European Parliament and the Council on the application of the Directive on the establishment of a European works council or a procedure in Community-scale undertakings and Community-scale groups of undertakings for the purposes of informing and consulting employees (Council Directive 94/45/EC of 22 September 1994) (29 May 2001).

PROCEDURE

The Committee on Legal Affairs and the Internal Market appointed Gary Titley draftsman at its meeting of 22 November 2000.

It considered the draft opinion at its meetings of 23 April 2001 and 29 May 2001.

At the latter meeting it adopted the following conclusions unanimously.

SHORT JUSTIFICATION

Background

Council Directive 94/45/EC of 22 September 1994[17] constituted the first application of Article 2(2) of the Social Agreement (now repealed and replaced by Articles 136–143 of the EC Treaty as a result of the Amsterdam Treaty). The United Kingdom did not sign up to the Social Agreement and so the directive did not apply to it. However, following the Amsterdam Treaty, Directive 97/74[18] extended the directive to that country and your draftsman is pleased to report that it has now been implemented by Regulations in the UK and Northern Ireland.[19]

This aspect of the implementation of the directive falls outside the scope of the Commission's report, which covers only the period to 22 September 1996.

Although the directive was generally transposed satisfactorily (by law or regulation, after consultation of the social partners, or, as in the case of Belgium, by collective agreement), proceedings had to be brought against Luxembourg[20] and a case has been brought against Italy for failing fully to implement the legislation. Portugal did not incorporate the directive into national law until 1999.

---

17.   L 254, 1994.
18.   *O.J.*, L 10, 1998.
19.   The Transnational Information and Consultation of Employees Regulations 1999, SI 1999 No 3323.
20.   Culminating in the judgment in Case C-430/98 Commission v. Luxembourg [1999] *ECR* I-7391.

The directive's aim is to improve workers' rights to be informed and consulted in multinational groups or companies operating in Europe. The "Community-scale undertakings" to which it applies have to employ at least 1000 workers across the Member States and have at least 150 workers employed in at least two Member States. The trade unions estimate that over 1100 multinationals employing some 15 million workers are affected.

The directive's approach is a voluntary one. Under Article 13, companies which had concluded voluntary agreements for the transnational information and consultation of their entire workforce before 22 September 1996 were exempt. With the directive in force, it is only if negotiations to conclude voluntary agreements via the Special Negotiating Body (SNB) are refused or fail that the directive's requirements on the composition, role and function of what might be termed the basic standard European Works Council (EWC) apply.

This allows the various national models for worker participation to continue in being, in accordance with the principle of subsidiarity.

Apart from promoting European solidarity and allowing ready discussion on working conditions and terms of employment across frontiers, the directive improves the flow of information to the workforce as a whole and worker consultation (see point 5 of the Annex[21]).

Recent research has shown that positive outcomes of the Community legislation include the ability of employee representatives to influence decisions (for instance, in the field of health and safety) and the possibility of better dialogue, both between the social partners and between employees in different countries. Works council members also felt that they had some influence on issues concerning the reorganisation of production and locations. However, although some enlightened companies are now realising that timely involvement of the EWC can be helpful in the event of restructuring (relocation of production, outsourcing, etc), EWCs are not invariably consulted on strategic issues and the annual meeting with central management does not fully satisfy the need for timely information and debate. There is reason to consider that the duty to consult and inform workers could usefully be stepped up. It is worth noting that in various cases prior to the adoption of the directive (e.g. Case T-96/92 Comité Central d'Entreprise de la Société Générale des Grandes Sources and Others v. Commission [1995] ECR II-1213) the Court of Justice held that works councils were parties concerned for the purposes of merger control proceedings, even though they were not to be regarded as individually concerned for that purpose, and this presupposes a duty to inform and consult on the part of the employer.

A further problem to which the Commission report adverts is the vagueness of the requirement for an information and consultation meeting to

---

21.   "Without prejudice to Article 8, the members of the European Works Council shall inform the representatives of the employees of the establishments or of the undertakings of a Community-scale group of undertakings or, in the absence of representatives the workforce as a whole, of the content and outcome of the information and consultation procedure carried out in accordance with the Annex."

be held with management "as soon as possible" in the event of exceptional circumstances affecting employees, particularly in the event of relocations, the closure of establishments or undertakings or collective redundancies (Annex, point 3). It is essential, in the interest of the objectives of the directive, legal certainty and the impact of such exceptional circumstances on workers' lives and local communities, to tighten up this requirement. It should be borne in mind that Article 27 of the Charter of Fundamental Rights provides that "Workers or their representatives must ... be guaranteed information and consultation in good time ... "

Lastly, your draftsman would draw attention to two areas in which wide discrepancies appear to exist between the different countries, namely the ways in which part-time employees are taken into account and the number of hours which employee representatives can take off work for works council activities. Greater convergence should be secured in any future revision of the directive.

CONCLUSIONS

The Committee on Legal Affairs and the Internal Market calls on the Committee on Employment and Social Affairs, as the committee responsible, to incorporate the following points in its motion for a resolution:

1. Commends the Commission on its detailed and timely report and trusts that the findings made therein and as a result of thorough consultations with interested parties will result, not only in proposals for revision of Directive 94/45, but also for co-ordination of the various provisions on information and consultation contained therein, in the general framework directive on information and consultation at national level and in the proposed directive on workers' involvement in the European Company Statute;

2. Calls on the Commission to make proposals for reinforcing and extending the scope of the duty to consult and inform the European Works Council on strategic issues, particularly in the event of restructuring operations;

3. Believes, especially in the light of Article 27 of the Charter of Fundamental Rights, that the European Works Council must be consulted in good time in the event of exceptional circumstances affecting employees, particularly in the event of relocations, the closure of establishments or undertakings or collective redundancies;

4. Suggests that the Commission come forward with a programme for promoting the training and exchanges of members of European Works Councils (language learning, training in negotiation skills and in the rudiments of company, employment and competition law), not only with a view to facilitating their tasks, but also with an eye to promoting European solidarity and understanding;

5. Considers that any revision of the directive should result in mandatory, rather than merely optional, coverage of merchant navy crews;

6. Takes the view that, in considering a revision of the directive, the Commission should consider adopting guidelines for penalties for infringement;

7. Expresses the hope that the process of revision of the directive will lead to a greater convergence in the approach adopted in the Member States and countries of the European Economic Area towards part-time workers and arrangements for time-off for employee representatives.

C. OPINION OF THE COMMITTEE ON INDUSTRY, EXTERNAL TRADE, RESEARCH AND ENERGY FOR THE COMMITTEE ON EMPLOYMENT AND SOCIAL AFFAIRS

on the report from the Commission to the European Parliament and the Council on the application of the Directive on the establishment of a European works council or a procedure in Community-scale undertakings and Community-scale groups of undertakings for the purposes of informing and consulting employees (Council Directive 94/45/EC of 22 September 1994) (30 May 2001)

PROCEDURE

The Committee on Industry, External Trade, Research and Energy appointed Harlem Désir draftsman at its meeting of 22 June 2000.

It considered the draft opinion at its meetings of 27 March, 25 April and 29 May 2001.

At the last meeting it adopted the following conclusions by 25 votes to 0, with 19 abstentions.

SHORT JUSTIFICATION

Council Directive 94/45/EC of 22 September 1994 laid down that: "Not later than 22 September 1999, the Commission shall, in consultation with the Member States and with management and labour at European level, review its operation". It is on the basis of that review and of a conference held in April 1999 with the social partners that the Commission delivered its report to Parliament and the Council on 4 April 2000.

The Commission emphasises that most of the Member States have transposed the Directive more or less within the two-year deadline, although some countries were quite late in doing so.

The report notes that the Directive has led to the establishment of European Works Councils (EWC) in some 600 Community-scale undertakings and groups of undertakings, i.e. in more than one-third of the undertakings concerned. Most EWCs (more than 400) were established on the basis of agreements already in force signed pursuant to Article 13, i.e. before the cut-off date for transposing the Directive into national law (22 September 1996).

The report highlights a number of deficiencies in the 1994 text:
– problems of interpretation with particular regard to:
– the concept of "controlling undertaking",
– geographical criteria,
– conditions for the renewal of agreements already in force,
– changes in the structure of the group,
– the concept of "expert".

The report also notes that *"some of the agreements [signed] seem to guarantee only a very low level of transnational consultation and information"*.

Finally, with regard to restructuring operations having a serious social impact, it notes that *"the problem [exists] of whether the present text is sufficiently clear with regard to ensuring that information is provided and consultation takes place within a reasonable time limit and in any event before a decision is taken"*.

It should not be the case that, notwithstanding the existence of the Directive, employees learn about decisions affecting them from the radio, with information to shareholders and company share-price appreciation being deemed more important than the fate of the workforce. Given the announcements of site closures or redundancies at Renault Vilvoorde, Danone, Corus and ABB-Alstom, not to mention Marks & Spencer, where management announced its restructuring plans to the EWC fifteen minutes before making them public, the review of this Directive makes very good sense. As the Commission emphasises, we need to know whether Europe is capable of providing a response to the problems of employees who are adversely affected by globalisation. That implies that employees' representatives must be given a chance to influence the decision-making process and, where appropriate, that alternative solutions must be sought which might limit the adverse social impact of restructuring. Your draftsman takes the view emphasised in the Commission report that the review of the Directive must take into account the connection between the various Community laws either in force or in the process of being adopted which concern information and consultation of employees:

- the European Works Council Directive
- the proposal for a Directive establishing a general framework for informing and consulting employees in the European Community
- the draft Directive concerning the involvement of workers in the European Company.

Your draftsman regrets that the Commission has not tackled the issue of thresholds which it was specifically asked to address. A lowering of those thresholds would be in line with developments in the business world in Europe.

CONCLUSIONS

The Committee on Industry, External Trade, Research and Energy calls on the Committee on Employment and Social Affairs, as the committee responsible, to incorporate the following points in its motion for a resolution:

1. Notes that the Directive has led to more than 600 agreements being signed but that, in a large number of Community-scale undertakings and groups of undertakings, no EWC has been established or agreement signed concerning the information and consultation of employees at European level;

2. Emphasises that social relations based on dialogue, genuine information and consultation of employees and their representatives will benefit collective negotiations and reduce the risk of conflict, and that it may also prove to be a factor for undertakings' success;

3. Calls on the Commission to notify those Member States which have not yet taken steps to transpose the Directive;

4. Shares the Commission's view that *"the problem [exists] of whether the present text is sufficiently clear with regard to ensuring that information is provided and consultation takes place within a reasonable time limit and in any event before a decision is taken"*;

5. Emphasises that in order to achieve genuine consultation of workers' representatives, it is necessary to give them high quality, regular and usable information in good time;

6. Notes that the definition of consultation as *"the establishment of dialogue and exchange of views"* has proved to be too vague to guarantee that consultation takes place in time for it to have an effect on negotiations, i.e. before decisions are taken, including in the cases referred to in the Annex to the Directive entitled "Subsidiary requirements" *"where there are exceptional circumstances affecting the employees' interests to a considerable extent, particularly in the event of relocations, the closure of establishments or undertakings or collective redundancies"*;

7. Emphasises that, for the application of the Directive in general, and not only in the cases referred to in the Annex under the heading "Subsidiary requirements", it should be guaranteed that, in the case of measures which affect the employees' interests to a considerable extent, EWCs should *"have the right to be informed"* and that, after an information and consultation meeting on the basis of a management report, EWCs should be able to deliver *"an opinion"* before any final decision is taken;

8. Recalls that, when it voted in April 1999 at first reading on the proposal for a Council directive establishing a general framework for informing and consulting employees in the European Community, the European Parliament clearly called for consultation to take place *"during the planning stage, so as to ensure the effectiveness of the step"*, such consultation to be carried out *"on the basis of information supplied by the employer"*, as well as on the basis of *"the opinion which the employees' representatives are entitled to formulate"* and with regard to which that are entitled *"to obtain a response, and the reasons for that response"*, the aim of consultation being *"to seek prior agreement"*;

9. Emphasises that, in the draft directive supplementing the Statute for a European Company, "consultation" is defined as *"the establishment of dialogue and exchange of views ... at a time, in a manner and with a content which allows the employees' representatives, on the basis of information provided, to express an opinion on the measures envisaged ... which may be taken into account in the decision-making process ... "*;

10. Emphasises that, in the draft directive supplementing the Statute for a European Company, "information" is defined as "the informing of the

body representative of the employees and/or employees' representatives ... at a time, in a manner and with a content which allows the employees' representatives to undertake an in-depth assessment of the possible impact and, where appropriate, prepare consultations with the competent organ (of the SE)";

11. Notes that the Directive on the European Works Council should, therefore, be revised in an effort to achieve consistency and in order to take account of the more recent and more precise wordings, which will give greater effectiveness to the concepts of consultation and information by enabling them to lead to genuine negotiations;

12. Recalls that the Directive on collective redundancies lays down that *"Employers shall notify the competent public authority in writing of any projected collective redundancies"* and *"forward to the workers' representatives a copy of the notification"*. The latter *"may send any comments they may have to the competent public authority"*; calls for the Directive on the European Works Council to make express reference to this right of EWCs to refer matters to the competent public authority in the case of measures which significantly affect employees' interests;

13. Takes the view that, in order to guarantee compliance with the provisions of the Directive, penalties for non-compliance should be consistent and have a deterrent effect and, in particular, that decisions taken in breach of the procedures for the information and consultation of employees should be annulled;

14. Takes the view that ensuring trade-union participation in the Special Negotiating Body (SNB) will guarantee the best conditions for the establishment of the European Works Council and for the smooth linking of employee representation at national and transnational level;

15. Emphasises the importance of training for EWC members, given the diversity of the national laws in force in the various undertakings or groups of undertakings as well as the need to offer language courses which will enable employees' representatives to exchange information at the various levels;

16. Emphasises the need to provide for possible consultation with one or more experts, with contractual negotiations concerning the cost of expert advice and any applicable ceiling being conducted on an individual basis with undertakings;

17. EWCs and employees' representatives at transnational level must be given the resources which they require to carry out their tasks, including resources to enable them to hold preparatory meetings. EWC members must be entitled to hold meetings with representatives of local employees. The EWC budget must be sufficient to cover its operating and translation costs and for it to report independently to employees on its activities. In order to reduce current disparities between the Member States as regards time credits granted (ranging from some 2 hours per month in Spain and Italy to 20 hours per month in France), the Directive should lay down a minimum time credit for EWC members;

18. Calls for the Directive to include a clause for the revision, after a certain period of time has elapsed, of agreements signed in accordance with Article 13;

19. Stresses, as the Commission points out in the report, that the Directive does not currently require agreements to contain an adjustment clause covering changes to the make-up of the undertaking; considers that it should be revised to ensure that agreements actually do cover all the undertaking's or group's workers at all times;

20. Emphasises that the three-year period required for the conclusion of an agreement with an SNB for the establishment of an EWC seems unduly long and will open the door to delaying tactics; calls for the Directive to provide that; if negotiations have not reached a successful conclusion within a period of 18 months, an EWC shall be established in application of the "Subsidiary requirements" which shall constitute minimum standards;

21. Calls for the revision of the thresholds adopted in 1994 which exclude from information and consultation at European level a large number of undertakings affected by the same transnational considerations as those which are currently eligible; proposes that the Directive shall apply to all undertakings which have more than 500 employees, including at least 100 employees in two Member States;

22. Hopes that consideration will be given, in conjunction with the social partners, to the addition of the concept of "participation" to the "information" and "consultation" of employees at Community level in order to involve employees and their representatives more fully in the major strategic choices which will determine the evolution of the undertaking, its development and its organisation.

D. DEBATES IN THE EUROPEAN PARLIAMENT (17 MAY 2001)
    WORKS COUNCILS AND REDUNDANCIES

Ghilardotti (PSE). – (IT) I was pleased to hear that for the next Council the Commission intends to insist that the Council assume its responsibilities with regard to the directive on employees' rights to information and consultation. As several Members have already pointed out, it is now three years since Parliament gave it its first reading. In these three years we have several times in this House debated problems of redundancies, mergers and company relocations, but the Council has never assumed any responsibility, has never had the courage to face up to this subject and make a decision, adding something to the laws and other instruments that the Union has and can use to strengthen its own intervention regarding companies' social responsibilities. Now it seems that some countries have dropped their reservations, and so the conditions are right for the next Council to take up a position.

The information and consultation problem is one that has something to do with the possibility of intervening in a preventive manner so that the consequences of unilateral company decisions are not such that they place jobs, working conditions or the living conditions of workers at risk. For this to happen, however, it is necessary to reach a precise agreement, and Parliament's positions from this point of view were highly specific even at first reading on the methods, times and content of consultations and information. In addition – and I am pleased that the Commission has remembered this – there is a fundamental instrument which, paradoxically, is regarded as a fundamental element in all laws except those concerning workers, i.e. that of penalties. There is no law on any subject that does not lay down penalties for breach of the law. Only in the case of workers' rights does this still not happen in Europe. The directive on the right to information and consultation does lay down sanctions, and I am pleased that the Commission is maintaining this position.

Parliament not only upholds the Commission's position but supports the Commission in its position and I believe this matter of penalties will not only be confirmed in the Council's positions on the directive but will extend to other legislation as well – works councils, mass redundancies – otherwise without a penalty instrument all these laws too will be less effective than we would like them to be.

Verheugen, Commission. – (DE) The health and safety rules applicable to me are obviously not being applied today. I have hardly sat down.

The recent persistent wave of redundancies by numerous large companies as the result of closures or restructuring measures has reached worrying proportions. Restructuring is often used as a euphemism for redundancies. These redundancies do not only affect the employees themselves, they also affect their families and sometimes, where they depend on one or two main employers, whole regions.

As much of the recent restructuring announced has taken place at European level, there is urgent need for the Community to act. A comprehensive Community concept should possibly combine innovative measures with an examination of existing instruments. I intend at this point to confine myself to the legal aspects.

First a word on quickly adopting new and updating existing legislation. In relation to the framework directive on informing and hearing workers, may I say that the Commission will complete its amended proposal on a general framework for informing and hearing workers in the next few days, so as to ensure that it can be quickly adopted in the Council. The Commission will press for the Council to adopt the directive on 11 June.

We hope that a consensus will be reached. However, if necessary, we shall endeavour to reach political agreement by a qualified majority. We cannot wait for ever, especially in the present climate of insecurity created by the restructuring plans of numerous companies.

I should like once again to emphasise a decisive aspect of the Commission proposal in this context, namely the question of sanctions. I know that Parliament emphatically supports this action and shares the Commission's satisfaction with the progress made recently in this sensitive area.

With Parliament's support and the Council's strong political will, we can wrap this process up by the end of the year, which will be a decisive step forward.

Now to the Statute for European Companies. We also achieved another important, long-awaited result at the end of last year: the Statute for European Companies with provisions for worker participation. One of the most excellent and positive aspects of the Statute is the fact that it contains joined up provisions on worker participation which reflect the progressive approach taken at national level in the proposal on informing and hearing workers. This will certainly help ensure that better account is taken of the social dimension when European companies are restructured.

I am positive that the European Parliament will do everything to ensure that this legal act is adopted immediately after the summer recess.

Finally, to the revision of the directive on European works councils. The Commission will revise the directive on European works councils in 2002 but will continue to examine the practical implementation of the directive in the run up to the revision.

Globalisation and industrial change bring social problems in their wake. However, they can also be a source of prosperity for people and regions, if the change is designed and controlled appropriately. The main concern for governments and the Community is to strike a balance between promoting corporate innovation and growth, on the one hand, and preparing people for change and, possibly, the necessary protective measures, on the other.

This was why my colleague, Mrs Diamantopoulou, announced a check list for corporate restructuring last week. This check list includes political instruments already available, namely legislation, monitoring procedures, financial help and tried and tested procedures. Governments and companies must make optimum use of these instruments or devise new instruments. Dialogue, transparency, suitable participation of workers, anticipation, risk prevention and developing employability are the key elements in a European response to this challenge. Let us do our very best to develop these legislative and other instruments which will help us to put our ideas into practice.

Menrad (PPE-DE). – (DE) I should like to thank the Commission for its explanation and also for telling us that the framework directive will soon be ready, as will the Statute for European Companies. However, I should like first and foremost to refer to the European works council project, which our group has fully supported. I think the Commission is right to criticise how companies are behaving at present. The Commission report on European works councils, which we are currently debating in the Committee on Employment and Social Affairs – we have held a hearing on the subject – is most interesting. It proves that works councils have, as a rule, fulfilled their duties. We found out, interestingly, that restructuring, which may be necessary on occasions, can be implemented more efficiently if employees are informed and involved. In countries with more codetermination, such as Germany, there are fewer disputes and hardly any strikes in connection with structural changes to the economy.

The spirit of cooperation and partnership which Parliament brought to bear at numerous points of the directive is such that closures and relocations cannot take place in the form of commando attacks but must be preceded by timely and comprehensive information for and consultation with the workers. This is often not the case. Ensuring there is timely information and consultation, before company decisions are taken, is a very important aspect and must be taken into account when the directive is revised. I hope that the Commission will introduce an initiative this year which at least ensures that the social partners are informed and involved.

The current rules must be tightened. It is not enough for sanctions to be imposed solely at national level; we also need measures at European level. As you rightly stressed, we need the framework directive, because in numerous cases restructuring takes place solely at national, rather than at transnational level.

The directives on mass redundancies and safeguarding employee rights during takeovers also belong here.

I would like to ask you, Commissioner, if there are any plans to revise these two directives as well?

I think that the Europe of the future is also a Europe of the workers. Information, consultation and codetermination rights are in keeping with the European Charter of Fundamental Rights.

Désir (PSE). – (FR) Over the last few months, a growing number of sudden decisions have been taken to make mass redundancies or to close down companies' sites. These decisions are usually taken without any consideration of alternative solutions for safeguarding jobs, and are sometimes taken by businesses making large profits, such as Danone, or they may even come about as a result of mergers, which have just been authorised by the Commission, as in the case of ABB Alstom Power. In several cases, employees learnt that they were to be made redundant on the radio, their representatives were only informed of the decision a few minutes before it was officially announced, and, in the case of Marks & Spencer, the decision was announced ten minutes before the opening of the Stock Exchange. I would like to welcome the Marks & Spencer employees' representatives, who are seated in the public gallery.

These events, like those which happened at Renault-Vilvoorde, have again highlighted the shortcomings of Community legislation, when it exists, and the urgent need to adopt, at long last, a general framework to guarantee workers' rights to information, consultation and collective negotiation, in order to safeguard their rights and to enable solutions to be found, other than those that put their jobs and future at risk. Employees faced with these decisions must be able to count upon the European Union, on its legislation and on its institutions.

The European Union cannot remain a framework within which the only restrictive rules are those of the internal market, competition and budgetary discipline, whilst social rules remain woolly, can be avoided and have no facility for imposing penalties if the rules are breached. I shall let Mrs Ghilardotti speak about the general framework on behalf of my group, and I shall focus on the two other aspects, which are the revision of the 1994 Directive on a European Work Council and procedures for mergers and acquisitions. The definitions of information and consultation given in the Directive on works councils are so vague that they provide no guarantee. To define consultation as "the exchange of views and establishment of dialogue" is far too imprecise. We therefore need another guarantee to ensure that consultation does indeed take place at the right time, in other words, before decisions are taken, during the working-out phase, to ensure that the works council may give an opinion, propose other solutions, and that negotiation can be based not only on the management's plan, but also on counter-proposals from workers' representatives. I believe that we must at last ensure the possibility of referral to a competent public authority on a national level, as already laid down in the 1998 directive on collective redundancies and, if required, on a European level, particularly in companies with a Europe-wide presence so that, if the procedure of information and prior consultation is disregarded, or if the decisions are blatantly unfounded and other solutions could be considered both on a social and an employment level, the competent public authority can declare the redundancy plan null and void. The 1994 Directive must therefore be revised – I share your view, Commissioner – otherwise this text, which was pioneering when it was adopted, will end up being obsolete in the light of the new drafts adopted by Council, on the European limited company, or by Parliament in 1999, at first reading, on the Directive on a general framework for informing and consulting employees. Genuine consultation obviously requires information to be readily available to workers' representatives and to be of practical value, such as the opportunity to hold meetings, to have access to experts, or to request support from unions.

My second and final point relates to mergers. I do believe that we should really be able to take the dimension of employment into account, and that is possible without amending the Treaties, simply by adapting legislation, because the Treaties already set the Commission the task of monitoring the effects of these decisions on employment. I therefore believe that the proposed questionnaire is essential but also that workers' representatives must be able to refer to the Commission if, in their view, the merger plan is putting jobs or industrial plants at risk. I also believe that it is not only the Commissioner for Competition, but also the Commissioner for Employment and Social Affairs who must, if necessary, be able to question the conditions specified if they do not provide adequate guarantees for job security.

Isler Béguin (Verts/ALE). – (FR) One year on from Lisbon, the outlook is bleak. The dream of a Europe in which the words "new economy" are synonymous with growth and full employment is fading. The suddenness and the increase in redundancy programmes have made employees think seriously about the delays in building a social Europe. All companies are affected: market leaders who are long established in their fields and which act as windows onto society, such as Ericsson, Danone and Philips; players that have appeared in the wake of the liberalisation of transport, such as AOM and Air Liberté, who are making their employees pay for their failed merger and companies who carry off all the prizes for showing contempt for their employees, such as Marks & Spencer, whose employees are demonstrating today in London. We offer our support to these employees, and to those that are here in the House. According to the Commission, a total of over a quarter of a million redundancies have been announced across the world in the last few weeks. The Commission has just announced its plan to introduce a package to provide effective legal guarantees to workers regarding information and consultation. This is good news at a time when employees who are up in arms are joined by a public which disapproves of unilateral action by employers. We have the responsibility of setting this high-speed train in motion. At the same time, we must quickly adopt the directive on the information and consultation of workers, in order to put an end to the scandalous practices of companies that challenge the social legislation of the Member States. We must revise the 1994 Works Councils Directive, give them real rights to receive advance notice of plans and to receive expert advice, and make them compulsory for all transnational companies of more than 500 employees. We must adopt the directive on worker involvement in the European company and ensure that their representatives participate in supervisory committees and boards of directors where the decisions are taken.

Lastly, we need to reform our legislation on mergers and acquisitions, which takes no account of their social and geographical impact. The objective we need to pursue is a European social law that is comprehensible, workable, progressive and on a par with competition law. Our objective is to have a Europe that works on two fronts: economic dynamism and genuine social democracy. The Commission has demonstrated its will to make progress on this issue. All we need to do now is persuade the Council.

Wurtz (GUE/NGL). – (FR) I insisted that we should have the opportunity to hold this debate in light of the tidal wave of restructuring programmes announced in countries across the Union. It is particularly timely today because, following the recent mobilisation of employees from the Danone group in Calais, the employees of Marks & Spencer are now holding a large European demonstration in London.

In the eyes of the public, Marks & Spencer, following its decision to close 38 shops and to make thousands of employees redundant has, like Danone, come to represent one of the most abhorrent symbols of the strategy known as "shareholder value", of shareholder law and of the social irresponsibility of major companies.

This is the eighth time since the Michelin affair in October 1999 that I have spoken in Parliament to warn the Council and the Commission of the urgent need to confirm the social responsibility of companies and to establish meaningful rights for employees. Until now, we have merely received evasive answers extending the due date and the long-awaited revised directive on informing and consulting workers has been our Loch Ness monster: everyone has been talking about it but no one has seen hide nor hair of it.

The European public is now demanding practical and meaningful measures. I feel that as far as the workers who are affected and many other people are concerned, the Union has staked part of its credibility on this issue.

Therefore, Commissioner, I would like you to give clear answers to three questions.

First of all, a draft, revised directive on informing and consulting workers has existed since 1998. You mentioned it yourself and it is cautious and to my mind, quite inadequate. Nevertheless, the Council, to this day, refuses to review it. If I have understood you properly, Commissioner, you are going to push for the Council of 11 June to override the veto exercised by the United Kingdom, Ireland, Denmark and even Germany, whose Chancellor has just tried to pass himself off as a European visionary. You also intend, if I have understood correctly, to introduce a system of penalties for companies who breach the directive's provisions. Have I understood correctly?

My second question is this: the directive on establishing a European works councils dates back to 1995. To this day, only a minority of companies concerned has implemented the directive. Incidentally, these bodies are basically talking shops without any real power. The Nice European Council stipulated that this directive should be revised, and I quote, "by 2002", which would require setting the procedure in motion immediately.

I feel that the Commission' s working programme for 2001 ignores this problem. Why is this the case, Commissioner, and what do you intend to do now? Do you plan to give this future works council real prerogatives, such as the right to suspend a restructuring plan and the time to examine an alternative project to the one laid down by the management?

Lastly, and with this point I shall conclude, the European Parliament has declared itself to be in favour of systematic verification that social and employment obligations are being met by every company that benefits from Community aid. Parliament has also requested that, each time the

Commission makes a statement on a company merger plan, it makes its assent conditional on the employees' rights being respected. What are your plans on this matter?

Gillig (PSE). – (FR) I hope that this evening's debate clearly demonstrates our will to produce a piece of work that is consistent and which will lead to the directives in this field being updated. As you pointed out, Commissioner, we can no longer wait a new crisis to be announced to reassure ourselves that the legal instruments from which employees should benefit are at last appropriate, effective and provide for penalties in the event that European-level regulations are not respected.

The Marks & Spencer employees, like those from the other companies mentioned by Harlem Désir, demand, as European citizens, that Europe establishes frameworks for protection and for organising collective action, which as we all know is the only guarantee of individual rights in the field of employment law. They are demanding that these frameworks be established, recognised and protected and they are placing great hope in your words, Commissioner. The Commission and Parliament should also, however, demonstrate their political will by making any further development of economic union and of any new regulations conditional on the implement-ation of social provisions that stipulate new forms of regulation such as those that we are expecting today with the revision of the directives that has been announced.

The workers of the European Union, Commissioner, must not suffer as a result of European integration.

They must instead be the main beneficiaries of it. Respect for workers' rights and the building of a social Europe are the pillars which, unless strengthened, could dash all our hopes for building democracy in our Union.

Verheugen, Commission. – (DE) The Commission sees this debate as important support for its initiatives. I have the feeling that a real political tail wind is blowing and that we are in full agreement on the objectives.

I should like to comment on the specific questions asked. First, Mr Menrad's question as to whether there are any plans to revise the directives on mass redundancies and takeovers as well. There are no plans to revise them, nor does the Commission consider it necessary, because the scope of the rules planned in the new directives on information and participation is such that the two directives which you mentioned will then be able to demonstrate their real worth. The requirements of the new directive relate to the subject of the two directives which you mentioned, and we therefore do not believe that these directives need to be revised.

As far as Mr Wurtz's question is concerned, the honourable Member understood me perfectly correctly. The Commission is firmly resolved to do everything in its power now to advance acceptance of the directive on information and participation and to meet the deadline which I mentioned. I did indeed say that, if a consensus cannot be achieved, we shall work on getting the directive adopted by a qualified majority. You also understood correctly that the Commission takes the view that this directive must contain sanctions.

You then asked if the directive on European works councils was to be revised. Yes, this is planned for 2002 and we have already begun to organise the preparations. As far as your third question on mergers is concerned, we still have to examine if and to what extent account must be taken of social aspects during mergers. The results of this examination are not yet ready.

PART II

THE EUROPEAN COMPANY STATUTE

1. Analysis

I. MORE THAN 30 YEARS OF DISCUSSION

The first proposal for a regulation on the statute for a European company (Societas Europaea, SE) dates from 1970; the proposal was amended in 1975.

Recently, the idea was revitalised with, on the one hand, a proposal for a Council regulation on the statute for a European Company, and on the other, a directive complementing the statute for a European Company with regard to the involvement of employees in the European Company, both of 25 August 1989.[1] In 1991, amended proposals were made.[2] The proposal remains, after more than 30 years, as controversial as it was in 1970.

In the reformulation of its proposals, the Commission took account of the new dimension by the Single Act of 1986, on the one hand, and of the dynamics of the 1992 project, on the other. The completion of the internal market and the improvement it must bring about in the economic and the social situation throughout the Community, mean not only that barriers to trade must be removed, but also that the structures of production must be adapted to the Community dimensions.

For this purpose it is essential that companies whose business is not limited to satisfying purely local needs should be able to plan and carry out the reorganisation of their business on a Community-wide scale. In practical terms companies still have to choose a form of company governed by a particular national law. The legal framework within which business must still be carried on in Europe, as it is still based entirely on national laws, no longer applies to the creation of groups consisting of companies from different Member States. It is thus essential to ensure as far as possible that the economic unit and the legal unit of business in Europe coincide.

The essential objective of the legal rules governing a European company is to make it possible for companies from different Member States to merge or to create a holding company, and to enable companies or other legal bodies carrying on economic activities and governed by the law of different Member States to form a joint subsidiary. Companies may be formed throughout the Community under the form of a European public limited company (SE). The capital of the SE shall be divided into shares. The liability of the shareholders for the debts and obligations of the company shall be limited to the amount

---

1.   *O.J.*, 16 October 1989 No. C-263.
2.   *O.J.*, 29 May 1991 and C-178/1, 8 July 1991. C-138.

R. Blanpain (ed.), Involvement of Employees in the European Union, 105–128.
© 2002 *Kluwer Law International. Printed in Great Britain.*

subscribed by them. The SE is a commercial company whatever the object of its undertaking. It shall have legal personality (Article 1 regulation). The capital of the SE amounts to no less than ECU 1,000,000 (Article 4). It should be pointed out that the statute is not legally binding, but voluntary: the companies are free to decide whether they choose it or not.

The proposed statute is legally based upon Article 95A of the EEC Treaty. This is of course important, since proposals based on Article 95A can be adopted by qualified majority. This is obviously a controversial point, certainly as regards taxes. It is also remarkable that workers' participation is the subject of a separate instrument, namely, a directive based upon Article 44 of the EEC Treaty, within the framework of freedom of establishment in which different directives aiming at the approximating of national legislation regarding limited liability companies have been enacted. We should also point out that the proposed directive retains the one-tier system as well as the two-tier system, similar to the proposed V^{th} directive, to which we basically refer as far as organs of the company and their competences are concerned. In a nutshell: the Vth directive aims at the coordination of national legalisations; the SE has a uniform European system as its target. Both proposals are inspired by the same principles regarding workers' participation.

II. MODELS OF PARTICIPATION

Workers' participation in the SE is regulated by the proposed directive of 25 August 1989, with the exception of Article 33 of the regulation of the same date, pursuant to which:

> "the administrative or management of each of the founder companies shall discuss with its workers' representatives the legal economic and employment implications of the formation of a SE holding company for the employees and any measures proposed to deal with them."

The "whereas" to the proposed directive indicates that in order to promote the economic and social objectives of the Community, arrangements should be made for employees to participate in the supervision and strategic development of the SE. The great diversity of rules and practices existing in the Member States regarding the manner in which employees' representatives participate make it possible to lay down uniform rules on the involvement of employees in the SE. This means that account should be taken of the specific characteristics of the laws of the Member States by establishing for the SE a framework comprising several models of participation, and authorising, firstly, Member States to choose the model best corresponding to their national traditions, and secondly, the management or administrative board, as the case may be, and the workers' representatives of the SE or of its founder companies to choose the model most suited to their social environment. The directive forms an indispensable complement to the provisions of the regulation and it is therefore necessary to ensure that the two sets of provisions are applied concomitantly.

An SE may not be formed unless one of the systems of the workers' participation has been chosen (Article 3(2)).

The involvement of employees means the participation "in the supervision and strategic development of the SE" (Article 2). A distinction must, however, be made between the registered office and the establishments of the SE. The status and duties of the workers' representatives in the establishment are determined by national law. Regarding the registered office, Member States can choose between four models, as they can for the Vth directive. Each Member State determines the manner in which the participation models shall be applied for an SE having its registered office in its territory (Article 3(4)). Each Member State may retain all models or restrict its choice to one or more models (Article 3(5)).

The models retained by the Commission were the following:
- the German model: at least one-third though not more than one-half of the members of the supervisory board or the administrative board are appointed by the employees or their representatives (model 1) (Article 4, 1st indent);
- the Dutch model: co-option by the board. However, the general meeting of shareholders or the workers' representatives may, on specific grounds, object to the appointment of a particular candidate. In such cases, the appointment may not be made until an independent body established under public law has declared the objection inadmissible (model 2) (Article 4, 2nd indent);
- a separate body shall represent the employees of the SE. The number of members of that body and the detailed rules governing their election or appointment shall be laid down in the statutes in consultation with the workers' representatives of the founder companies in accordance with the law or practices of the Member States (Article 5(1)). These representatives have rights to information and consultation comparable to those provided for in the proposed V[th] directive (model 3);
- another model may be established by means of an agreement concluded between the management boards and the administrative boards of the founder companies and the employees or their representatives in those companies. The parties to the negotiation may be assisted by experts of their choice at the expense of the founder companies. The agreement may be concluded for a fixed period and renegotiated at the expiry of that period. However, the agreement concluded shall remain in force until the entry into force of the new agreement. Where the two parties to the agreement so decide, or where no such agreement can be reached, a standard model provided by the law of the State shall apply. This model shall ensure, for the employees, at least the rights of information and consultation as mentioned (Article 6) (model 4).

The model to be applied shall be determined by an agreement concluded between the management board and the administrative boards of the founder companies and the workers' representatives of those companies, as provided by the laws and practices of the Member States. Where no agreement can be reached, the management and the administrative boards shall choose the model applicable to the SE (Article 3(1)). A chosen model can always be replaced by another by means of an agreement. The workers' representatives of the SE shall be elected in accordance with systems that appropriately take into account the number of staff they represent. All the employees must be able to participate in the vote (Article 7).

Initially, the workers' representatives of the SE shall be appointed by the workers' representatives of the founder companies in proportion to the number of employees they represent (Article 8). The workers' representatives receive such financial material resources as enable them to meet and perform their duties in an appropriate manner (Article 9).

Employee participation in the capital or in the profits or losses of the SE may be organised by means of a collective agreement (Article 11).

In a Communication on worker information and consultation of 14 November 1995,[3] the Commission relaunched the debate on workers' participation and indicated possible directions for Community action:

"Various options are possible.

Option 1: maintain the status quo

This option would mean continuing the discussions in the Council on the basis of the existing proposals and maintaining the fragmented approach to Community action on employee information, consultation and involvement. The main disadvantage of this option is that as things stand, it seems to offer little hope of progress.

Option 2: global approach

This option involves a change in the way of looking at the whole question. Instead of attempting to establish, at Community level, sets of specific rules for each entity to be covered by Community rules on company law, attempts would be made to establish a general framework at European level on informing and consulting employees. This would make it possible to withdraw the proposals for directives annexed to the proposals for regulations on the statute for a European company, a European association, a European co-operative society and a European mutual society. The same would apply to the social provisions in the proposal for the "*fifth directive*" and the "*Vredeling proposal*".

Given that the European Community already has a legal framework for employee information and consultation at transnational level, this global approach would mean quite simply that a Community instrument on information and consultation at national level would have to be adopted. Before taking this approach, a number of questions need to be answered: Would it be in keeping with the principles of subsidiarity and proportionality? What would be the nature of the proposal (approximation of legislation or

---

3.   COM(95) 547 final.

establishment of minimum requirements)? and, lastly. Which legal basis should be used (Treaty or Maastricht Social Agreement)?

The main advantage of this option is that it is a step towards simplifying Community law and European social policy. It could also make it easier – and, in fact, might even be necessary – to achieve progress with the above-mentioned proposals, since the businesses concerned which are of purely national scale would then be covered by this general framework.

Option 3: immediate action on the proposals concerning the statute for a European company, a European association, a European co-operative society and a European mutual society

If the global approach set out above is adopted, immediate steps could be taken to unlock these proposals, especially the proposal on the statute for a European company, the adoption of which is particularly urgent. This would be justified by the importance of this instrument for the organisation of companies at European level and by the urgent need to find a legal vehicle which meets the needs of major trans-European transport infrastructure projects (the Member States have indicated that they will need two years to introduce the implementing provisions for the Statute, in spite of its immediate legal effect).

This could be done in two ways:

The above-mentioned proposals for directives would be withdrawn on the same condition, *mutatis mutandis*, as that set out in Article 136 of the proposal for a regulation on the statute for a European company, which stipulates that no European company, European association, European co-operative society or European mutual society could be set up in a Member State which had not transposed the *"European Works-Councils"* Directive. This solution would have the advantage of maintaining the compulsory link between the establishment of these organisations and their application of the procedures for employee information and consultation, which has always been a key element in these proposals. It would also prevent discrimination between these organisations depending on the Member State in which they decided to locate their registered office.

No conditions would be attached to the withdrawal of these proposals. In this case, only the Community provisions in force (the *"European Works Councils"*, *"collective redundancies"* and *"business transfers"* Directives) would be applicable to the organisations concerned, as appropriate.

The disadvantage of this sub-option is that one Member State is not covered by the *"European Works Councils"* Directive. This would mean that the European companies, European associations, European co-operative societies and European mutual societies which are of multinational scale and have their registered offices in this Member State would not be subject to the same obligations in the area of transnational information and consultation of employees, as would be the case for organisations with their registered office in another Member State.

The arguments set out above are provided as a contribution to the discussion which the Commission would like to see developed among the Member States, in the EP and the ESC and between the social partners at Community level.

The Commission reaffirms that it is open to any way of achieving the objectives at the heart of this debate. These are, first, to put an end to the unacceptable situation of never-ending institutional discussion of the above-mentioned proposals and, second, to supplement the Community legal framework in the area of employee information and consultation and to make it more coherent and effective.

The Commission would like to receive the comments and views of the Member States, the EP, the ESC and the social partners at European level on these matters. It is particularly interested in knowing their views on the options set out in this communication."

The discussion was given a new lease of life, thanks to the expert group, presided over by Mr. E. Davignon, a leading industrialist and former vice-president of the European Commission. The group of experts on "European systems of worker involvement" was set up in November 1996. The group was given the following as its main task by the Commission: to examine the type of involvement rules to be applied to the European Company. It delivered its final report in May 1997.

The proposals of the Davignon group (1997)[4] can be summarised as follows. The group decided to limit its discussions to three of the four ways of setting up a European Company set out in the draft ECS:
– the merger of existing companies;
– the creation of a joint holding company; and
– the creation of a joint subsidiary.

The conversion of existing national public limited liability companies was not retained, in order to avoid the possibility of becoming a European Company in order to escape national systems.

All European Companies, whatever their number of employees, would have a system of worker involvement.[5] It follows the route of the EWC since it recommends that negotiation should be the primary method of establishing the worker involvement system. Only if these negotiations fail would a set of statutory "reference rules" apply.

The report provides for detailed recommendations on the negotiating procedure for the European Company's worker involvement arrangements.

The employees would be represented by a negotiating body, made up of workers' representatives appointed "in accordance with national practices and procedures". Workers' representatives are entitled to the services of experts.

---

4. "European Company Statute revisited, *European Works Council Bulletin*", 1997, 10, pp. 8–13.

5. "All arrangements allowing workers' representatives to take part in company decision-making processes with a view to ensuring the collective expression and permanent consideration of their interests in the context of decisions concerning the management and economic and financial development of the company."

The content of the agreement would be flexible, but the report gives an indicative list of what the content of the agreement might be. Again, there is a parallel with the EWC.

If no agreement is reached, a set of reference rules will apply.

There are two forms of involvement:
- information and consultation through a group of employee representatives;
- the representation of employees on the European Company's board.

Workers' representatives would be members of the management board or supervisory board. Workers' representatives would make up one-fifth of the total members of the board in question, with a minimum of two members. The employee representatives on the board would be full members.

The report was welcomed by the Council, by the EP and by the social partners.

III. BOARD-LEVEL PARTICIPATION AGREED AT AVENTIS[6]

An agreement (7 March 2001) on European board-level employee participation was concluded between Aventis management, the German chemical workers' trade union, IG BCE, the French chemical workers' Unions affiliated to CGT and CFDT and the European Mine, Chemical and Energy Workers' Federation (EMCEF). Aventis, which has its headquarters in Strasbourg, France, was created in 1999 following the merger of the German chemicals multinational, Hoechst AG and the French Rhône-Poulenc SA. The company employs some 95,000 people in more than 120 countries.

The agreement, hailed as the first of its kind, especially in the light of the European Company Statute, provides for a total of six worker representatives to sit on the supervisory board of Aventis. Four of these six representatives (two French and two German) are full members of the board, nominated by trade unions and voted onto the board by the company's shareholder assembly. The two remaining worker representatives are, in line with French law, appointed by the works council. Under the terms of the agreement, EMCEF will nominate the candidate for one of these seats and, in return for the French works council agreeing to this, it will have the right to be represented on the Aventis European Works Council (or European Dialogue Committee). The four regular worker representatives will have the same rights as the 10 shareholder representatives on the board, whereas the works council representative will attend in a consultative capacity and the EMCEF representative will attend as a guest.

---

6.   *www.eurofound.ie*

IV. NICE SUMMIT (7–10 DECEMBER 2000): THE BREAKTHROUGH

The European Council of Nice reached agreement on the European Company Statute. According to the Nice summit conclusions, the agreement, in order to take into account different national employment relations systems, allows Member States the option of whether or not to transpose into their national law the fall-back reference provisions (which apply where no agreement can be reached between management and employee representatives) relating to board-level employee participation applicable to European companies constituted by merger. In order for a European company to be registered in a Member State which has not transposed these reference provisions, either: an agreement must have been concluded on the arrangements for worker involvement in that company, including board-level participation; or none of the companies involved in the merger must have been governed by board-level participation rules prior to the registration of the European company.[7]

In December 2000, the EU Council of Ministers on the worker involvement provisions relating to the European Company Statute reached political unanimous agreement.

The draft directive and the regulation on the company law aspects of the Statute are forwarded to the European Parliament for an opinion. The texts will subsequently be sent back to the Council of Ministers for adoption. The draft directive and regulation will come into force three years after adoption. The draft directive will require negotiations between management and employee representatives in each European company over the worker involvement arrangements to be applied, with statutory reference provisions applying where no agreement is reached.[8]

V. ADOPTION: 8 OCTOBER 2001

Two documents of the Council of the EU relate to the European company: a Council regulation on the Statute for a European Company (SE)[9] and a Council directive supplementing the Statute for a European Company with regard to the involvement of employees.[10] Arrangements for the involvement of employees are to be established in every SE. The Employment and Social Affairs Council of 8 October 2001 adopted both texts.[11] The Council adopted the two legislative proposals on SE without taking on board any of the amendments tabled in the European Parliament.

We summarise the provisions in both instruments relating to the involvement of employees.

---

7.   Andrea Broughton, *www.eurofound.ie*
8.   "Agreement on European Company Statute and working time in road transport industry", *www.eurofound.ie*
9.   14886/00 (1 February 2001).
10.   14732/00 (1 February 2001).
11.   *O.J.*, 10 November 2001, L 294.

A. Definitions

The Directive contains a number of definitions, amongst which, for the purposes of this directive:

– *"Employees' representatives"* means the employees' representatives provided for by national law and/or practice;
– *"Representative Body* (RB)"* means the body representative of the employees set up by the agreements or in accordance with the provisions of the Annex, with the purpose of informing and consulting the employees of an SE and its subsidiaries and establishments situated in the Community and, where applicable, of exercising participation rights in relation to the SE;
– *"Special Negotiating Body* (SNB)"* means the body established to negotiate with the competent body of the participating companies regarding the establishment of arrangements for the involvement of employees within the SE;
– *"Involvement of employees"* means any mechanism, including information, consultation and participation, through which employees' representatives may exercise an influence on decisions to be taken within the company;
– *"Information"* means the informing of the body representative of the employees and/or employees' representatives by the competent organ of the SE on questions which concern the SE itself and any of its subsidiaries or establishments situated in another Member State or which exceed the powers of the decision-making organs in a single Member State at a time, in a manner and with a content which allows the employees' representatives to undertake an in-depth assessment of the possible impact and, where appropriate, prepare consultations with the competent organ of the SE;
– *"Consultation"* means the establishment of dialogue and exchange of views between the body representative of the employees and/or the employees' representatives and the competent organ of the SE, at a time, in a manner and with a content which allows the employees' representatives, on the basis of information provided, to express an opinion on measures envisaged by the competent organ which may be taken into account in the decision-making process within the SE;
– *"Participation"* means the influence of the body representative of the employees and/or the employees' representatives in the affairs of a company by way of:
  – the right to elect or appoint some of the members of the company's supervisory or administrative organ; or
  – the right to recommend and/or oppose the appointment of some or all of the members of the company's supervisory or administrative organ.

B. Formation of an SE

The following formations are, according to the Regulation (Title II), possible:

- formation by means of a merger. In the case of a merger by acquisition, the acquiring company shall take the form of an SE when the merger takes place. In the case of a merger by the formation of a new company, the SE shall be the newly formed company;
- formation of a holding SE: public and private limited-liability companies may promote the formation of a holding SE provided that each of at least two of them:
  - is governed by the law of a different Member Stale, or
  - has for at least two years had a subsidiary company governed by the law of another Member State or an establishment situated in another Member State;
- formation of a subsidiary SE: companies and firms formed under the law of a Member State with registered offices and head offices within the Community may form a subsidiary SE by subscribing for its shares, provided that each of at least two of them:
  - is governed by the law of a different Member Slate, or
  - has for at least two years had a subsidiary company governed by the law of another Member State or an establishment situated in another Member State;
- conversion of an existing public-liability company into an SE: a public limited-liability company, formed under the law of a Member State, that has its registered office and head office within the Community, may be transformed into an SE if for at east two years it has had a subsidiary company governed by the law of another Member State.

C. Structure of the SE

An SE shall comprise:
(a) a general meeting of shareholders, and
(b) either a supervisory organ and a management organ (two-tier system) or an administrative organ (one-tier system) depending on the form adopted in the statutes.

1. The two-tier system

In a two-tier system, the management organ shall be responsible for managing the SE. The member or members of the management organ shall be appointed and removed by the supervisory organ.

The supervisory organ shall supervise the work of the management organ. It may not itself exercise the power to manage the SE. The members of the supervisory organ are appointed by the general meeting. The management organ shall report to the supervisory organ at least once every three months on the progress and foreseeable development of the SE's business. The supervisory organ elects a chairman from among its members. If employees appoint half of the members, only a member appointed by the general meeting of shareholders may be elected chairman.

2. The one-tier system

The administrative organ shall manage the SE. The administrative organ will consist of at least three members where employee participation is regulated in accordance with the Directive. The administrative organ shall elect a chairman from among its members. If half of the members are appointed by employees, only a member appointed by the general meeting of shareholders may be elected chairman.

D. Workers' involvement

According to the Directive arrangements for the involvement of employees have to be established in every SE in accordance with either a negotiating procedure, or in the absence of this, by standard rules.

1. The negotiating procedure

a. Creation of an snb
When management draw up a plan for the establishment of an SE, it must as soon as possible after publishing the draft terms take the necessary steps[12] to start negotiations with the representatives of the companies' employees on arrangements for the involvement of employees in the SE.

(1) Composition
For this purpose, an SNB representative of the employees of the participating companies and concerned subsidiaries or establishments is *created* in accordance with the following provisions:
(a)   in electing or appointing members of the SNB, it must be ensured:
i.   that these members are elected or appointed in proportion to the number of employees employed in each Member State by allocating in respect of a Member State one seat for each portion of employees employed in that Member State which equals 10 per cent, or a fraction thereof, of the number of employees employed in all the Member States taken together;
ii.   that in the case of an SE formed by way of merger, there are such further additional members from each Member State as may be necessary in order to ensure that the SNB includes at least one member representing each participating company which is registered and has employees in that

---

12.   Including providing information about the identity of the participating companies, concerned subsidiaries or establishments, and the number of their employees.

Member State and which it is proposed will cease to exist as a separate legal entity following the registration of the SE, insofar as:

— the number of such additional members does not exceed 20 per cent of the number of members designated by virtue of point (i); and

— the composition of the SNB does not entail a double representation of the employees concerned. If the number of such companies is higher than the number of additional seats, these additional seats shall be allocated to companies in different Member States by decreasing order of the number of employees they employ.

(b)   Member States shall determine the method to be used for the election or appointment of the members of the SNB who are to be elected or appointed in their territories. They shall take the necessary measures to ensure that, as far as possible, such members shall include at least one member representing each participating company that has employees in the Member State concerned.

Such measures must not increase the overall number of members. Member States may provide that such members may include representatives of trade unions whether or not they are employees.

Without prejudice to national legislation and/or practice laying down thresholds for the establishing of a representative body (RB), Member States shall provide that employees in undertakings or establishments in which there are no employees' representatives through no fault of their own have the right to elect or appoint members of the SNB.

(2)   Arrangements for involvement

The SNB and management determine, by written agreement, arrangements for the involvement of employees within the SE. To this end the SNB will be informed of the plan and the actual process of establishing the SE, up to its registration.

(3)   Rules for decision-making

The SNB shall take decisions by an absolute majority of its members, provided that such a majority also represents an absolute majority of the employees.[13]

---

13.   Each member shall have one vote. However, should the result of the negotiations lead to a reduction of participation rights, the majority required for a decision to approve such an agreement shall be the votes of two thirds of the members of the SNB representing at least two-thirds of the employees, including the votes of members representing employees employed in at least two Member States,

— in the case of an SE to be established by way of merger, if participation covers at least 25 per cent of the overall number of employees of the participating companies, or

— in the case of an SE to be established by way of creating a holding company or forming a subsidiary, if participation covers at least 50 per cent of the overall number of employees of the participating companies.

Reduction of participation rights means a proportion of members of the organs of the SE within the meaning of Article 2(k), which is lower than the highest proportion existing within the participating companies.

(4)   Experts

For the purpose of the negotiations, the SNB may request experts of its choice, for example representatives of appropriate Community-level trade union organisations, to assist it with its work. Such experts may be present at negotiation meetings in an advisory capacity at the request of the SNB, where appropriate to promote coherence and consistency at Community level. The SNB may decide to inform the representatives of appropriate external organisations, including trade unions, of the start of the negotiations.

(5)   Opt-out

The SNB may decide by majority vote[14] not to open negotiations or to terminate negotiations already opened, and to rely on the rules on information and consultation of employees in force in the Member States where the SE has employees. Such a decision shall stop the procedure to conclude an agreement. Where such a decision has been taken, none of the provisions of the standard rules will apply.

The SNB will be reconvened on the written request of at least 10 per cent of the employees of the SE, or their representatives, at the earliest two years after the abovementioned decision, unless the parties agree to negotiations being reopened sooner. If the SNB decides to reopen negotiations with the management but no agreement is reached as a result of those negotiations, none of the provisions of the standard rules will apply.

(6)   Expenses

Any expenses relating to the functioning of the SNB and, in general, to negotiations, are borne by the participating companies so as to enable the SNB to carry out its task in an appropriate manner. In compliance with this principle, Member States may lay down budgetary rules regarding the operation of the SNB. They may in particular limit the funding to cover one expert only.

b.   Content of the agreement

Without prejudice to the autonomy of the parties,[15] the agreement has to specify:

(a)   the scope of the agreement;

---

14.   The majority required to decide not to open or to terminate negotiations shall be the votes of two-thirds of the members representing at least two-thirds of the employees, including the votes of members representing employees employed in at least two Member States. In the case of an SE established by way of transformation, this paragraph shall not apply if there is participation in the company to be transformed.

15.   Without prejudice to Article 13(3)(a), in the case of an SE established by means of transformation, the agreement shall provide for at least the same level of all elements of employee involvement as the ones existing within the company to be transformed into an SE.

(b)   the composition, number of members and allocation of seats on the RB in connection with arrangements for the information and consultation of the employees of the SE and its subsidiaries and establishments;

(c)   the functions and the procedure for the information and consultation of the RB;

(d)   the frequency of meetings of the RB;

(e)   the financial and material resources to be allocated to the RB;

(f)   if, during negotiations, the parties decide to establish one or more information and consultation procedures instead of an RB, the arrangements for implementing those procedures;

(g)   if, during negotiations, the parties decide to establish arrangements for participation, the substance of those arrangements including (if applicable) the number of members in the SE's administrative or supervisory body which the employees will be entitled to elect, appoint, recommend or oppose, the procedures as to how these members may be elected, appointed, recommended or opposed by the employees, and their rights;

(h)   the date of entry into force of the agreement and its duration; cases where the agreement should be renegotiated and the procedure for its renegotiation.

The agreement is not, unless provision is made otherwise therein, be subject to the standard rules.

c.   Duration of negotiations

Negotiations shall commence as soon as the SNB is established and may continue for six months thereafter. The parties may, however, decide, by joint agreement, to extend negotiations beyond that period up to a total of one year from the establishment of the SNB.

d.   Spirit of cooperation

Management and the SNB must negotiate in a spirit of cooperation with a view to reaching an agreement on arrangements for the involvement of the employees within the SE.

e.   Legislation applicable to the negotiation procedure

As a general rule, the legislation applicable to the negotiation procedure is the legislation of the Member State in which the registered office of the SE is to be situated.

2.   Standard rules

Member States must lay down standard rules on employee involvement, which must satisfy the provisions set out in the Annex of the Directive. These are as follows.

a. Composition of the body representative of the employees

A representative body (RB) is to be set up in accordance with the following rules:

(a) The RB is composed of employees of the SE and its subsidiaries and establishments elected or appointed from their number by the employees' representatives or, in the absence thereof, by the entire body of employees.

(b) The election or appointment of members of the RB is to be carried out in accordance with national legislation and/or practice. Member States must lay down rules to ensure that the number of members of, and allocation of seats on, the RB will be adapted to take account of changes occurring within the SE and its subsidiaries and establishments.

(c) Where its size so warrants, the RB will elect a select committee from among its members, comprising at most three members.

(d) The RB shall adopt its rules of procedure.

(e) The members of the RB are elected or appointed in proportion to the number of employees employed in each Member State by the participating companies and concerned subsidiaries or establishments, by allocating in respect of a Member State one seat per each portion of employees employed in that Member State which equals 10 per cent, or a fraction thereof, of the number of employees employed by the participating companies and concerned subsidiaries or establishments in all the Member States taken together.

(f) The competent organ of the SE must be informed of the composition of the RB.

(g) Four years after the RB is established, it must examine whether to open negotiations for the conclusion of an agreement or to continue to apply the standard rules.

If a decision has been taken to negotiate an agreement, the term "SNB" is replaced by "RB". Where, by the deadline by which the negotiations come to an end, no agreement has been concluded, the arrangements initially adopted in accordance with the standard rules will continue to apply.

b. Standard rules for information and consultation

The competence and powers of the RB set up in an SE are governed by the following rules:

(a) The competence of the RB is limited to questions that concern the SE itself and any of its subsidiaries or establishments situated in another Member State or which exceed the powers of the decision-making organs in a single Member State.

(b) The RB has the right to be informed and consulted and, for that purpose, to meet with the management of the SE at least once a year, on the basis of regular reports on the progress of the business of the SE and its prospects. The local managements shall be informed accordingly.

Management must provide the RB with the agenda for meetings of the administrative, or, where appropriate, the management and supervisory organ, and with copies of all documents submitted to the general meeting of its shareholders. The meeting shall relate in particular to the structure, economic and financial situation, the probable development of the business and of production and sales, the situation and probable trend of employment, investments, and substantial changes concerning organisation, introduction of new working methods or production processes, transfers of production, mergers, cut-backs or closures of undertakings, establishments or important parts thereof, and collective redundancies.

(c) Where there are exceptional circumstances affecting the employees' interests to a considerable extent, particularly in the event of relocations, transfers, the closure of establishments or undertakings or collective redundancies, the RB has the right to be informed. The RB or, where it so decides, in particular for reasons of urgency, the select committee, has the right to meet at its request the competent organ of the SE or any more appropriate level of management within the SE having its own powers of decision, so as to be informed and consulted on measures significantly affecting employees' interests.

Where management decides not to act in accordance with the opinion expressed by the RB, this body shall have the right to a further meeting with the competent organ of the SE with a view to seeking agreement.

In the case of a meeting organised with the select committee, those members of the RB who represent employees who are directly concerned by the measures in question also have the right to participate.

The meetings referred to above do not affect the prerogatives of the competent organ.

(d) Member States may lay down rules on the chairing of information and consultation meetings. Before any meeting with management, the RB or the select committee are entitled to meet without the representatives of management being present.

(e) The members of the RB will inform the representatives of the employees of the content and outcome of the information and consultation procedures.

(f) The RB or the select committee may be assisted by experts of its choice.

(g) The members of the RB are entitled to time off for training without loss of wages.

(h) The costs of the RB are borne by the SE, which will provide the body's members with the financial and material resources needed to enable them to perform their duties in an appropriate manner.

In particular, the SE will, unless otherwise agreed, bear the cost of organising meetings and providing interpretation facilities and the accommodation and travelling expenses of members of the RB and the select committee.

In compliance with these principles, the Member States may lay down budgetary rules regarding the operation of the RB. They may in particular limit funding to cover one expert only.

c.   Standard rules for participation
Employee participation in an SE is governed by the following provisions:
(a)   In the case of an SE established by transformation, if the rules of a
      Member State relating to employee participation in the administrative or
      supervisory body applied before registration, all aspects of employee
      participation shall continue to apply to the SE. Point (b) shall apply
      mutatis mutandis to that end.
(b)   In other cases of the establishing of an SE, the employees have the right to
      elect, appoint, recommend or oppose the appointment of a number of
      members of the administrative or supervisory body of the SE equal to the
      highest proportion in force in the participating companies concerned
      before registration of the SE.

If none of the participating companies was governed by participation
rules before registration of the SE, the latter is not be required to establish
provisions for employee participation.

The RB shall decide on the allocation of seats within the administrative
or supervisory body among the members representing the employees from the
various Member States or on the way in which the SE's employees may
recommend or oppose the appointment of the members of these bodies
according to the proportion of the SE's employees in each Member State. If the
employees of one or more Member States are not covered by this proportional
criterion, the RB shall appoint a member from one of those Member States, in
particular the Member State of the SE's registered office where that is
appropriate. Each Member State may determine the allocation of the seats it is
given within the administrative or supervisory body.

Every member of the administrative body or, where appropriate, the
supervisory body of the SE who has been elected, appointed or recommended
by the RB or, depending on the circumstances, by the employees, is a full
member with the same rights and obligations as the members representing the
shareholders, including the right to vote.

d.   The application of standard rules
The standard rules as laid down by the legislation of the Member State in
which the registered office of the SE is to be situated shall apply from the date
of the registration of the SE where either:
(a)   the parties so agree; or
(b)   no agreement has been concluded by the deadline, and:
–   the management of each of the participating companies decides to accept
      the application of the standard rules in relation to the SE and so to
      continue with its registration of the SE; and
–   the SNB has not taken the decision not to open negotiations.

Moreover, the standard rules regarding participation, fixed by the
national legislation of the Member State of registration, will apply only:

(a) in the case of an SE established by transformation, if the rules of a Member State relating to employee participation in the administrative or supervisory body applied to a company transformed into an SE;

(b) in the case of an SE established by merger:

- if, before registration of the SE, one or more forms of participation applied in one or more of the participating companies covering at least 25 per cent of the total number of employees in all the participating companies; or

- if, before registration of the SE, one or more forms of participation applied in one or more of the participating companies covering less than 25 per cent of the total number of employees in all the participating companies and if the SNB so decides;

(c) in the case of an SE established by setting up a holding company or establishing a subsidiary:

- if, before registration of the SE, one or more forms of participation applied in one or more of the participating companies covering at least 50 per cent of the total number of employees in all the participating companies; or

- if, before registration of the SE, one or more forms of participation applied in one or more of the participating companies covering less than 50 per cent of the total number of employees in all the participating companies and if the SNB so decides.

If there was more than one form of participation within the various participating companies, the SNB shall decide which of those forms must be established in the SE. Member States may fix the rules that are applicable in the absence of any decision on the matter for an SE registered in their territory. The SNB shall inform the competent organs of the participating companies of any decisions taken pursuant to this paragraph.

Member States may provide that the reference provisions concerning "standard rules for participation" do not apply in the case provided for in case of merger.

3. *Miscellaneous provisions*

a. *Reservation and confidentiality*

Member States must provide that members of the SNB or the RB, and experts who assist them, are not authorised to reveal any information which as been given to them in confidence.

The same applies to employees' representatives in the context of an information and consultation procedure. This obligation continues to apply, wherever the persons referred to may be, even after the expiry of their terms of office.

Each Member State will provide, in specific cases and under the conditions and limits laid down by national legislation, that an SE or a participating company established in its territory is not obliged to transmit information where its nature is such that, according to objective criteria, to do so would seriously harm the functioning of the SE (or, as the case may be, the participating company) or its subsidiaries and establishments, or would be prejudicial to them.

A Member State may make such dispensation subject to prior administrative or judicial authorisation.

Each Member State may lay down particular provisions for SEs in its territory which pursue directly and essentially the aim of ideological guidance with respect to information and the expression of opinions, on condition that, on the date of adoption of this Directive, such provisions already exist in the national legislation.

In doing so Member States will make provision for administrative or judicial appeal procedures which the employees' representatives may initiate when an SE or participating company demands confidentiality or does not give information. Such procedures may include arrangements designed to protect the confidentiality of the information in question.

b. Operation of the RB and Procedure for the Information and Consultation of Employees

The competent organ of the SE and the RB work together in a spirit of cooperation with due regard for their reciprocal rights and obligations. The same applies to cooperation between the supervisory or administrative organ of the SE and the employees' representatives in conjunction with a procedure for the information and consultation of employees.

c. Protection of employees' representatives

The members of the SNB, the members of the RB, any employees' representatives exercising functions under the information and consultation procedure and any employees' representatives in the supervisory or administrative organ of an SE, who are employees of the SE, its subsidiaries or establishments or of a participating company will, in the exercise of their functions, enjoy the same protection and guarantees provided for employees' representatives by the national legislation and/or practice in force in their country of employment.

This applies in particular to attendance at meetings of the SNB or RB, any other meeting in the case of an information and conciliation procedure or any meeting of the administrative or supervisory organ, and to the payment of wages for members employed by a participating company or the SE or its subsidiaries or establishments during a period of absence necessary for the performance of their duties.

d. Misuse of procedures

Member States must take appropriate measures in conformity with Community law with a view to preventing the misuse of an SE for the purpose of depriving employees of rights to employee involvement or withholding such rights.

e. Compliance with this Directive

Each Member State must ensure that the management of establishments of an SE and the supervisory or administrative organs of subsidiaries and of participating companies which are situated within its territory and the employees' representatives or, as the case may be, the employees themselves, abide by the obligations laid down by this Directive, regardless of whether or not the SE has its registered office within its territory.

Member States must provide for appropriate measures in the event of failure to comply with this Directive; in particular they shall ensure that administrative or legal procedures are available to enable the obligations deriving from this Directive to be enforced.

f. Link between this directive and other provisions

Where an SE is a Community-scale undertaking or a controlling undertaking of a Community-scale group of undertakings within the meaning of Directives on EWCs, the provisions of these Directives and the provisions transposing them into national legislation shall not apply to them or to their subsidiaries.

However, where the SNB decides not to open negotiations or to terminate negotiations already opened, the EWC directives and the provisions transposing them into national legislation shall apply.

Provisions on the participation of employees in company bodies provided for by national legislation and/or practice, other than those implementing this Directive, will not apply to companies covered by this Directive.

This Directive shall not prejudice:

(a) the existing rights to involvement of employees provided for by national legislation and/or practice in the Member States as enjoyed by employees of the SE and its subsidiaries and establishments, other than participation in the bodies of the SE;

(b) the provisions on participation in the bodies laid down by national legislation and/or practice applicable to the subsidiaries of the SE.

In order to preserve these rights Member States may take the necessary measures to guarantee that the structures of employee representation in participating companies, which will cease to exist as separate legal entities, are maintained after the registration of the SE.

Some Preliminary Observations

1. In gauging the meaning and importance of the establishment of SE for the "involvement of employees", one has first to keep in mind that such establishment remains a voluntary affair for the companies concerned, and depends on whether they see advantages in creating an SE. Much will depend on the possible tax incentives that will go along with the setting up of an SE: are companies allowed to deduct the debts incurred in one country from the profits made in another Member State?

2. The Directive foresees various forms of workers' involvement, namely:

– information;

– consultation; and

– participation: sitting on the boards of companies.

3. The method of introducing information and consultation and participation is very similar to the procedures laid down in the 1994 Directive on EWCs. Either the parties involved conclude an agreement or standard rules are imposed.
4. In the case of an agreement, an SNB will negotiate to set up an RB or a procedure and/or a formula of employees' representatives sitting in the board(s) of companies.
5. If no agreement is reached, standard rules will apply. These standards rules provide for information and consultation to be exercised through an RB, similar to the rights of EWCs. Regarding employees sitting on boards, this will be the case if such formulas already exist at national level in (the) companies concerned and if Member States do not opt out from the participation rights, as they can do in the case of the establishment of an SE by way of a merger.
6. When the Directive on involvement of employees applies, the rules concerning EWCs do not apply.
7. It is also significant that, as for the EWCs, a spirit of cooperation between the parties concerned should prevail.
8. Trade unions are expressed referred to for the composition of SNB as possible experts.
9. Furthermore, this Directive remains more or less silent regarding the moment at which information must be given concerning restructurings. Even such expressions as "in good time" or "in appropriate time" have been left out.

2. Legislation

I. COUNCIL DIRECTIVE 2001/86/EC OF 8 OCTOBER 2001.[1]
    SUPPLEMENTING THE STATUTE FOR A EUROPEAN COMPANY
    WITH REGARD TO THE INVOLVEMENT OF EMPLOYEES

THE COUNCIL OF THE EUROPEAN UNION,

Having regard to the Treaty establishing the European Community, and in particular Article 308 thereof,

Having regard to the amended proposal from the Commission,[2]

Having regard to the Opinion of the European Parliament,[3]

Having regard to the Opinion of the Economic and Social Committee,[4]

Whereas:

1. In order to attain the objectives of the Treaty, Council Regulation (EC) No 2157/2001,[5] establishes a Statute for a European Company (SE).

2. That Regulation aims at creating a uniform legal framework within which companies from different Member States should be able to plan and carry out the reorganisation of their business on a Community scale.

3. In order to promote the social objectives of the Community, special provisions have to be set, notably in the field of employee involvement, aimed at ensuring that the establishment of an SE does not entail the disappearance or reduction of practices of employee involvement existing within the companies participating in the establishment of an SE. This objective should be pursued through the establishment of a set of rules in this field, supplementing the provisions of the Regulation.

4. Since the objectives of the proposed action, as outlined above, cannot be sufficiently achieved by the Member States, in that the object is to establish a set of rules on employee involvement applicable to the SE, and can therefore, by reason of the scale and impact of the proposed action, be better achieved at Community level, the Community may adopt measures, in accordance with the principle of subsidiarity as set out in

---

1. Adopted 8 October 2001.
2. *O.J.*, C 138, 29 May 1991.
3. *O.J.*, C 342, 20 December 1993.
4. *O.J.*, C 342, 20 December 1993.
5. *O.J.*, 10 November 2001.

R. Blanpain (ed.), Involvement of Employees in the European Union, 129–178.
© 2002 *Kluwer Law International. Printed in Great Britain.*

Article 5 of the Treaty. In accordance with the principle of proportionality, as set out in that Article, this Directive does not go beyond what is necessary to achieve these objectives.

5.   The great diversity of rules and practices existing in the Member States as regards the manner in which employees' representatives are involved in decision-making within companies makes it inadvisable to set up a single European model of employee involvement applicable to the SE.

6.   Information and consultation procedures at transnational level should nevertheless be ensured in all cases of creation of an SE.

7.   If and when participation rights exist within one or more companies establishing an SE, they should be preserved through their transfer to the SE, once established, unless the parties decide otherwise.

8.   The concrete procedures of employee transnational information and consultation, as well as, if applicable, participation, to apply to each SE should be defined primarily by means of an agreement between the parties concerned or, in the absence thereof, through the application of a set of subsidiary rules.

9.   Member States should still have the option of not applying the standard rules relating to participation in the case of a merger, given the diversity of national systems for employee involvement. Existing systems and practices of participation where appropriate at the level of participating companies must in that case be maintained by adapting registration rules.

10. The voting rules within the special body representing the employees for negotiation purposes, in particular when concluding agreements providing for a level of participation lower than the one existing within one or more of the participating companies, should be proportionate to the risk of disappearance or reduction of existing systems and practices of participation. That risk is greater in the case of an SE established by way of transformation or merger than by way of creating a holding company or a common subsidiary.

11. In the absence of an agreement subsequent to the negotiation between employees' representatives and the competent organs of the participating companies, provision should be made for certain standard requirements to apply to the SE, once it is established. These standard requirements should ensure effective practices of transnational information and consultation of employees, as well as their participation in the relevant organs of the SE if and when such participation existed before its establishment within the participating companies.

12. Provision should be made for the employees' representatives acting within the framework of the Directive to enjoy, when exercising their functions, protection and guarantees which are similar to those provided to employees' representatives by the legislation and/or practice of the country of employment. They should not be subject to any discrimination as a result of the lawful exercise of their activities and should enjoy adequate protection as regard dismissal and other sanctions.

13. The confidentiality of sensitive information should be preserved even after the expiry of the employees' representatives' terms of office and provision should be made to allow the competent organ of the SE to withhold information which would seriously harm, if subject to public disclosure, the functioning of the SE.

14. Where an SE and its subsidiaries and establishments are subject to Council Directive 94/45/EC of 22 September 1994 on the establishment of a European Works Council or a procedure in Community-scale undertakings and Community-scale groups of undertakings for the purposes of informing and consulting employees,[6] the provisions of that Directive and the provision transposing it into national legislation should not apply to it nor to its subsidiaries and establishments, unless the special negotiating body decides not to open negotiations or to terminate negotiations already opened.

15. This Directive should not affect other existing rights regarding involvement and need not affect other existing representation structures, provided for by Community and national laws and practices.

16. Member States should take appropriate measures in the event of failure to comply with the obligations laid down in this Directive.

17. The Treaty has not provided the necessary powers for the Community to adopt the proposed Directive, other than those provided for in Article 308.

18. It is a fundamental principle and stated aim of this Directive to secure employees' acquired rights as regards involvement in company decisions. Employee rights in force before the establishment of SEs should provide the basis for employee rights of involvement in the SE (the "before and after" principle). Consequently, that approach should apply not only to the initial establishment of an SE but also to structural changes in an existing SE and to the companies affected by structural change processes.

19. Member States should be able to provide that representatives of trade unions may be members of a special negotiating body regardless of whether they are employees of a company participating in the establishment of an SE. Member States should in this context in particular be able to introduce this right in cases where trade union representatives have the right to be members of, and to vote in, supervisory or administrative company organs in accordance with national legislation.

20. In several Member States, employee involvement and other areas of industrial relations are based on both national legislation and practice which in this context is understood also to cover collective agreements at various national, sectoral and/or company levels,

HAS ADOPTED THIS DIRECTIVE:

---

6. *O.J.*, L 254, 30 September 1994. Directive as last amended by Directive 97/74/EC (*O.J.*, L 10, 16 January 1998).

SECTION I
GENERAL

Article 1
Objective

1. This Directive governs the involvement of employees in the affairs of European public limited-liability companies (Societas Europaea, hereinafter referred to as "SE"), as referred to in Regulation (EC) No 2157/2001.
2. To this end, arrangements for the involvement of employees shall be established in every SE in accordance with the negotiating procedure referred to in Articles 3 to 6 or, under the circumstances specified in Article 7, in accordance with the Annex.

Article 2
Definitions

For the purposes of this Directive:
(a) "SE" means any company established in accordance with Regulation (EC) No 2157/2001;
(b) "Participating companies" means the companies directly participating in the establishing of an SE;
(c) "Subsidiary" of a company means an undertaking over which that company exercises a dominant influence defined in accordance with Article 3(2) to (7) of Directive 94/45/EC;
(d) "Concerned subsidiary or establishment" means a subsidiary or establishment of a participating company which is proposed to become a subsidiary or establishment of the SE upon its formation;
(e) "Employees' representatives" means the employees' representatives provided for by national law and/or practice;
(f) "Representative body" means the body representative of the employees set up by the agreements referred to in Article 4 or in accordance with the provisions of the Annex, with the purpose of informing and consulting the employees of an SE and its subsidiaries and establishments situated in the Community and, where applicable, of exercising participation rights in relation to the SE;
(g) "Special negotiating body" means the body established in accordance with Article 3 to negotiate with the competent body of the participating companies regarding the establishment of arrangements for the involvement of employees within the SE;
(h) "Involvement of employees" means any mechanism, including information, consultation and participation, through which employees' representatives may exercise an influence on decisions to be taken within the company;

(i)   "Information" means the informing of the body representative of the employees and/or employees' representatives by the competent organ of the SE on questions which concern the SE itself and any of its subsidiaries or establishments situated in another Member State or which exceed the powers of the decision-making organs in a single Member State at a time, in a manner and with a content which allows the employees' representatives to undertake an in-depth assessment of the possible impact and, where appropriate, prepare consultations with the competent organ of the SE;

(j)   "Consultation" means the establishment of dialogue and exchange of views between the body representative of the employees and/or the employees' representatives and the competent organ of the SE, at a time, in a manner and with a content which allows the employees' representatives, on the basis of information provided, to express an opinion on measures envisaged by the competent organ which may be taken into account in the decision-making process within the SE;

(k)   "Participation" means the influence of the body representative of the employees and/or the employees' representatives in the affairs of a company by way of:

–   the right to elect or appoint some of the members of the company's supervisory or administrative organ; or

–   the right to recommend and/or oppose the appointment of some or all of the members of the company's supervisory or administrative organ.

SECTION II
NEGOTIATING PROCEDURE

Article 3
Creation of a special negotiating body

1.   Where the management or administrative organs of the participating companies draw up a plan for the establishment of an SE, they shall as soon as possible after publishing the draft terms of merger or creating a holding company or after agreeing a plan to form a subsidiary or to transform into an SE, take the necessary steps, including providing information about the identity of the participating companies, concerned subsidiaries or establishments, and the number of their employees, to start negotiations with the representatives of the companies' employees on arrangements for the involvement of employees in the SE.

2.   For this purpose, a special negotiating body representative of the employees of the participating companies and concerned subsidiaries or establishments shall be created in accordance with the following provisions:

(a)   in electing or appointing members of the special negotiating body, it must be ensured:

i.   that these members are elected or appointed in proportion to the number of employees employed in each Member State by the participating companies and concerned subsidiaries or establishments, by allocating in respect of a Member State one seat per each portion of employees employed in that Member State which equals 10%, or a fraction thereof, of the number of employees employed by the participating companies and concerned subsidiaries or establishments in all the Member States taken together;

ii.   that in the case of an SE formed by way of merger, there are such further additional members from each Member State as may be necessary in order to ensure that the special negotiating body includes at least one member representing each participating company which is registered and has employees in that Member State and which it is proposed will cease to exist as a separate legal entity following the registration of the SE, insofar as:

–   the number of such additional members does not exceed 20% of the number of members designated by virtue of point (i); and

–   the composition of the special negotiating body does not entail a double representation of the employees concerned.

      If the number of such companies is higher than the number of additional seats available pursuant to the first subparagraph, these additional seats shall be allocated to companies in different Member States by decreasing order of the number of employees they employ.

(b)   Member States shall determine the method to be used for the election or appointment of the members of the special negotiating body who are to be elected or appointed in their territories. They shall take the necessary measures to ensure that, as far as possible, such members shall include at least one member representing each participating company which has employees in the Member State concerned. Such measures must not increase the overall number of members.

      Member States may provide that such members may include representatives of trade unions whether or not they are employees of a participating company or concerned subsidiary or establishment.

      Without prejudice to national legislation and/or practice laying down thresholds for the establishing of a representative body, Member States shall provide that employees in undertakings or establishments in which there are no employees' representatives through no fault of their own have the right to elect or appoint members of the special negotiating body.

3.   The special negotiating body and the competent organs of the participating companies shall determine, by written agreement, arrangements for the involvement of employees within the SE.

      To this end, the competent organs of the participating companies shall inform the special negotiating body of the plan and the actual process of establishing the SE, up to its registration.

4. Subject to paragraph 6, the special negotiating body shall take decisions by an absolute majority of its members, provided that such a majority also represents an absolute majority of the employees. Each member shall have one vote. However, should the result of the negotiations lead to a reduction of participation rights, the majority required for a decision to approve such an agreement shall be the votes of two thirds of the members of the special negotiating body representing at least two thirds of the employees, including the votes of members representing employees employed in at least two Member States,

–   in the case of an SE to be established by way of merger, if participation covers at least 25% of the overall number of employees of the participating companies, or

–   in the case of an SE to be established by way of creating a holding company or forming a subsidiary, if participation covers at least 50% of the overall number of employees of the participating companies.

    Reduction of participation rights means a proportion of members of the organs of the SE within the meaning of Article 2(k), which is lower than the highest proportion existing within the participating companies.

5. For the purpose of the negotiations, the special negotiating body may request experts of its choice, for example representatives of appropriate Community-level trade union organisations, to assist it with its work. Such experts may be present at negotiation meetings in an advisory capacity at the request of the special negotiating body, where appropriate to promote coherence and consistency at Community level. The special negotiating body may decide to inform the representatives of appropriate external organisations, including trade unions, of the start of the negotiations.

6. The special negotiating body may decide by the majority set out below not to open negotiations or to terminate negotiations already opened, and to rely on the rules on information and consultation of employees in force in the Member States where the SE has employees. Such a decision shall stop the procedure to conclude the agreement referred to in Article 4. Where such a decision has been taken, none of the provisions of the Annex shall apply.

    The majority required to decide not to open or to terminate negotiations shall be the votes of two thirds of the members representing at least two thirds of the employees, including the votes of members representing employees employed in at least two Member States.

    In the case of an SE established by way of transformation, this paragraph shall not apply if there is participation in the company to be transformed.

    The special negotiating body shall be reconvened on the written request of at least 10% of the employees of the SE, its subsidiaries and establishments, or their representatives, at the earliest two years after the abovementioned decision, unless the parties agree to negotiations being reopened sooner. If the special negotiating body decides to reopen negotiations with the management but no agreement is reached as a result of those negotiations, none of the provisions of the Annex shall apply.

7.   Any expenses relating to the functioning of the special negotiating body and, in general, to negotiations shall be borne by the participating companies so as to enable the special negotiating body to carry out its task in an appropriate manner.

In compliance with this principle, Member States may lay down budgetary rules regarding the operation of the special negotiating body. They may in particular limit the funding to cover one expert only.

Article 4
Content of the agreement

1.   The competent organs of the participating companies and the special negotiating body shall negotiate in a spirit of cooperation with a view to reaching an agreement on arrangements for the involvement of the employees within the SE.
2.   Without prejudice to the autonomy of the parties, and subject to paragraph 4, the agreement referred to in paragraph 1 between the competent organs of the participating companies and the special negotiating body shall specify:
(a)   the scope of the agreement;
(b)   the composition, number of members and allocation of seats on the representative body which will be the discussion partner of the competent organ of the SE in connection with arrangements for the information and consultation of the employees of the SE and its subsidiaries and establishments;
(c)   the functions and the procedure for the information and consultation of the representative body;
(d)   the frequency of meetings of the representative body;
(e)   the financial and material resources to be allocated to the representative body;
(f)   if, during negotiations, the parties decide to establish one or more information and consultation procedures instead of a representative body, the arrangements for implementing those procedures;
(g)   if during negotiations the parties decide to establish arrangements for participation, the substance of those arrangements including (if applicable) the number of members in the SE's administrative or supervisory body which the employees will be entitled to elect, appoint, recommend or oppose, the procedures as to how these members may be elected, appointed, recommended or opposed by the employees, and their rights;
(h)   the date of entry into force of the agreement and its duration, cases where the agreement should be renegotiated and the procedure for its renegotiation.

3. The agreement shall not, unless provision is made otherwise therein, be subject to the standard rules referred to in the Annex.
4. Without prejudice to Article 13(3)(a), in the case of an SE established by means of transformation, the agreement shall provide for at least the same level of all elements of employee involvement as the ones existing within the company to be transformed into an SE.

Article 5
Duration of negotiations

1. Negotiations shall commence as soon as the special negotiating body is established and may continue for six months thereafter.
2. The parties may decide, by joint agreement, to extend negotiations beyond the period referred to in paragraph 1, up to a total of one year from the establishment of the special negotiating body.

Article 6
Legislation applicable to the negotiation procedure

Except where otherwise provided in this Directive, the legislation applicable to the negotiation procedure provided for in Articles 3 to 5 shall be the legislation of the Member State in which the registered office of the SE is to be situated.

Article 7
Standard rules

1. In order to achieve the objective described in Article 1, Member States shall, without prejudice to paragraph 3 below, lay down standard rules on employee involvement which must satisfy the provisions set out in the Annex.

    The standard rules as laid down by the legislation of the Member State in which the registered office of the SE is to be situated shall apply from the date of the registration of the SE where either:

(a) the parties so agree; or
(b) by the deadline laid down in Article 5, no agreement has been concluded, and:
–   the competent organ of each of the participating companies decides to accept the application of the standard rules in relation to the SE and so to continue with its registration of the SE; and
–   the special negotiating body has not taken the decision provided in Article 3(6).

2. Moreover, the standard rules fixed by the national legislation of the Member State of registration in accordance with part 3 of the Annex shall apply only:

(a) in the case of an SE established by transformation, if the rules of a Member State relating to employee participation in the administrative or supervisory body applied to a company transformed into an SE;

(b) in the case of an SE established by merger:

– if, before registration of the SE, one or more forms of participation applied in one or more of the participating companies covering at least 25% of the total number of employees in all the participating companies; or

– if, before registration of the SE, one or more forms of participation applied in one or more of the participating companies covering less than 25% of the total number of employees in all the participating companies and if the special negotiating body so decides;

(c) in the case of an SE established by setting up a holding company or establishing a subsidiary:

– if, before registration of the SE, one or more forms of participation applied in one or more of the participating companies covering at least 50% of the total number of employees in all the participating companies; or

– if, before registration of the SE, one or more forms of participation applied in one or more of the participating companies covering less than 50% of the total number of employees in all the participating companies and if the special negotiating body so decides.

If there was more than one form of participation within the various participating companies, the special negotiating body shall decide which of those forms must be established in the SE. Member States may fix the rules which are applicable in the absence of any decision on the matter for an SE registered in If there was more than one form of participation within the various participating companies, the special their territory. The special negotiating body shall inform the competent organs of the participating companies of any decisions taken pursuant to this paragraph.

3. Member States may provide that the reference provisions in part 3 of the Annex shall not apply in the case provided for in point (b) of paragraph 2.

SECTION III
MISCELLANEOUS PROVISIONS

Article 8
Reservation and confidentiality

1. Member States shall provide that members of the special negotiating body or the representative body, and experts who assist them, are not authorised to reveal any information which as been given to them in confidence.

The same shall apply to employees' representatives in the context of an information and consultation procedure.

This obligation shall continue to apply, wherever the persons referred to may be, even after the expiry of their terms of office.

2. Each Member State shall provide, in specific cases and under the conditions and limits laid down by national legislation, that the supervisory or administrative organ of an SE or of a participating company established in its territory is not obliged to transmit information where its nature is such that, according to objective criteria, to do so would seriously harm the functioning of the SE (or, as the case may be, the participating company) or its subsidiaries and establishments or would be prejudicial to them.

A Member State may make such dispensation subject to prior administrative or judicial authorisation.

3. Each Member State may lay down particular provisions for SEs in its territory which pursue directly and essentially the aim of ideological guidance with respect to information and the expression of opinions, on condition that, on the date of adoption of this Directive, such provisions already exist in the national legislation.

4. In applying paragraphs 1, 2 and 3, Member States shall make provision for administrative or judicial appeal procedures which the employees' representatives may initiate when the supervisory or administrative organ of an SE or participating company demands confidentiality or does not give information.

Such procedures may include arrangements designed to protect the confidentiality of the information in question.

Article 9
Operation of the representative body and procedure for the information and consultation of employees

The competent organ of the SE and the representative body shall work together in a spirit of cooperation with due regard for their reciprocal rights and obligations.

The same shall apply to cooperation between the supervisory or administrative organ of the SE and the employees' representatives in conjunction with a procedure for the information and consultation of employees.

Article 10
Protection of employees' representatives

The members of the special negotiating body, the members of the representative body, any employees' representatives exercising functions under the information and consultation procedure and any employees' representatives in the supervisory or administrative organ of an SE who are employees of the SE, its subsidiaries or establishments or of a participating company shall, in the exercise of their functions, enjoy the same protection and guarantees provided for employees' representatives by the national legislation and/or practice in force in their country of employment.

This shall apply in particular to attendance at meetings of the special negotiating body or representative body, any other meeting under the agreement referred to in Article 4(2)(f) or any meeting of the administrative or supervisory organ, and to the payment of wages for members employed by a participating company or the SE or its subsidiaries or establishments during a period of absence necessary for the performance of their duties.

Article 11
Misuse of procedures

Member States shall take appropriate measures in conformity with Community law with a view to preventing the misuse of an SE for the purpose of depriving employees of rights to employee involvement or withholding such rights.

Article 12
Compliance with this Directive

1. Each Member State shall ensure that the management of establishments of an SE and the supervisory or administrative organs of subsidiaries and of participating companies which are situated within its territory and the employees' representatives or, as the case may be, the employees themselves abide by the obligations laid down by this Directive, regardless of whether or not the SE has its registered office within its territory.
2. Member States shall provide for appropriate measures in the event of failure to comply with this Directive; in particular they shall ensure that administrative or legal procedures are available to enable the obligations deriving from this Directive to be enforced.

Article 13
Link between this Directive and other provisions

1. Where an SE is a Community-scale undertaking or a controlling undertaking of a Community-scale group of undertakings within the meaning of Directive 94/45/EC or of Directive 97/74/EC[7] extending the

_____

7.   *O.J.*, 10, 16 January 1998.

said Directive to the United Kingdom, the provisions of these Directives and the provisions transposing them into national legislation shall not apply to them or to their subsidiaries.

However, where the special negotiating body decides in accordance with Article 3(6) not to open negotiations or to terminate negotiations already opened, Directive 94/45/EC or Directive 97/74/EC and the provisions transposing them into national legislation shall apply.

2. Provisions on the participation of employees in company bodies provided for by national legislation and/or practice, other than those implementing this Directive, shall not apply to companies established in accordance with Regulation (EC) No 2157/2001 and covered by this Directive.

3. This Directive shall not prejudice:

(a) the existing rights to involvement of employees provided for by national legislation and/or practice in the Member States as enjoyed by employees of the SE and its subsidiaries and establishments, other than participation in the bodies of the SE;

(b) the provisions on participation in the bodies laid down by national legislation and/or practice applicable to the subsidiaries of the SE.

4. In order to preserve the rights referred to in paragraph 3, Member States may take the necessary measures to guarantee that the structures of employee representation in participating companies which will cease to exist as separate legal entities are maintained after the registration of the SE.

Article 14
Final provisions

1. Member States shall adopt the laws, regulations and administrative provisions necessary to comply with this Directive no later than three years from the date of adoption of this Directive, or shall ensure by that date at the latest that management and labour introduce the required provisions by way of agreement, the Member States being obliged to take all necessary steps enabling them at all times to guarantee the results imposed by this Directive. They shall forthwith inform the Commission thereof.

2. When Member States adopt these measures, they shall contain a reference to this Directive or shall be accompanied by such reference on the occasion of their official publication. The methods of making such reference shall be laid down by the Member States.

Article 15
Review by the Commission

Not later than 8 October 2007, the Commission shall, in consultation with the Member States and with management and labour at Community level, review the procedures for applying this Directive, with a view to proposing suitable amendments to the Council where necessary.

Article 16
Entry into force

This Directive shall enter into force on the date of its publication in the Official Journal of the European Communities.

Article 17
Addressees

This Directive is addressed to the Member States.

ANNEX

Standard Rules
        (referred to in Article 7)

Part 1: Composition of the body representative of the employees

In order to achieve the objective described in Article 1, and in the cases referred to in Article 7, a representative body shall be set up in accordance with the following rules:

(a)   The representative body shall be composed of employees of the SE and its subsidiaries and establishments elected or appointed from their number by the employees' representatives or, in the absence thereof, by the entire body of employees.

(b)   The election or appointment of members of the representative body shall be carried out in accordance with national legislation and/or practice.
       Member States shall lay down rules to ensure that the number of members of, and allocation of seats on, the representative body shall be adapted to take account of changes occurring within the SE and its subsidiaries and establishments.

(c)   Where its size so warrants, the representative body shall elect a select committee from among its members, comprising at most three members.

(d)   The representative body shall adopt its rules of procedure.

(e)   The members of the representative body are elected or appointed in proportion to the number of employees employed in each Member State by the participating companies and concerned subsidiaries or establishments, by allocating in respect of a Member State one seat per each portion of employees employed in that Member State which equals 10%, or a fraction thereof, of the number of employees employed by the participating companies and concerned subsidiaries or establishments in all the Member States taken together.

(f) The competent organ of the SE shall be informed of the composition of the representative body.

(g) Four years after the representative body is established, it shall examine whether to open negotiations for the conclusion of the agreement referred to in Articles 4 and 7 or to continue to apply the standard rules adopted in accordance with this Annex.

Articles 3(4) to (7) and 4 to 6 shall apply, mutatis mutandis, if a decision has been taken to negotiate an agreement according to Article 4, in which case the term "special negotiating body" shall be replaced by "representative body". Where, by the deadline by which the negotiations come to an end, no agreement has been concluded, the arrangements initially adopted in accordance with the standard rules shall continue to apply.

Part 2: Standard rules for information and consultation

The competence and powers of the representative body set up in an SE shall be governed by the following rules:

(a) The competence of the representative body shall be limited to questions which concern the SE itself and any of its subsidiaries or establishments situated in another Member State or which exceed the powers of the decision-making organs in a single Member State.

(b) Without prejudice to meetings held pursuant to point (c), the representative body shall have the right to be informed and consulted and, for that purpose, to meet with the competent organ of the SE at least once a year, on the basis of regular reports drawn up by the competent organ, on the progress of the business of the SE and its prospects. The local managements shall be informed accordingly.

The competent organ of the SE shall provide the representative body with the agenda for meetings of the administrative, or, where appropriate, the management and supervisory organ, and with copies of all documents submitted to the general meeting of its shareholders.

The meeting shall relate in particular to the structure, economic and financial situation, the probable development of the business and of production and sales, the situation and probable trend of employment, investments, and substantial changes concerning organisation, introduction of new working methods or production processes, transfers of production, mergers, cut-backs or closures of undertakings, establishments or important parts thereof, and collective redundancies.

(c) Where there are exceptional circumstances affecting the employees' interests to a considerable extent, particularly in the event of relocations, transfers, the closure of establishments or undertakings or collective redundancies, the representative body shall have the right to be informed.

The representative body or, where it so decides, in particular for reasons of urgency, the select committee, shall have the right to meet at its request, the competent organ of the SE or any more appropriate level of management within the SE having its own powers of decision, so as to be informed and consulted on measures significantly affecting employees' interests.

Where the competent organ decides not to act in accordance with the opinion expressed by the representative body, this body shall have the right to a further meeting with the competent organ of the SE with a view to seeking agreement.

In the case of a meeting organised with the select committee, those members of the representative body who represent employees who are directly concerned by the measures in question shall also have the right to participate.

The meetings referred to above shall not affect the prerogatives of the competent organ.

(d) Member States may lay down rules on the chairing of information and consultation meetings.

Before any meeting with the competent organ of the SE, the representative body or the select committee, where necessary enlarged in accordance with the third subparagraph of paragraph (c), shall be entitled to meet without the representatives of the competent organ being present.

(e) Without prejudice to Article 8, the members of the representative body shall inform the representatives of the employees of the SE and of its subsidiaries and establishments of the content and outcome of the information and consultation procedures.

(f) The representative body or the select committee may be assisted by experts of its choice.

(g) Insofar as this is necessary for the fulfilment of their tasks, the members of the representative body shall be entitled to time off for training without loss of wages.

(h) The costs of the representative body shall be borne by the SE, which shall provide the body's members with the financial and material resources needed to enable them to perform their duties in an appropriate manner.

In particular, the SE shall, unless otherwise agreed, bear the cost of organising meetings and providing interpretation facilities and the accommodation and travelling expenses of members of the representative body and the select committee.

In compliance with these principles, the Member States may lay down budgetary rules regarding the operation of the representative body. They may in particular limit funding to cover one expert only.

Part 3: Standard rules for participation

Employee participation in an SE shall be governed by the following provisions:

(a) In the case of an SE established by transformation, if the rules of a Member State relating to employee participation in the administrative or supervisory body applied before registration, all aspects of employee participation shall continue to apply to the SE. Point (b) shall apply mutatis mutandis to that end.

(b) In other cases of the establishing of an SE, the employees of the SE, its subsidiaries and establishments and/or their representative body shall have the right to elect, appoint, recommend or oppose the appointment of a number of members of the administrative or supervisory body of the SE equal to the highest proportion in force in the participating companies concerned before registration of the SE.

If none of the participating companies was governed by participation rules before registration of the SE, the latter shall not be required to establish provisions for employee participation.

The representative body shall decide on the allocation of seats within the administrative or supervisory body among the members representing the employees from the various Member States or on the way in which the SE's employees may recommend or oppose the appointment of the members of these bodies according to the proportion of the SE's employees in each Member State. If the employees of one or more Member States are not covered by this proportional criterion, the representative body shall appoint a member from one of those Member States, in particular the Member State of the SE's registered office where that is appropriate. Each Member State may determine the allocation of the seats it is given within the administrative or supervisory body.

Every member of the administrative body or, where appropriate, the supervisory body of the SE who has been elected, appointed or recommended by the representative body or, depending on the circumstances, by the employees shall be a full member with the same rights and obligations as the members representing the shareholders, including right to vote.

II. COUNCIL REGULATION (EC) NO 2157/2001 OF ON THE STATUTE FOR A EUROPEAN COMPANY (SE)

THE COUNCIL OF THE EUROPEAN UNION,

Having regard to the Treaty establishing the European Community, and in particular Article 308 thereof,

Having regard to the proposal from the Commission,[8]

---

8.   *O.J.*, 263, 16 October 1989 and *O.J.*, C 176, 8 July 1991.

Having regard to the Opinion of the European Parliament,[9]
Having regard to the Opinion of the Economic and Social Committee,[10]
Whereas:

1. The completion of the internal market and the improvement it brings about in the economic and social situation throughout the Community mean not only that barriers to trade must be removed, but also that the structures of production must be adapted to the Community dimension. For that purpose it is essential that companies the business of which is not limited to satisfying purely local needs should be able to plan and carry out the reorganisation of their business on a Community scale.

2. Such reorganisation presupposes that existing companies from different Member States are given the option of combining their potential by means of mergers. Such operations can be carried out only with due regard to the rules of competition laid down in the Treaty.

3. Restructuring and cooperation operations involving companies from different Member States give rise to legal and psychological difficulties and tax problems. The approximation of Member States' company law by means of Directives based on Article 44 of the Treaty can overcome some of those difficulties. Such approximation does not, however, release companies governed by different legal systems from the obligation to choose a form of company governed by a particular national law.

4. The legal framework within which business must be carried on in the Community is still based largely on national laws and therefore no longer corresponds to the economic framework within which it must develop if the objectives set out in Article 18 of the Treaty are to be achieved. That situation forms a considerable obstacle to the creation of groups of companies from different Member States.

5. Member States are obliged to ensure that the provisions applicable to European companies under this Regulation do not result either in discrimination arising out of unjustified different treatment of European Companies compared with public limited-liability companies or in disproportionate restrictions on the formation of a European Company or on the transfer of its registered office.

6. It is essential to ensure as far as possible that the economic unit and the legal unit of business in the Community coincide. For that purpose, provision should be made for the creation, side by side with companies governed by a particular national law, of companies formed and carrying on business under the law created by a Community Regulation directly applicable in all Member States.

7. The provisions of such a Regulation will permit the creation and management of companies with a European dimension, free from the obstacles arising from the disparity and the limited territorial application of national company law.

---

9.   *O.J.*, C.
10.   *O.J.*, C 124, 21 May 1990.

8.   The Statute for a European public limited-liability Company (hereafter referred to as "SE") is among the measures to be adopted by the Council before 1992 listed in the Commission's White Paper on completing the internal market, approved by the European Council that met in Milan in June 1985. The European Council that met in Brussels in 1987 expressed the wish to see such a Statute created swiftly.

9.   Since the Commission's submission in 1970 of a proposal for a Regulation on the Statute for a European public limited-liability Company, amended in 1975, work on the approximation of national company law has made substantial progress, so that on those points where the functioning of an SE does not need uniform Community rules reference may be made to the law governing public limited-liability companies in the Member State where it has its registered office.

10. Without prejudice to any economic needs that may arise in the future, if the essential objective of legal rules governing SEs is to be attained, it must be possible at least to create such a company as a means both of enabling companies from different Member States to merge or to create a holding company and of enabling companies and other legal persons carrying on economic activities and governed by the laws of different Member States to form joint subsidiaries.

11. In the same context it should be possible for a public limited-liability company with a registered office and head office within the Community to transform itself into an SE without going into liquidation, provided it has a subsidiary in a Member State other than that of its registered office.

12. National provisions applying to public limited-liability companies that offer their securities to the public and to securities transactions should also apply where an SE is formed by means of an offer of securities to the public and to SEs wishing to utilise such financial instruments.

13. The SE itself must take the form of a company with share capital, that being the form most suited, in terms of both financing and management, to the needs of a company carrying on business on a European scale. In order to ensure that such companies are of reasonable size, a minimum amount of capital should be set so that they have sufficient assets without making it difficult for small and medium-sized undertakings to form SEs.

14. An SE must be efficiently managed and properly supervised. It must be borne in mind that there are at present in the Community two different systems for the administration of public limited-liability companies. Although an SE should be allowed to choose between the two systems, the respective responsibilities of those responsible for management and those responsible for supervision should be clearly defined.

15. Having regard to the approximation effected by the Fourth Council Directive (78/660/EEC) of 25 July 1978 based on Article 54(3)(g) of the Treaty on the annual accounts of certain types of companies[11] and the

---

11.   *O.J.*, L 222, 14 August 1978. Directive as last amended by Directive 99/60/EC (*O.J.*, L 162, 26 June 1999).

Seventh Council Directive (83/349/EEC) of 13 June 1983 based on Article 54(3)(g) of the Treaty on consolidated accounts,[12] the provisions of those Directives may be made applicable to SEs and such companies may be allowed to choose between the options offered by those provisions.

16. Under the rules and general principles of private international law, where one undertaking controls another governed by a different legal system, its ensuing rights and obligations as regards the protection of minority shareholders and third parties are governed by the law governing the controlled undertaking, without prejudice to the obligations imposed on the controlling undertaking by its own law, for example the requirement to prepare consolidated accounts.

17. Without prejudice to the consequences of any subsequent coordination of the laws of the Member States, specific rules for SEs are not at present required in this field. The rules and general principles of private international law should therefore be applied both where an SE exercises control and where it is the controlled company.

18. The rule thus applicable where an SE is controlled by another undertaking should be specified, and for this purpose reference should be made to the law governing public limited-liability companies in the State in which the SE has its registered office.

19. Each Member State must be required to apply the sanctions applicable to public limited-liability companies governed by its law in respect of infringements of this Regulation.

20. The rules on the involvement of employees in the European Company are laid down in Directive 2001/86/EC,[13] and those provisions thus form an indissociable complement to this Regulation and must be applied concomitantly.

21. This Regulation does not cover other areas of law such as taxation, competition, intellectual property or insolvency. The provisions of the Member States' law and of Community law are therefore applicable in the above areas and in other areas not covered by this Regulation.

22. Directive 2001/86/EC is designed to ensure that employees have a right of involvement in issues and decisions affecting the life of their SE. Other social and labour legislation questions, in particular the right of employees to information and consultation as regulated in the Member States, are governed by the national provisions applicable, under the same conditions, to public limited-liability companies.

23. The entry into force of this Regulation must be deferred so that each Member State may incorporate into its national law the provisions of Directive 2001/86/EC and set up in advance the necessary machinery for the formation and operation of SEs with registered offices within its territory, so that the Regulation and the Directive may be applied concomitantly.

---

12.   O.J., L 193, 18 July 19831. Directive as last amended by the 1994 Act of Accession.
13.   See p. 22 of this *Official Journal*.

24. A company the head office of which is not in the Community should be allowed to participate in the formation of an SE provided that company is formed under the law of a Member State, has its registered office in that Member State and has a real and continuous link with a Member State's economy according to the principles established in the 1962 General Programme for the abolition of restrictions on freedom of establishment. Such a link exists in particular if a company has an establishment in that Member State and conducts operations therefrom.

25. The SE should be enabled to transfer its registered office to another Member State. Adequate protection of the interests of minority share-holders who oppose the transfer, of creditors and of holders of other rights should be proportionate. Such transfer should not affect the rights originating before the transfer.

26. This Regulation is without prejudice to any provision which may be inserted in the 1968 Brussels Convention or in any text adopted by Member States or by the Council to replace such Convention, relating to the rules of jurisdiction applicable in the case of transfer of the registered offices of a public limited-liability company from one Member State to another.

27. Activities by financial institutions are regulated by specific directives and the national law implementing those directives and additional national rules regulating those activities apply in full to an SE.

28. In view of the specific Community character of an SE, the "real seat" arrangement adopted by this Regulation in respect of SEs is without prejudice to Member States' laws and does not pre-empt any choices to be made for other Community texts on company law.

29. The Treaty does not provide, for the adoption of this Regulation, powers of action other than those of Article 308 thereof.

30. Since the objectives of the intended action, as outlined above, cannot be adequately attained by the Member States in as much as a European public limited-liability company is being established at European level and can therefore, because of the scale and impact of such company, be better attained at Community level, the Community may take measures in accordance with the principle of subsidiarity enshrined in Article 5 of the Treaty. In accordance with the principle of proportionality as set out in the said Article, this Regulation does not go beyond what is necessary to attain these objectives,

HAS ADOPTED THIS REGULATION:

TITLE I

GENERAL PROVISIONS

Article 1

1. A company may be set up within the territory of the Community in the form of a European public limited-liability company (Societas Europaea or SE) on the conditions and in the manner laid down in this Regulation.
2. The capital of an SE shall be divided into shares. No shareholder shall be liable for more than the amount he has subscribed.
3. An SE shall have legal personality.
4. Employee involvement in an SE shall be governed by the provisions of Directive 2001/86/EC.

Article 2

1. Public limited-liability companies such as referred to in Annex I, formed under the law of a Member State, with registered offices and head offices within the Community may form an SE by means of a merger provided that at least two of them are governed by the law of different Member States.
2. Public and private limited-liability companies such as referred to in Annex II, formed under the law of a Member State, with registered offices and head offices within the Community may promote the formation of a holding SE provided that each of at least two of them:
(a) is governed by the law of a different Member State, or
(b) has for at least two years had a subsidiary company governed by the law of another Member State or an establishment situated in another Member State.
3. Companies and firms within the meaning of the second paragraph of Article 48 of the Treaty and other legal bodies governed by public or private law, formed under the law of a Member State, with registered offices and head offices within the Community may form a subsidiary SE by subscribing for its shares, provided that each of at least two of them:
(a) is governed by the law of a different Member State, or
(b) has for at least two years had a subsidiary company governed by the law of another Member State or an establishment situated in another Member State.
4. A public limited-liability company, formed under the law of a Member State, which has its registered office and head office within the Community may be transformed into an SE if for at least two years it has had a subsidiary company governed by the law of another Member State.

5. A Member State may provide that a company the head office of which is not in the Community may participate in the formation of an SE provided that company is formed under the law of a Member State, has its registered office in that Member State and has a real and continuous link with a Member State's economy.

Article 3

1. For the purposes of Article 2(1), (2) and (3), an SE shall be regarded as a public limited-liability company governed by the law of the Member State in which it has its registered office.
2. An SE may itself set up one or more subsidiaries in the form of SEs. The provisions of the law of the Member State in which a subsidiary SE has its registered office that require a public limited-liability company to have more than one shareholder shall not apply in the case of the subsidiary SE. The provisions of national law implementing the Twelfth Council Company Law Directive (89/667/EEC) of 21 December 1989 on single-member private limited-liability companies[14] shall apply to SEs "mutatis mutandis".

Article 4

1. The capital of an SE shall be expressed in euros.
2. The subscribed capital shall not be less than EUR 120.000.
3. The laws of a Member State requiring a greater subscribed capital for companies carrying on certain types of activity shall apply to SEs with registered offices in that Member State.

Article 5

Subject to Article 4(1) and (2), the capital of an SE, its maintenance and changes thereto, together with its shares, bonds and other similar securities shall be governed by the provisions which would apply to a public limited-liability company with a registered office in the Member State in which the SE is registered.

---

14.   *O.J.*, L 395, 30 December 1989. Directive as last amended by the 1994 Act of Accession.

Article 6

For the purposes of this Regulation, "the statutes of the SE" shall mean both the instrument of incorporation and, where they are the subject of a separate document, the statutes of the SE.

Article 7

The registered office of an SE shall be located within the Community, in the same Member State as its head office. A Member State may in addition impose on SEs registered in its territory the obligation of locating their head office and their registered office in the same place.

Article 8

1. The registered office of an SE may be transferred to another Member State in accordance with paragraphs 2 to 13. Such a transfer shall not result in the winding up of the SE or in the creation of a new legal person.
2. The management or administrative organ shall draw up a transfer proposal and publicise it in accordance with Article 13, without prejudice to any additional forms of publication provided for by the Member State of the registered office. That proposal shall state the current name, registered office and number of the SE and shall cover:
(a) the proposed registered office of the SE;
(b) the proposed statutes of the SE including, where appropriate, its new name;
(c) any implication the transfer may have on employees' involvement;
(d) the proposed transfer timetable;
(e) any rights provided for the protection of shareholders and/or creditors.
3. The management or administrative organ shall draw up a report explaining and justifying the legal and economic aspects of the transfer and explaining the implications of the transfer for shareholders, creditors and employees.
4. An SE's shareholders and creditors shall be entitled, at least one month before the general meeting called upon to decide on the transfer, to examine at the SE's registered office the transfer proposal and the report drawn up pursuant to paragraph 3 and, on request, to obtain copies of those documents free of charge.
5. A Member State may, in the case of SEs registered within its territory, adopt provisions designed to ensure appropriate protection for minority shareholders who oppose a transfer.
6. No decision to transfer may be taken for two months after publication of the proposal. Such a decision shall be taken as laid down in Article 59.

7. Before the competent authority issues the certificate mentioned in paragraph 5, the SE shall satisfy it that, in respect of any liabilities arising prior to the publication of the transfer proposal, the interests of creditors and holders of other rights in respect of the SE (including those of public bodies) have been adequately protected in accordance with requirements laid down by the Member State where the SE has its registered office prior to the transfer.

A Member State may extend the application of the first subparagraph to liabilities that arise (or may arise) prior to the transfer.

The first and second subparagraphs shall be without prejudice to the application to SEs of the national legislation of Member States concerning the satisfaction or securing of payments to public bodies.

8. In the Member State in which an SE has its registered office the court, notary or other competent authority shall issue a certificate attesting to the completion of the acts and formalities to be accomplished before the transfer.

9. The new registration may not be effected until the certificate referred to in paragraph 8 has been submitted, and evidence produced that the formalities required for registration in the country of the new registered office have been completed.

10. The transfer of an SE's registered office and the consequent amendment of its statutes shall take effect on the date on which the SE is registered, in accordance with Article 12, in the register for its new registered office.

11. When the SE's new registration has been effected, the registry for its new registration shall notify the registry for its old registration. Deletion of the old registration shall be effected on receipt of that notification, but not before.

12. The new registration and the deletion of the old registration shall be publicised in the Member States concerned in accordance with Article 13.

13. On publication of an SE's new registration, the new registered office may be relied on as against third parties. However, as long as the deletion of the SE's registration from the register for its previous registered office has not been publicised, third parties may continue to rely on the previous registered office unless the SE proves that such third parties were aware of the new registered office.

14. The laws of a Member State may provide that, as regards SEs registered in that Member State, the transfer of a registered office which would result in a change of the law applicable shall not take effect if any of that Member State's competent authorities opposes it within the two-month period referred to in paragraph 6. Such opposition may be based only on grounds of public interest.

Where an SE is supervised by a national financial supervisory authority according to Community directives the right to oppose the change of registered office applies to this authority as well.

Review by a judicial authority shall be possible.

15. An SE may not transfer its registered office if proceedings for winding up, liquidation, insolvency or suspension of payments or other similar proceedings have been brought against it.

16. An SE which has transferred its registered office to another Member State shall be considered, in respect of any cause of action arising prior to the transfer as determined in paragraph 10, as having its registered office in the Member States where the SE was registered prior to the transfer, even if the SE is sued after the transfer.

Article 9

1. An SE shall be governed:
(a) by this Regulation,
(b) where expressly authorised by this Regulation, by the provisions of its statutes

    or

(c) in the case of matters not regulated by this Regulation or, where matters are partly regulated by it, of those aspects not covered by it, by:
i.   the provisions of laws adopted by Member States in implementation of Community measures relating specifically to SEs;
ii. the provisions of Member States' laws which would apply to a public limited-liability company formed in accordance with the law of the Member State in which the SE has its registered office;
iii. the provisions of its statutes, in the same way as for a public limited-liability company formed in accordance with the law of the Member State in which the SE has its registered office.

2. The provisions of laws adopted by Member States specifically for the SE must be in accordance with Directives applicable to public limited-liability companies referred to in Annex I.

3. If the nature of the business carried out by an SE is regulated by specific provisions of national laws, those laws shall apply in full to the SE.

Article 10

Subject to this Regulation, an SE shall be treated in every Member State as if it were a public limited-liability company formed in accordance with the law of the Member State in which it has its registered office.

Article 11

1. The name of an SE shall be preceded or followed by the acronym "SE".
2. Only SEs may include the acronym "SE" in their name.

3. Nevertheless, companies, firms and other legal entities registered in a Member State before the date of entry into force of this Regulation in the names of which the acronym "SE" appears shall not be required to alter their names.

Article 12

1. Every SE shall be registered in the Member State in which it has its registered office in a register designated by the law of that Member State in accordance with Article 3 of the First Council Directive (68/151/EEC) of 9 March 1968 on coordination of safeguards which, for the protection of the interests of members and others, are required by Member States of companies within the meaning of the second paragraph of Article 58 of the Treaty, with a view to making such safeguards equivalent throughout the Community.[15]

2. An SE may not be registered unless an agreement on arrangements for employee involvement pursuant to Article 4 of Directive 2001/86/EC has been concluded, or a decision pursuant to Article 3(6) of the Directive has been taken, or the period for negotiations pursuant to Article 5 of the Directive has expired without an agreement having been concluded.

3. In order for an SE to be registered in a Member State which has made use of the option referred to in Article 7(3) of Directive 2001/86/EC, either an agreement pursuant to Article 4 of the Directive must have been concluded on the arrangements for employee involvement, including participation, or none of the participating companies must have been governed by participation rules prior to the registration of the SE.

4. The statutes of the SE must not conflict at any time with the arrangements for employee involvement which have been so determined. Where new such arrangements determined pursuant to the Directive conflict with the existing statutes, the statutes shall to the extent necessary be amended.

    In this case, a Member State may provide that the management organ or the administrative organ of the SE shall be entitled to proceed to amend the statutes without any further decision from the general shareholders meeting.

Article 13

Publication of the documents and particulars concerning an SE which must be publicised under this Regulation shall be effected in the manner laid down in the laws of the Member State in which the SE has its registered office in accordance with Directive 68/151/EEC.

---

15.   *O.J.*, L 65, 14 March 1968. Directive as last amended by the 1994 Act of Accession.

Article 14

1. Notice of an SE's registration and of the deletion of such a registration shall be published for information purposes in the Official Journal of the European Communities after publication in accordance with Article 13. That notice shall state the name, number, date and place of registration of the SE, the date and place of publication and the title of publication, the registered office of the SE and its sector of activity.
2. Where the registered office of an SE is transferred in accordance with Article 8, notice shall be published giving the information provided for in paragraph 1, together with that relating to the new registration.
3. The particulars referred to in paragraph 1 shall be forwarded to the Official Publications Office of the European Communities within one month of the publication referred to in Article 13.

TITLE II

FORMATION

SECTION 1
GENERAL

Article 15

1. Subject to this Regulation, the formation of an SE shall be governed by the law applicable to public limited-liability companies in the State in which the SE establishes its registered office.
2. The registration of an SE shall be publicised in accordance with Article 13.

Article 16

1. An SE shall acquire legal personality on the date on which it is registered in the register referred to in Article 12.
2. If acts have been performed in an SE's name before its registration in accordance with Article 12 and the SE does not assume the obligations arising out of such acts after its registration, the natural persons, companies, firms or other legal entities which performed those acts shall be jointly and severally liable therefor, without limit, in the absence of agreement to the contrary.

SECTION 2
FORMATION BY MERGER

Article 17

1. An SE may be formed by means of a merger in accordance with Article
    2(1).
2. Such a merger may be carried out in accordance with:
(a) the procedure for merger by acquisition laid down in Article 3(1) of the
    Third Council Directive (78/855/EEC) of 9 October 1978 based on Article
    54(3)(g) of the Treaty concerning mergers of public limited-liability
    companies[16] or
(b) the procedure for merger by the formation of a new company laid down
    in Article 4(1) of the said Directive.

In the case of a merger by acquisition, the acquiring company shall take
the form of an SE when the merger takes place. In the case of a merger by the
formation of a new company, the SE shall be the newly formed company.

Article 18

For matters not covered by this section or, where a matter is partly covered by
it, for aspects not covered by it, each company involved in the formation of an
SE by merger shall be governed by the provisions of the law of the Member
State to which it is subject that apply to mergers of public limited-liability
companies in accordance with Directive 78/855/EEC.

Article 19

The laws of a Member State may provide that a company governed by the law
of that Member State may not take part in the formation of an SE by merger if
any of that Member State's competent authorities opposes it before the issue of
the certificate referred to in Article 25(2).

Such opposition may be based only on grounds of public interest.
Review by a judicial authority shall be possible.

Article 20

1. The management or administrative organs of merging companies shall
    draw up draft terms of merger. The draft terms of merger shall include the
    following particulars:

---

16. *O.J.*, L 295, 20 October 1978, p. 36. Directive as last amended by the 1994 Act of
     Accession.

(a)   the name and registered office of each of the merging companies together with those proposed for the SE;
(b)   the share-exchange ratio and the amount of any compensation;
(c)   the terms for the allotment of shares in the SE;
(d)   the date from which the holding of shares in the SE will entitle the holders to share in profits and any special conditions affecting that entitlement;
(e)   the date from which the transactions of the merging companies will be treated for accounting purposes as being those of the SE;
(f)   the rights conferred by the SE on the holders of shares to which special rights are attached and on the holders of securities other than shares, or the measures proposed concerning them;
(g)   any special advantage granted to the experts who examine the draft terms of merger or to members of the administrative, management, supervisory or controlling organs of the merging companies;
(h)   the statutes of the SE;
(i)   information on the procedures 86 which arrangements for employee involvement are determined pursuant to Directive 2001/86/EC.
2.   The merging companies may include further items in the draft terms of merger.

Article 21

For each of the merging companies and subject to the additional requirements imposed by the Member State to which the company concerned is subject, the following particulars shall be published in the national gazette of that Member State:
(a)   the type, name and registered office of every merging company;
(b)   the register in which the documents referred to in Article 3(2) of Directive 68/151/EEC are filed in respect of each merging company, and the number of the entry in that register;
(c)   an indication of the arrangements made in accordance with Article 24 for the exercise of the rights of the creditors of the company in question and the address at which complete information on those arrangements may be obtained free of charge;
(d)   an indication of the arrangements made in accordance with Article 24 for the exercise of the rights of minority shareholders of the company in question and the address at which complete information on those arrangements may be obtained free of charge;
(e)   the name and registered office proposed for the SE.

Article 22

As an alternative to experts operating on behalf of each of the merging companies, one or more independent experts as defined in Article 10 of

Directive 78/855/EEC, appointed for those purposes at the joint request of the companies by a judicial or administrative authority in the Member State of one of the merging companies or of the proposed SE, may examine the draft terms of merger and draw up a single report to all the shareholders.

The experts shall have the right to request from each of the merging companies any information they consider necessary to enable them to complete their function.

Article 23

1. The general meeting of each of the merging companies shall approve the draft terms of merger.
2. Employee involvement in the SE shall be decided pursuant to Directive 2001/86/EC. The general meetings of each of the merging companies may reserve the right to make registration of the SE conditional upon its express ratification of the arrangements so decided.

Article 24

1. The law of the Member State governing each merging company shall apply as in the case of a merger of public limited-liability companies, taking into account the cross-border nature of the merger, with regard to the protection of the interests of:
(a) creditors of the merging companies;
(b) holders of bonds of the merging companies;
(c) holders of securities, other than shares, which carry special rights in the merging companies.
2. A Member State may, in the case of the merging companies governed by its law, adopt provisions designed to ensure appropriate protection for minority shareholders who have opposed the merger.

Article 25

1. The legality of a merger shall be scrutinised, as regards the part of the procedure concerning each merging company, in accordance with the law on mergers of public limited-liability companies of the Member State to which the merging company is subject.
2. In each Member State concerned the court, notary or other competent authority shall issue a certificate conclusively attesting to the completion of the pre-merger acts and formalities.
3. If the law of a Member State to which a merging company is subject provides for a procedure to scrutinise and amend the share-exchange ratio, or a procedure to compensate minority shareholders, without

159

preventing the registration of the merger, such procedures shall only apply if the other merging companies situated in Member States which do not provide for such procedure explicitly accept, when approving the draft terms of the merger in accordance with Article 23(1), the possibility for the shareholders of that merging company to have recourse to such procedure. In such cases, the court, notary or other competent authorities may issue the certificate referred to in paragraph 2 even if such a procedure has been commenced. The certificate must, however, indicate that the procedure is pending. The decision in the procedure shall be binding on the acquiring company and all its shareholders.

Article 26

1. The legality of a merger shall be scrutinised, as regards the part of the procedure concerning the completion of the merger and the formation of the SE, by the court, notary or other authority competent in the Member State of the proposed registered office of the SE to scrutinise that aspect of the legality of mergers of public limited-liability companies.
2. To that end each merging company shall submit to the competent authority the certificate referred to in Article 25(2) within six months of its issue together with a copy of the draft terms of merger approved by that company.
3. The authority referred to in paragraph 1 shall in particular ensure that the merging companies have approved draft terms of merger in the same terms and that arrangements for employee involvement have been determined pursuant to Directive 2001/86/EC.
4. That authority shall also satisfy itself that the SE has been formed in accordance with the requirements of the law of the Member State in which it has its registered office in accordance with Article 15.

Article 27

1. A merger and the simultaneous formation of an SE shall take effect on the date on which the SE is registered in accordance with Article 12.
2. The SE may not be registered until the formalities provided for in Articles 25 and 26 have been completed.

Article 28

For each of the merging companies the completion of the merger shall be publicised as laid down by the law of each Member State in accordance with Article 3 of Directive 68/151/EEC.

Article 29

1. A merger carried out as laid down in Article 17(2)(a) shall have the following consequences ipso jure and simultaneously:
(a) all the assets and liabilities of each company being acquired are transferred to the acquiring company;
(b) the shareholders of the company being acquired become shareholders of the acquiring company;
(c) the company being acquired ceases to exist;
(d) the acquiring company adopts the form of an SE.
2. A merger carried out as laid down in the second indent of Article 17(2)(b) shall have the following consequences ipso jure and simultaneously:
(a) all the assets and liabilities of the merging companies are transferred to the SE;
(b) the shareholders of the merging companies become shareholders of the SE;
(c) the merging companies cease to exist.
3. Where, in the case of a merger of public limited-liability companies, the law of a Member State requires the completion of any special formalities before the transfer of certain assets, rights and obligations by the merging companies becomes effective against third parties, those formalities shall apply and shall be carried out either by the merging companies or by the SE following its registration.
4. The rights and obligations of the participating companies on terms and conditions of employment arising from national law, practice and individual employment contracts or employment relationships and existing at the date of the registration shall, by reason of such registration be transferred to the SE upon its registration.

Article 30

A merger as provided for in Article 2(1) may not be declared null and void once the SE has been registered.

The absence of scrutiny of the legality of the merger pursuant to Articles 25 and 26 may be included among the grounds for the winding-up of the SE.

Article 31

1. Where a merger within the meaning of the first indent of Article 17(2) is carried out by a company which holds all the shares and other securities conferring the right to vote at general meetings of another company, neither Article 20(1)(b), (c) and (d), Article 29(1)(b) nor Article 22 shall apply. National law governing each merging company and mergers of

public limited-liability companies in accordance with Article 24 of Directive 78/855/EEC shall nevertheless apply.

2. Where a merger by acquisition is carried out by a company which holds 90% or more but not all of the shares and other securities conferring the right to vote at general meetings of another company, reports by the management or administrative body, reports by an independent expert or experts and the documents necessary for scrutiny shall be required only to the extent that the national law governing either the acquiring company or the company being acquired so requires.

Member States may, however, provide that this paragraph may apply where a company holds shares conferring 90% or more but not all of the voting rights.

SECTION 3
FORMATION OF A HOLDING SE

Article 32

1. A holding SE may be formed in accordance with Article 2(2).
    A company promoting the formation of a holding SE in accordance with Article 2(2) shall continue to exist.
2. The management or administrative organs of the companies which promote such an operation shall draw up, in the same terms, draft terms for the formation of the holding SE. The draft terms shall include a report explaining and justifying the legal and economic aspects of the formation and indicating the implications for the shareholders and for the employees of the adoption of the form of a holding SE. The draft terms shall also set out the particulars provided for in Article 20(1)(a), (b), (c), (f), (g), (h) and (i) and shall fix the minimum proportion of the shares in each of the companies promoting the operation which the shareholders must contribute to the formation of the holding SE. That proportion shall be shares conferring more than 50% of the permanent voting rights.
3. For each of the companies promoting the operation, the draft terms for the formation of the holding SE shall be publicised in the manner laid down in each Member State's national law in accordance with Article 3 of Directive 68/151/EEC at least one month before the date of the general meeting called to decide thereon.
4. One or more experts independent of the companies promoting the operation, appointed or approved by a judicial or administrative authority in the Member State to which each company is subject in accordance with national provisions adopted in implementation of Directive 78/855/EEC, shall examine the draft terms of formation drawn up in accordance with paragraph 2 and draw up a written report for the shareholders of each company. By agreement between the companies

promoting the operation, a single written report may be drawn up for the shareholders of all the companies by one or more independent experts, appointed or approved by a judicial or administrative authority in the Member State to which one of the companies promoting the operation or the proposed SE is subject in accordance with national provisions adopted in implementation of Directive 78/855/EEC.

5. The report shall indicate any particular difficulties of valuation and state whether the proposed share-exchange ratio is fair and reasonable, indicating the methods used to arrive at it and whether such methods are adequate in the case in question.

6. The general meeting of each company promoting the operation shall approve the draft terms of formation of the holding SE.

    Employee involvement in the holding SE shall be decided pursuant to Directive 2001/86/EC. The general meetings of each company promoting the operation may reserve the right to make registration of the holding SE conditional upon its express ratification of the arrangements so decided.

7. These provisions shall apply mutatis mutandis to private limited-liability companies.

Article 33

1. The shareholders of the companies promoting such an operation shall have a period of three months in which to inform the promoting companies whether they intend to contribute their shares to the formation of the holding SE. That period shall begin on the date upon which the terms for the formation of the holding SE have been finally determined in accordance with Article 32.

2. The holding SE shall be formed only if, within the period referred to in paragraph 1, the shareholders of the companies promoting the operation have assigned the minimum proportion of shares in each company in accordance with the draft terms of formation and if all the other conditions are fulfilled.

3. If the conditions for the formation of the holding SE are all fulfilled in accordance with paragraph 2, that fact shall, in respect of each of the promoting companies, be publicised in the manner laid down in the national law governing each of those companies adopted in implementation of Article 3 of Directive 68/151/EEC.

    Shareholders of the companies promoting the operation who have not indicated whether they intend to make their shares available to the promoting companies for the purpose of forming the holding SE within the period referred to in paragraph 1 shall have a further month in which to do so.

4. Shareholders who have contributed their securities to the formation of the SE shall receive shares in the holding SE.

5. The holding SE may not be registered until it is shown that the formalities referred to in Article 32 have been completed and that the conditions referred to in paragraph 2 have been fulfilled.

Article 34

A Member State may, in the case of companies promoting such an operation, adopt provisions designed to ensure protection for minority shareholders who oppose the operation, creditors and employees.

SECTION 4
FORMATION OF A SUBSIDIARY SE

Article 35

An SE may be formed in accordance with Article 2(3).

Article 36

Companies, firms and other legal entities participating in such an operation shall be subject to the provisions governing their participation in the formation of a subsidiary in the form of a public limited-liability company under national law.

SECTION 5
CONVERSION OF AN EXISTING PUBLIC-LIABILITY COMPANY INTO AN SE

Article 37

1. An SE may be formed in accordance with Article 2(4).
2. Without prejudice to Article 11 the conversion of a public limited-liability company into an SE shall not result in the winding up of the company or in the creation of a new legal person.
3. The registered office may not be transferred from one Member State to another pursuant to Article 8 at the same time as the conversion is effected.
4. The management or administrative organ of the company in question shall draw up draft terms of conversion and a report explaining and justifying the legal and economic aspects of the conversion and indicating

the implications for the shareholders and for the employees of the adoption of the form of an SE.

5. The draft terms of conversion shall be publicised in the manner laid down in each Member State's law in accordance with Article 3 of Directive 68/151/EEC at least one month before the general meeting called upon to decide thereon.

6. Before the general meeting referred to in paragraph 7 one or more independent experts appointed or approved, in accordance with the national provisions adopted in implementation of Article 10 of Directive 78/855/EEC, by a judicial or administrative authority in the Member State to which the company being converted into an SE is subject shall certify in compliance with Directive (EEC) 77/91[17] mutatis mutandis that the company has net assets at least equivalent to its capital plus those reserves which must not be distributed under the law or the Statutes.

7. The general meeting of the company in question shall approve the draft terms of conversion together with the statutes of the SE. The decision of the general meeting shall be passed as laid down in the provisions of national law adopted in implementation of Article 7 of Directive 78/855/EEC.

8. Member States may condition a conversion to a favourable vote of a qualified majority or unanimity in the organ of the company to be converted within which employee participation is organised.

9. The rights and obligations of the company to be converted on terms and conditions of employment arising from national law, practice and individual employment contracts or employment relationships and existing at the date of the registration shall, by reason of such registration be transferred to the SE.

TITLE III

STRUCTURE OF THE SE

Article 38

Under the conditions laid down by this Regulation an SE shall comprise:
(a) a general meeting of shareholders and

---

17. Second Council Directive 77/91/EEC of 13 December 1976 on coordination of safeguards which, for the protection of the interests of members and others, are required by Member States of companies within the meaning of the second paragraph of Article 58 of the Treaty, in respect of the formation of public limited liability companies and the maintenance and alteration of their capital, with a view to making such safeguards equivalent (OJ L 26, 31 January 1977, p. 1). Directive as last amended by the 1994 Act of Accession.

(b)   either a supervisory organ and a management organ (two-tier system) or an administrative organ (one-tier system) depending on the form adopted in the statutes.

SECTION 1
TWO-TIER SYSTEM

Article 39

1.   The management organ shall be responsible for managing the SE. A Member State may provide that a managing director or managing directors shall be responsible for the current management under the same conditions as for public limited-liability companies that have registered offices within that Member State's territory.
2.   The member or members of the management organ shall be appointed and removed by the supervisory organ.
     A Member State may, however, require or permit the statutes to provide that the member or members of the management organ shall be appointed and removed by the general meeting under the same conditions as for public limited-liability companies that have registered offices within its territory.
3.   No person may at the same time be a member of both the management organ and the supervisory organ of the same SE. The supervisory organ may, however, nominate one of its members to act as a member of the management organ in the event of a vacancy. During such a period the functions of the person concerned as a member of the supervisory organ shall be suspended. A Member State may impose a time limit on such a period.
4.   The number of members of the management organ or the rules for determining it shall be laid down in the SE's statutes. A Member State may, however, fix a minimum and/or a maximum number.
5.   Where no provision is made for a two-tier system in relation to public limited-liability companies with registered offices within its territory, a Member State may adopt the appropriate measures in relation to SEs.

Article 40

1.   The supervisory organ shall supervise the work of the management organ. It may not itself exercise the power to manage the SE.
2.   The members of the supervisory organ shall be appointed by the general meeting. The members of the first supervisory organ may, however, be appointed by the statutes. This shall apply without prejudice to Article

47(4) or to any employee participation arrangements determined pursuant to the Directive 2001/86/EC.

3. The number of members of the supervisory organ or the rules for determining it shall be laid down in the statutes. A Member State may, however, stipulate the number of members of the supervisory organ for SEs registered within its territory or a minimum and/or a maximum number.

Article 41

1. The management organ shall report to the supervisory organ at least once every three months on the progress and foreseeable development of the SE's business.
2. In addition to the regular information referred to in paragraph 1, the management organ shall promptly pass the supervisory organ any information on events likely to have an appreciable effect on the SE.
3. The supervisory organ may require the management organ to provide information of any kind which it needs to exercise supervision in accordance with Article 40(1). A Member State may provide that each member of the supervisory organ also be entitled to this facility.
4. The supervisory organ may undertake or arrange for any investigations necessary for the performance of its duties.
5. Each member of the supervisory organ shall be entitled to examine all information submitted to it.

Article 42

The supervisory organ shall elect a chairman from among its members. If half of the members are appointed by employees, only a member appointed by the general meeting of shareholders may be elected chairman.

SECTION 2
THE ONE-TIER SYSTEM

Article 43

1. The administrative organ shall manage the SE. A Member State may provide that a managing director or managing directors shall be responsible for the day-to-day management under the same conditions as for public limited-liability companies that have registered offices within that Member State's territory.
2. The number of members of the administrative organ or the rules for determining it shall be laid down in the SE's statutes. A Member State

may, however, set a minimum and, where necessary, a maximum number of members.

3. The administrative organ shall, however, consist of at least three members where employee participation is regulated in accordance with Directive 2001/86/EC.

4. The member or members of the administrative organ shall be appointed by the general meeting. The members of the first administrative organ may, however, be appointed by the statutes. This shall apply without prejudice to Article 47(4) or to any employee participation arrangements determined pursuant to Directive 2001/86/EC.

5. Where no provision is made for a one-tier system in relation to public limited-liability companies with registered offices within its territory, a Member State may adopt the appropriate measures in relation to SEs.

Article 44

1. The administrative organ shall meet at least once every three months at intervals laid down by the statutes to discuss the progress and foreseeable development of the SE's business.

2. Each member of the administrative organ shall be entitled to examine all information submitted to it.

Article 45

The administrative organ shall elect a chairman from among its members. If half of the members are appointed by employees, only a member appointed by the general meeting of shareholders may be elected chairman.

SECTION 3
RULES COMMON TO THE ONE-TIER AND TWO-TIER SYSTEMS

Article 46

1. Members of company organs shall be appointed for a period laid down in the statutes not exceeding six years.

2. Subject to any restrictions laid down in the statutes, members may be reappointed once or more than once for the period determined in accordance with paragraph 1.

Article 47

1. An SE's statutes may permit a company or other legal entity to be a member of one of its organs, provided that the law applicable to public limited-liability companies in the Member State in which the SE's registered office is situated does not provide otherwise.
2. That company or other legal entity shall designate a natural person to exercise its functions on the organ in question.
3. No person may be a member of any SE organ or a representative of a member within the meaning of paragraph 1 who:
(a) is disqualified, under the law of the Member State in which the SE's registered office is situated, from serving on the corresponding organ of a public limited-liability company governed by the law of that Member State, or
(b) is disqualified from serving on the corresponding organ of a public limited-liability company governed by the law of a Member State owing to a judicial or administrative decision delivered in a Member State.
4. An SE's statutes may, in accordance with the law applicable to public limited-liability companies in the Member State in which the SE's registered office is situated, lay down special conditions of eligibility for members representing the shareholders.
5. This Regulation shall not affect national law permitting a minority of shareholders or other persons or authorities to appoint some of the members of a company organ.

Article 48

1. An SE's statutes shall list the categories of transactions which require authorisation of the management organ by the supervisory organ in the two-tier system or an express decision by the administrative organ in the one-tier system.

   A Member State may, however, provide that in the two-tier system the supervisory organ may itself make certain categories of transactions subject to authorisation.
2. A Member State may determine the categories of transactions which must at least be indicated in the statutes of SEs registered within its territory.

Article 49

The members of an SE's organs shall be under a duty, even after they have ceased to hold office, not to divulge any information which they have concerning the SE the disclosure of which might be prejudicial to the company's interests, except where such disclosure is required or permitted under national law provisions applicable to public limited-liability companies or is in the public interest.

Article 50

1. Unless otherwise provided by this Regulation or the statutes, the internal rules relating to quorums and decision-taking in SE organs shall be as follows:
(a) quorum: at least half of the members must be present or represented;
(b) decision-taking: a majority of the members present or represented.
(c) Where there is no relevant provision in the statutes, the chairman of each organ shall have a casting vote in the event of a tie. There shall be no provision to the contrary in the statutes, however, where half of the supervisory organ consists of employees' representatives.
(d) Where employee participation is provided for in accordance with Directive 2001/86/EC, a Member State may provide that the supervisory organ's quorum and decision-making shall, by way of derogation from the provisions referred to in paragraphs 1 and 2, be subject to the rules applicable, under the same conditions, to public limited-liability companies governed by the law of the Member State concerned.

Article 51

Members of an SE's management, supervisory and administrative organs shall be liable, in accordance with the provisions applicable to public limited-liability companies in the Member State in which the SE's registered office is situated, for loss or damage sustained by the SE following any breach on their part of the legal, statutory or other obligations inherent in their duties.

SECTION 4
GENERAL MEETING

Article 52

The general meeting shall decide on matters for which it is given sole responsibility by:
(a) this Regulation or
(b) the legislation of the Member State in which the SE's registered office is situated adopted in implementation of Directive 2001/86/EC.

Furthermore, the general meeting shall decide on matters for which responsibility is given to the general meeting of a public limited-liability company governed by the law of the Member State in which the SE's registered office is situated, either by the law of that Member State or by the SE's statutes in accordance with that law.

Article 53

Without prejudice to the rules laid down in this section, the organisation and conduct of general meetings together with voting procedures shall be governed by the law applicable to public limited-liability companies in the Member State in which the SE's registered office is situated.

Article 54

1. An SE shall hold a general meeting at least once each calendar year, within six months of the end of its financial year, unless the law of the Member State in which the SE's registered office is situated applicable to public limited-liability companies carrying on the same type of activity as the SE provides for more frequent meetings. A Member State may, however, provide that the first general meeting may be held at any time in the eighteen months following an SE's incorporation.
2. General meetings may be convened at any time by the management organ, the administrative organ, the supervisory organ or any other organ or competent authority in accordance with the national law applicable to public limited-liability companies in the Member State in which the SE's registered office is situated.

Article 55

1. One or more shareholders who together hold at least 10% of an SE's subscribed capital may request the SE to convene a general meeting and draw up the agenda therefore; the SE's statutes or national legislation may provide for a smaller proportion under the same conditions as those applicable to public limited-liability companies.
2. The request that a general meeting be convened shall state the items to be put on the agenda.
3. If, following a request made under paragraph 1, a general meeting is not held in due time and, in any event, within two months, the competent judicial or administrative authority within the jurisdiction of which the SE's registered office is situated may order that a general meeting be convened within a given period or authorise either the shareholders who have requested it or their representatives to convene a general meeting. This shall be without prejudice to any national provisions which allow the shareholders themselves to convene general meetings.

Article 56

One or more shareholders who together hold at least 10% of an SE's subscribed capital may request that one or more additional items be put on the agenda of any general meeting. The procedures and time limits applicable to such requests shall be laid down by the national law of the Member State in which the SE's registered office is situated or, failing that, by the SE's statutes. The above proportion may be reduced by the statutes or by the law of the Member State in which the SE's registered office is situated under the same conditions as are applicable to public limited-liability companies.

Article 57

Save where this Regulation or, failing that, the law applicable to public limited-liability companies in the Member State in which an SE's registered office is situated requires a larger majority, the general meeting's decisions shall be taken by a majority of the votes validly cast.

Article 58

The votes cast shall not include votes attaching to shares in respect of which the shareholder has not taken part in the vote or has abstained or has returned a blank or spoilt ballot paper.

Article 59

1. Amendment of an SE's statutes shall require a decision by the general meeting taken by a majority which may not be less than two-thirds of the votes cast, unless the law applicable to public limited-liability companies in the Member State in which an SE's registered office is situated requires or permits a larger majority.
2. A Member State may, however, provide that where at least half of an SE's subscribed capital is represented, a simple majority of the votes referred to in paragraph 1 shall suffice.
3. Amendments to an SE's statutes shall be publicised in accordance with Article 13.

Article 60

1. Where an SE has two or more classes of shares, every decision by the general meeting shall be subject to a separate vote by each class of shareholders whose class rights are affected thereby.

2. Where a decision by the general meeting requires the majority of votes specified in Article 59(1) or (2), that majority shall also be required for the separate vote by each class of shareholders whose class rights are affected by the decision.

TITLE IV

ANNUAL ACCOUNTS AND CONSOLIDATED ACCOUNTS

Article 61

Subject to Article 62 an SE shall be governed by the rules applicable to public limited-liability companies under the law of the Member State in which its registered office is situated as regards the preparation of its annual and, where appropriate, consolidated accounts including the accompanying annual report and the auditing and publication of those accounts.

Article 62

1. An SE which is a credit or financial institution shall be governed by the rules laid down in the national law of the Member State in which its registered office is situated in implementation of Directive 2000/12/EC of the European Parliament and of the Council of 20 March 2000 relating to the taking up and pursuit of the business of credit institutions[18] as regards the preparation of its annual and, where appropriate, consolidated accounts, including the accompanying annual report and the auditing and publication of those accounts.
2. An SE which is an insurance undertaking shall be governed by the rules laid down in the national law of the Member State in which its registered office is situated in implementation of Council Directive 91/674/EEC of 19 December 1991 on the annual accounts and consolidated accounts of insurance undertakings[19] as regards the preparation of its annual and, where appropriate, consolidated accounts including the accompanying annual report and the auditing and publication of those accounts.

---

18.   *O.J.*, L 126, 26 May 2000.
19.   *O.J.*, L 374, 31 December 1991.

TITLE V

WINDING UP, LIQUIDATION, INSOLVENCY AND CESSATION OF PAYMENTS

Article 63

As regards winding up, liquidation, insolvency, cessation of payments and similar procedures, an SE shall be governed by the legal provisions which would apply to a public limited-liability company formed in accordance with the law of the Member State in which its registered office is situated, including provisions relating to decision-making by the general meeting.

Article 64

1. When an SE no longer complies with the requirement laid down in Article 7, the Member State in which the SE's registered office is situated shall take appropriate measures to oblige the SE to regularise its position within a specified period either:
(a) by re-establishing its head office in the Member State in which its registered office is situated or
(b) by transferring the registered office by means of the procedure laid down in Article 8.
2. The Member State in which the SE's registered office is situated shall put in place the measures necessary to ensure that an SE which fails to regularise its position in accordance with paragraph (1) is liquidated.
3. The Member State in which the SE's registered office is situated shall set up a judicial remedy with regard to any established infringement of Article 7. That remedy shall have a suspensory effect on the procedures laid down in paragraphs 1 and 2.
4. Where it is established on the initiative of either the authorities or any interested party that an SE has its head office within the territory of a Member State in breach of Article 7, the authorities of that Member State shall immediately inform the Member State in which the SE's registered office is situated.

Article 65

Without prejudice to provisions of national law requiring additional publication, the initiation and termination of winding up, liquidation, insolvency or suspension of payment procedures and any decision to continue operating shall be publicised in accordance with Article 13.

Article 66

1. An SE may be converted into a public limited-liability company governed by the law of the Member State in which its registered office is situated. No decision on conversion may be taken before two years have elapsed since its registration or before the first two sets of annual accounts have been approved.

2. The conversion of an SE into a public limited-liability company shall not result in the winding up of the company or in the creation of a new legal person.

3. The management or administrative organ of the SE shall draw up draft terms of conversion and a report explaining and justifying the legal and economic aspects of the conversion and indicating the implications of the adoption of the public limited-liability company for the shareholders and for the employees.

4. The draft terms of conversion shall be publicised in the manner laid down in each Member State's law in accordance with Article 3 of Directive 68/151/EEC at least one month before the general meeting called to decide thereon.

5. Before the general meeting referred to in paragraph 6, one or more independent experts appointed or approved, in accordance with the national provisions adopted in implementation of Article 10 of Directive 78/855/EEC, by a judicial or administrative authority in the Member State to which the SE being converted into a public limited-liability company is subject shall certify that the company has assets at least equivalent to its capital.

6. The general meeting of the SE shall approve the draft terms of conversion together with the statutes of the public limited-liability company. The decision of the general meeting shall be passed as laid down in the provisions of national law adopted in implementation of Article 7 of Directive 78/855/EEC.

TITLE VI

ADDITIONAL AND TRANSITIONAL PROVISIONS

Article 67

1. If and so long as the third phase of EMU does not apply to it each Member State may make SEs with registered offices within its territory subject to the same provisions as apply to public limited-liability companies covered by its legislation as regards the expression of their capital. An SE may, in any case, express its capital in euro as well. In that

event the national currency/euro conversion rate shall be that for the last day of the month preceding that of the formation of the SE.

2. If and so long as the third phase of EMU does not apply to the Member State in which an SE has its registered office, the SE may, however, prepare and publish its annual and, where appropriate, consolidated accounts in euros. The Member State may require that the SE's annual and, where appropriate, consolidated accounts be prepared and published in [the] national currency under the same conditions as those laid down for public limited-liability companies governed by the law of that Member State. This shall not prejudge the additional possibility for an SE of publishing its annual and, where appropriate, consolidated accounts in euros in accordance with Council Directive 90/604/EEC of 8 November 1990 amending Directive 78/60/EEC on annual accounts and Directive 83/349/EEC on consolidated accounts as concerns the exemptions for small and medium-sized companies and the publication of accounts in ecus.[20]

TITLE VII

FINAL PROVISIONS

Article 68

1. The Member States shall make such provision as is appropriate to ensure the effective application of this Regulation.
2. Each Member State shall designate the competent authorities within the meaning of Articles 8, 25, 26, 54, 55 and 64. It shall inform the Commission and the other Member States accordingly.

Article 69

Five years at the latest after the entry into force of this Regulation, the Commission shall forward to the Council and the European Parliament a report on the application of the Regulation and proposals for amendments, where appropriate. The report shall, in particular, analyse the appropriateness of:

(a) allowing the location of an SE's head office and registered office in different Member States;
(b) broadening the concept of merger in Article 17(2) in order to admit also other types of merger than those defined in Articles 3(1) and 4(1) of Directive 78/855/EEC;

---

20.   *O.J.*, L 317, 16 November 1990.

(c)   revising the jurisdiction clause in Article 8(12) in the light of any provision which may have been inserted in the 1968 Brussels Convention or in any text adopted by Member States or by the Council to replace such Convention;

(d)   allowing provisions in the statutes of an SE adopted by a Member State in execution of authorisations given to the Member States by this Regulation or laws adopted to ensure the effective application of this Regulation in respect to the SE which deviate from or are complementary to these laws, even when such provisions would not be authorised in the statutes of a public limited-liability company having its registered office in the Member State.

Article 70

This Regulation shall enter into force on 8 October 2004.

This Regulation shall be binding in its entirety and directly applicable in all Member States.

3. Documents

I. EUROPEAN PARLIAMENT. REPORT ON THE DRAFT COUNCIL REGULATION ON THE STATUTE FOR A EUROPEAN COMPANY (SE) (14886/2000 – C5-0092/2001 – 1989/0218(CNS)) (26 JUNE 2001)

Procedural page

On 30 June 1970 the Commission submitted its initial proposal for a regulation on a European Company. This proposal was amended in 1975. On 25 August 1989 the Commission submitted further proposals for a regulation on the Statute for a European Company and an associated directive on the involvement of employees in the European Company,[1] which were amended in 1991 (COM(1991) 174).[2]

The 1989 and 1991 proposals were based on Article 54 (the current Article 44) of the EC Treaty, which provided for the cooperation procedure. Once the Maastricht Treaty had come into force the proposals were placed under the codecision procedure.

At the sitting of 24 January 1991, Parliament adopted its position on the proposals at first reading and confirmed that position on 2 December 1993 and again on 27 October 1999.

The Council subsequently decided that the proper legal basis for the proposals was Article 308 of the EC Treaty, which provides for consultation of the European Parliament.

By letter of 9 March 2001 the Council consulted Parliament again under Article 308 of the EC Treaty, on the draft Council regulation on the Statute for a European Company (SE) (14886/2000–1989/0218 (CNS)).

At the sitting of 15 March 2001 the President of Parliament announced that she had referred this Council text to the Committee on Legal Affairs and the Internal Market as the committee responsible and the Committee on Economic and Monetary Affairs and Committee on Employment and Social Affairs for their opinions (C5-0092/2001).

The Committee on Legal Affairs and the Internal Market had appointed Hans-Peter Mayer rapporteur at its meeting of 29 February 2000.

---

1.   *O.J.*, C 263, 16 October 1989.
2.   *O.J.*, C 138, 14 May 1991.

R. Blanpain (ed.), *Involvement of Employees in the European Union*, 179–216.
© 2002 *Kluwer Law International. Printed in Great Britain.*

The committee considered the draft Council regulation and draft report at its meetings of 26 July 1994, 29 February 2000 and 27 February, 5 March, 23 April, 14 May, 29 May and 26 June 2001. At the last meeting it adopted the draft legislative resolution unanimously.

The opinion of the Committee on Employment and Social Affairs is attached; the Committee on Economic and Monetary Affairs decided on 16 June 2001 not to deliver an opinion.

Legislative proposal

Draft Council regulation on the Statute for a European Company (SE) (14886/2000 – C5-0092/2001 – 1989/0218(CNS))
The proposal is amended as follows:

Text proposed by the Council[3]	Amendments by Parliament
Amendment 1 Citations	
THE COUNCIL OF THE EUROPEAN UNION,	*THE EUROPEAN PARLIAMENT AND THE COUNCIL OF THE EUROPEAN UNION,*
Having regard to the Treaty establishing the European Community, and in particular Article *308* thereof,	Having regard to the Treaty establishing the European Community, and in particular Article *95* thereof,
Having regard to the proposal from the Commission,[4]	Having regard to the proposal from the Commission,
Having regard to the Opinion of the European Parliament,[5]	*Deleted*
Having regard to the Opinion of the Economic and Social Committee 3,	Having regard to the Opinion of the Economic and Social Committee, *Pursuant to the procedure laid down in Article 251 of the EC Treaty,*

Justification

In contrast to the Commission text, the proposal amended by the Council has the wrong legal basis.

Amendment 2 Recital 7 a (new)	*With a view to creating a uniform legal framework for the functioning of SEs, this Regulation should aim at minimising reference to differing national rules and laws, which may result in discrepancies in the treatment of SEs registered in different Member States.*

---

3.   *O.J.*, not yet published.
4.   *O.J.*, C 263, 16 October 1989 and *O.J.*, C 176, 8 July 1991.
5.   *O.J.*, C 124, 21 May 1990.

Text proposed by the Council	Amendments by Parliament

Justification

The current proposal still refers to too great an extent to national legislation, which means that, effectively, there is not one uniform SE but 15 different systems, whilst a single internal market allowing free competition should be the objective. Barriers to competition should be removed as far as possible.

Amendment 3
Recital 8

| The Statute for a European public limited-liability Company (hereafter referred to as "SE") is among the measures to be adopted by the Council before 1992 listed in the Commission's White Paper on completing the internal market, approved by the European Council that met in Milan in June 1985. The European Council that met in Brussels in 1987 expressed the wish to see such a Statute created swiftly. | The Statute for a European public limited-liability Company (hereafter referred to as "SE") is among the measures to be adopted by the Council before 1992 listed in the Commission's White Paper on completing the internal market, approved by the European Council that met in Milan in June 1985. The European Council that met in Brussels in 1987 expressed the wish to see such a Statute created swiftly. *The Commission then submitted its proposal in 1989[6] on which Parliament delivered its opinion at first reading in 1991.[7] The Commission amended its proposal in 1991[8] and consulted Parliament again.[9] In 1993 Parliament confirmed its opinion from first reading.[10]* |

Justification

The recital suppresses substantial parts of the legislative procedure hitherto.

Amendment 4
Recital 9

| Since the Commission's submission in 1970 of a proposal for a Regulation on the Statute for a European public limited-liability Company, amended in 1975, work on the approximation of national company law has made substantial progress, so that on those points where the functioning of an SE does not need uniform Community rules reference may be made to the law governing public limited-liability companies in the Member State where it has its registered office. | Since the Commission's submission in 1970 of a proposal for a Regulation on the Statute for a European public limited-liability Company, amended in 1975, work on the approximation of national company law has made substantial progress, so that on those points where *in the first instance* the functioning of an SE does not *necessarily* need uniform Community rules reference may *provisionally* be made to the law governing public limited-liability companies in the Member State where it has its registered office. |

Justification

The rules contained in the proposal are essentially rules on the formation of SEs. Substantial areas are left untouched. This should not be a permanent state of affairs. To ensure that the legal construct of the SE is standard in all Member States, national peculiarities need to be avoided. The Commission is therefore called upon to table appropriate proposals after an introductory period.

---

6.   *O.J.*, C 263, 16 October 1989.
7.   *O.J.*, C 148, 29 February 1991.
8.   *O.J.*, C 176, 8 July 1991.
9.   COM(1993) 570.
10.   *O.J.*, C 342, 20 December 1993.

Text proposed by the Council	Amendments by Parliament

Amendment 5
Recital 21

This Regulation does not cover other areas of law such as *taxation*, competition, intellectual property or insolvency. The provisions of the Member States' law and of Community law are therefore applicable in the above areas and in other areas not covered by this Regulation.

This Regulation does not cover other areas of law such as competition, intellectual property or insolvency. The provisions of the Member States' law and of Community law are therefore applicable in the above areas and in other areas not covered by this Regulation. *With regard to fiscal matters and accounting approaches, standard rules on taxation are required; the Commission will submit appropriate proposals.*

Justification

It is essential for fiscal accompanying rules to be adopted after a transitional period of three years following the entry into force of the regulation and the directive. The success of the SE as an autonomous legal form depends not least on resolving the problems of fiscal law which affect SEs in particular because of their links with different tax systems. The Commission is therefore requested to submit proposals promptly.

Amendment 6
Recital 21 a (new)

A long-term solution has to be found to problems arising out of unequal taxation burdens on SEs registered in different Member States.

Justification

The existence of major differences between national tax systems impedes free competition, precisely because of national differences affecting businesses within the internal market. For that reason, it will be necessary to endeavour in future to coordinate tax systems at the European level.

Amendment 7
Recital 22

Directive 2001/... /EC is designed to ensure that employees have a right of involvement in issues and decisions affecting the life of their SE. Other social and labour legislation questions, in particular the right of employees to information and consultation as regulated in the Member States, are governed by the national provisions applicable, under the same conditions, to public limited-liability companies.

Directive 2001/... /EC is designed to ensure that employees have a right of involvement in issues and decisions affecting the life of their SE. Other social and labour legislation questions, in particular the right of employees to information and consultation as regulated in the Member States, are governed by the national provisions applicable, under the same conditions, to public limited-liability companies. *Nevertheless, a guarantee that acquired rights of involvement will be preserved, regardless of any subsequent transfer of the SE's registered offices, is essential.*

Justification

It is essential to preserve workers' acquired rights of involvement, regardless of the nature of such rights.

Text proposed by the Council	Amendments by Parliament

Amendment 8
Recital 23

The entry into force of this Regulation must be deferred so that each Member State may incorporate into its national law the provisions of Directive 2001/86/EC and set up in advance the necessary machinery for the formation and operation of SEs with registered offices within its territory, so that the Regulation and the Directive may be applied concomitantly.

The entry into force of this Regulation must be deferred so that each Member State may incorporate into its national law the provisions of Directive 2001/... /EC and set up in advance the necessary machinery for the formation and operation of Ses with registered offices within its territory, so that the Regulation and the Directive may be applied concomitantly. *However, provision should be made for the formation of an SE when only those Member States are affected which have ensured transposition of this Regulation and Council Directive 2001/... /EC[11] prior to the end of the period of deferral.*

Justification

Provision should be made for the SE to be used immediately by companies of those Member States which have already integrated the SE in their legal systems. This would also create an incentive for speedier transposition.

Amendment 9
Recital 29

The Treaty does not provide, for the adoption of this Regulation, powers of action other than those of Article *308* thereof.

The Treaty does not provide, for the adoption of this Regulation, powers of action other than those of Article *95* thereof.

Justification

See justification for Amendment 1.

Amendment 10
Article 8, paragraph 2, letter c

Any implication the transfer may have on employees' involvement;

any implication the transfer may have on employees' involvement *and the measures to protect existing forms of involvement*;

Justification

In the event of transfer of an SE, existing forms of involvement must not be curtailed. The transfer plan must therefore include those measures required to safeguard existing forms of involvement.

---

11.   Council Directive of 8 October 2001 supplementing the statute for a European Company in respect of workers' involvement, *O.J.*, 10 November 2001.

Text proposed by the Council	Amendments by Parliament

Amendment 11
Article 12(1)

1. Every SE shall be registered in the Member State in which it has its registered office in a register designated by the law of that Member State in accordance with Article 3 of the First Council Directive (68/151/EEC) of 9 March 1968 on coordination of safeguards which, for the protection of the interests of members and others, are required by Member States of companies within the meaning of the second paragraph of Article *58* of the Treaty, with a view to making such safeguards equivalent throughout the Community.[12]

1. Every SE shall be registered in the Member State in which it has its registered office in a register designated by the law of that Member State in accordance with Article 3 of the First Council Directive (68/151/EEC) of 9 March 1968 on coordination of safeguards which, for the protection of the interests of members and others, are required by Member States of companies within the meaning of the second paragraph of Article *48* of the Treaty, with a view to making such safeguards equivalent throughout the Community.

Justification

Reference should be to Article 48 of the Treaty.

Amendment 12
Article 20, paragraph 1, letter i

Information on the procedures by which arrangements for employee involvement are determined pursuant to Directive 2001/86/EC.

Information on the procedures by which arrangements for employee involvement are determined pursuant to Directive 2001/86/EC, *in particular measures to protect existing forms of involvement.*

Justification

In the event of merger of two SEs, existing forms of involvement must not be curtailed. The transfer plan must therefore include those measures required to safeguard existing forms of involvement.

Amendment 13
Article 39, paragraph 5

Where no provision is made for a two-tier system in relation to public limited-liability companies with registered offices within its territory, a Member State *may* adopt the appropriate measures in relation to SEs.

Where no provision is made for a two-tier system in relation to public limited-liability companies with registered offices within its territory, a Member State *shall* adopt the appropriate measures in relation to SEs.

Justification

Freedom to choose between the single-tier and two-tier systems means that scope for a single-tier system must be created not only in Member States which have hitherto had a two-tier system. With a view to safeguarding acquired forms of worker involvement, appropriate facilities must be created in Member States which hitherto have had a single-tier system only.

---

12.   *O.J.*, L 65, 14 March 1968, p. 8. Directive as last amended by the 1994 Act of Accession.

Text proposed by the Council	Amendments by Parliament

Amendment 14
Article 43, paragraph 4

Where no provision is made for a one-tier system in relation to public limited-liability companies with registered offices within its territory, a Member State *may* adopt the appropriate measures in relation to SEs.

Where no provision is made for a one-tier system in relation to public limited-liability companies with registered offices within its territory, a Member State *shall* adopt the appropriate measures in relation to SEs.

Justification

Freedom to choose between the single-tier and two-tier systems means that scope for a single-tier system must be created in Member States which have hitherto had a two-tier system. The question of safeguarding acquired rights of worker involvement is dependent on this and must be regulated in the merger plan.

Amendment 15
Article 68, paragraph 1

The Member States shall make such provision as is appropriate to ensure the effective application of this Regulation.

The Member States shall make such provision as is appropriate to ensure the effective application of this Regulation. *The Member States may provide for an SE to be formed if the Member States in question have already ensured the effective application of this Regulation and of Council Directive 2001/86/EC.*[13]

Justification

See justification for Amendment 8

Amendment 16
Article 69, paragraph 1

Five years at the latest after the entry into force of this Regulation, the Commission shall forward to the Council and the European Parliament a report on the application of the Regulation and proposals for amendments, where appropriate. The report shall, in particular, analyse the appropriateness of:

Three years at the latest after the entry into force of this Regulation, the Commission shall forward to the Council and the European Parliament a report on the application of the Regulation and proposals for amendments, where appropriate. The report shall, in particular, analyse the *impact of this Regulation on small and medium-sized enterprises, in particular any obstacles to their forming an SE, and* the appropriateness of:

(a) allowing the location of an SE's head office and registered office in different Member States;
(b) broadening the concept of merger in Article 17(2) in order to admit also other types of merger than those defined in Articles 3(1) and 4(1) of Directive 78/855/EEC;

(a) allowing the location of an SE's head office and registered office in different Member States;
(b) broadening the concept of merger in Article 17(2) in order to admit also other types of merger than those defined in Articles 3(1) and 4(1) of Directive 78/855/EEC;

---

13. Council Directive of 8 October 2001 supplementing the Statute for a European Company in respect of workers' involvement, *O.J.*, 10 November 2001.

Text proposed by the Council	Amendments by Parliament
(c) revising the jurisdiction clause in Article 8(12) in the light of any provision which may have been inserted in the 1968 Brussels Convention or in any text adopted by Member States or by the Council to replace such Convention; (d) allowing provisions in the statutes of an SE adopted by a Member State in execution of authorisations given to the Member States by this Regulation or laws adopted to ensure the effective application of this Regulation in respect to the SE which deviate from or are complementary to these laws, even when such provisions would not be authorised in the statutes of a public limited-liability company having its registered office in the Member State.	(c) revising the jurisdiction clause in Article 8(12) in the light of any provision which may have been inserted in the 1968 Brussels Convention or in any text adopted by Member States or by the Council to replace such Convention; (d) allowing provisions in the statutes of an SE adopted by a Member State in execution of authorisations given to the Member States by this Regulation or laws adopted to ensure the effective application of this Regulation in respect to the SE which deviate from or are complementary to these laws, even when such provisions would not be authorised in the statutes of a public limited-liability company having its registered office in the Member State. *(e) approximating the fiscal rules applicable to SEs in order to solve the problems resulting from links with different systems of taxation.*

Justification

3 years:

A shorter deadline is proposed for making an initial evaluation, in order to avoid shortcomings impeding for too long the proper functioning of the regulation.

Small and medium-sized companies:

The regulation currently takes too little account of SMEs, which provide a great deal of employment and are the driving force behind a large section of the European economy.

See also justification for Amendment 5.

Draft legislative resolution

European Parliament legislative resolution on the Draft Council regulation on the Statute for a European Company (SE) (14886/2000 – C5-0092/2001 – 1989/0218(CNS)) (Consultation procedure – renewed consultation)

The European Parliament,

- having regard to the Draft Council regulation (14886/2000[14]),
- having regard to the Commission proposal to the Council (COM(1989) 268)[15] amended in 1991 by COM(1991) 174,[16]
- having regard to its position at first reading of 24 January 1991[17] confirmed on 2 December 1993[18] and 27 October 1999,[19]

---

14. Not yet published.
15. *O.J.*, C 263, 16 October 1989.
16. *O.J.*, C 138, 29 May 1991.
17. *O.J.*, C 48, 25 February 1991.
18. *O.J.*, C 342, 20 December 1993.
19. *O.J.*, C 154.

- having been consulted by the Council again under Article 308 of the EC Treaty (C5-0092/2001),
- having regard to Rule 67 and 71(2) of its Rules of Procedure,
- having regard to the report of the Committee on Legal Affairs and the Internal Market and the opinion of the Committee on Employment and Social Affairs (A5-0243/2001),

1. Approves the Council draft as amended;
2. Calls on the Commission to alter its proposal accordingly, pursuant to Article 250(2) of the EC Treaty;
3. Calls on the Council to notify Parliament should it intend to depart from the text approved by Parliament;
4. Asks to be consulted again if the Council intends to amend the draft regulation substantially;
5. Instructs its President to forward its position to the Council and Commission.

Explanatory statement

1. Decision of general principle

The idea of creating a European form of company obeying the same supranational rules in all Member States is almost as old as the European Union itself. The Societas Europaea (SE) is the flagship of European company law. The foundation stones were laid in the late 1950s when there were calls for uniform legislation. In 1970 the Commission submitted a proposal for a regulation on the statute of an SE. It contained uniform law down to the last detail. However, it ran into opposition because of diverging forms of company law in the Member States. As a result, in 1989 the Commission submitted an entirely new proposal for a regulation which excluded social and labour law, fiscal law, law on competition, protection of industrial property rights, insolvency law and industrial constitution law. However, the Member States were unable to agree on a common form of workers' participation.

Finally, on 20 December 2000, at the European Council summit in Nice, political agreement was reached on a Council regulation on the statute of the SE and a directive on worker participation.

2. The legal base

The first proposal for a statute of the SE was based on the current Article 308, which provides only for Parliament to be consulted. The 1989 proposal was in two parts: the regulation was based on the present Article 95 and the directive on the present Article 44(2)(g). The Nice proposals are both based on Article 308 with the result that, once again, Parliament is simply consulted.

Article 95 is just as appropriate a legal basis for the regulation as Article 308. For the purposes of democratic legitimacy – and in line with decisions of the Court of Justice – in such cases the legal base giving Parliament most say should be chosen.

In order that the SE can be applied speedily – which is something that industry is waiting for – the rapporteur proposes that the procedure be completed under Article 308 (consultation) as soon as possible. However, Parliament reserves the right, following adoption by the Council, to bring a case before the Court to examine the legal base.

3.   The regulation

a.   Statutory sources, company formation, capital and registered offices

Article 9 covers the statutory sources: firstly, the text of the regulation itself, secondly, company law of the Member States and, thirdly, the statutes of the SE.

Pursuant to Article 2 and 3, there are five different ways in which an SE can be established: two public limited-liability companies, with registered offices and head offices within the Community and formed under the law of a Member State, may form an SE by means of a merger; two national public or private limited-liability companies may set up a holding SE; companies within the meaning of the second paragraph of Article 48 of the Treaty and other legal bodies governed by public or private law may form a subsidiary SE; a public limited-liability company formed under the law of a Member State may be transformed into an SE if, for at least two years, it has had a subsidiary company; finally, an SE may set up a subsidiary company, also in the form of an SE. The common feature is that the SE must impact on at least two Member States.

The capital of the SE is in Euro and must be at least EUR 120.

The registered offices must be in the Member State where the head offices are located.

b.   Bodies

There are two different systems of managing limited-liability companies under the company law of the Member States. The "single" system in Britain, for example, provides solely for an administrative body. The "dual" system, applicable in Germany, for example, provides for a supervisory body and a management body. European unification requires that both systems be available in each country. Hence, companies can choose the single or the dual approach. This means, for example, that employee participation will be possible even in the single system. This will present national parliaments with complex tasks.

c. Transfer of place of business to another member state
Hitherto, company law of the Member States has been such that national companies can only transfer their place of business if they are dissolved and reformed in other Member State. With an SE a transfer will not result in the company being dissolved or in a new legal entity being created. However, a transfer plan has to be drawn up and made public. The management or administrative body of the SE also has to draw up a report on the consequences of the transfer.

The report must be made available to shareholders and creditors. After a certain period the general meeting decides on the transfer. The transfer takes legal effect as soon as the SE is entered in the register of the new location, following which the entry in the previous registry is deleted.

4. The directive

The directive will enter into force at the same time as the regulation. The rapporteur is Mr Miller. In connection with the regulation, the most important feature is protection of acquired rights of participation of the employees, whatever form that may take, and regardless of the subsequent location of the SE's registered offices.

5. The need for SEs

The shortcomings in the regulation and the complex nature of the directive lead to the question: do we actually need SEs? The answer is clearly "yes". It is not the need for SEs that is in doubt, but the way in which they are structured.

Although companies operate on a transnational basis today, they still face considerable legal and other difficulties. Despite approximation by European directives, company law still displays considerable differences. The growing together of what used to be separate markets means that we must finally create organisational forms which reflect the new situation in Europe. The obstacles to mobility for companies operating Europe-wide need to be removed.

However, there are serious shortcomings to the nature of the SEs. The directive on employee participation is fairly complex and it also enables all national rules on participation to be transferred to any other Member State. This will have serious legal consequences which are difficult to foresee.

It follows that SEs will differ from one Member State to another. There will not be one European SE, but an SE with French, Spanish or German features, for example. Furthermore, even within the same Member State a variety of different SEs will be created covering the full range of possible forms. It goes without saying that this will have its disadvantages – of a legal, actual and financial nature. In effect this will make access to SE status difficult for small and medium-sized businesses in particular.

Companies from Member States which do not have a tradition of worker participation are unlikely to want to adopt maximum participation. There is a risk, therefore, that German companies will in effect be unable to enter into a merger with companies from Member States where there is no employee participation. This will have a substantial discriminatory effect on such companies.

Furthermore, it is essential that in parallel with the entry into force of the directive and the regulation and after a transitional period of three years in which national legislation is to be enacted, accompanying fiscal rules are also adopted. The precise nature of the SE will, naturally be determined in part by fiscal legislation (e.g. accounting for profits and losses). The Commission and the national governments are therefore called upon to adopt the requisite accompanying fiscal rules by the year 2003 in order to give full shape to the new legal form of the SE.

There is one further point which the rapporteur believes is important. It should be possible for the SE to be used even before the end of the transitional period by companies in countries which have already transposed the entire package in their national law. This would provide a certain incentive for countries which are lagging behind.

As a general rule, the same consideration applies as applies to any case of approximation of laws and standardisation: it is long-term success which counts. Sooner or later the first step has to be taken so that the SE as a legal form can actually be created. In my opinion, in the course of time national peculiarities in interpretation of the law will increasingly become of secondary importance since the SE requires uniform rules if it is to function properly. Here, too, the post-Nice process comes into play: improvements have to be made.

In conclusion, I advocate launching the SE on its maiden voyage. This will show where repairs are still needed so that one day it will fulfil our hopes and become the flagship.

II. OPINION OF THE COMMITTEE ON EMPLOYMENT AND SOCIAL AFFAIRS FOR THE COMMITTEE ON LEGAL AFFAIRS AND THE INTERNAL MARKET ON THE PROPOSAL FOR A COUNCIL REGULATION ON THE STATUTE FOR A EUROPEAN COMPANY (SE), 21 JUNE 2001

Procedure

The Committee on Employment and Social Affairs appointed Toine Manders draftsman at its meeting of 15 February 2001.

It considered the draft opinion at its meetings of 20 March 2001, 29 May 2001 and 21 June 2001. At the last meeting it adopted the following amendments by 35 votes to 0, with 5 abstentions.

Short justification

A Statute for a European Company was already being discussed more than 30 years ago. In 1959 it became increasingly clear to Dutch lawyers that a statute for a European Company was needed. One of those lawyers was Mr Sanders who, on becoming professor at Rotterdam's Erasmus University, delivered an inaugural lecture entitled "Towards a European limited company?", in which he called for the concept of a European company to be established. On that occasion he established the term SE. The Commission subsequently asked him to produce a blueprint. Multinational companies wished to spread their business activities over a number of European countries. For such companies to be forced to set up a national company structure in each Member State is counter-productive and a source of frustration. Fragmentation of this kind is, moreover, inappropriate in the context of the internal market, which was completed in 2001.

It was not until 1970 that the first proposal was presented by the Commission. This proposal introduced the term "Societas Europaea" for the European Company, based on a uniform definition comprehensible to all Europeans. The concept was elaborated in great detail by the Commission at that time, with the original proposal extending to as many as 284 articles. The proposals have since been reduced to their essence, set out in 70 articles.

There is currently a great need for an SE, as more and more companies are operating across borders as a result of the completion of the internal market and the globalisation of business activities under the impact of information and communications technology such as the Internet. Some organisations maintain that the statute for an SE would save European businesses EUR 30 million a year.

There is at present no European company law but only national laws laid down in each Member State in this area. That may perhaps be the reason why for a long time it has not been possible to reach an agreement on this proposal, the delay being attributable, namely, to the different cultures existing in this area in the Member States.

It is to be welcomed that a common position has now finally been found by the Nice European Council. In this connection, reference should be made to the legal basis which was changed in the course of the negotiations at Nice from Article 95 (ex Article 44) of the Treaty to Article 308: on paper, a small change, but one which in fact has major implications for Parliament. On the basis of Article 95 (ex Article 44) Parliament had the right of codecision, whilst its role is now confined to advising and giving an opinion. In spite of the fact that democratic control by the EP is being disregarded in this respect, your draftsman takes the view that we should welcome the foundations laid here. In order to avoid this fragile common position falling apart, your draftsman has confined himself to making as few amendments as possible. Greater clarification can perhaps be provided later.

However, a number of issues have not been sufficiently dealt with in connection with this report. The statute for the SE pays little attention to the specific interests of small and medium-sized companies. It would be appropriate for more account to be taken of this category of businesses in future.

Although an oblique reference is made to small and medium-sized companies in recital 13 ("In order to ensure that such companies are of reasonable size, a minimum amount of capital should be set so that they have sufficient assets without making it difficult for small and medium-sized undertakings to form SEs."), it is important that more attention be given to such companies. European small and medium-sized companies provide a great deal of employment and are the driving force behind a large section of the European economy.

If we wish the statute for the SE to work fully effectively in future, we must also look at the different systems of taxation. The various systems will need to be harmonised in such a way that, for example, investment, depreciation, profit, losses, various cost items and, above all, obligations under administrative provisions are dealt with in the same way by SEs in different Member States.

This is primarily in order to ensure equality before the law in Europe, and to avoid national judges invoking national laws to review legal acts of SEs.

Adopting this regulation and the Menrad report (directive 2001/... /EC on the involvement of employees) means making a start to a formal SE, which can be improved over the longer term, if necessary, on the basis of experience in practice and under pressure from the market. It is advisable that an evaluation be carried out three years after entry into force, ensuring that a review of the way in which the statute is functioning is made in the not too distant future. We must avoid it being another thirty years before the statute functions fully satisfactorily.

An effective SE is in the interests of business, employment and consumers. Last but not least, the SE will strengthen not only the internal market but, above all, the European idea.

Amendments

The Committee on Employment and Social Affairs calls on the Committee on Legal Affairs and the Internal Market, as the committee responsible, to incorporate the following amendments in its report:

Text proposed by the Council[20]	Amendments by Parliament
Amendment 1 Recital 7 a (new)	*With a view to creating a uniform legal framework for the functioning of SEs, this Regulation should aim at minimising reference to differing national rules and laws, which may result in discrepancies in the treatment of SEs registered in different Member States.*

20.   Not yet published.

Text proposed by the Council	Amendments by Parliament

Justification
The current proposal still refers to too great an extent to national legislation, which means that, effectively, there is not one uniform SE but 15 different systems, whilst a single internal market allowing free competition should be the objective. Barriers to competition should be removed as far as possible.

Amendment 2
Recital 21 a (new)

A long-term solution has to be found to problems arising out of unequal taxation burdens on SEs registered in different Member States.

Justification

The existence of major differences between national tax systems impedes free competition, precisely because of national differences affecting businesses within the internal market. For that reason, it will be necessary to endeavour in future to coordinate tax systems at the European level.

Amendment 3
Article 69

Five years at the latest after the entry into force of this Regulation, the Commission shall forward to the Council and the European Parliament a report on the application of the Regulation and proposals for amendments, where appropriate. The report shall, in particular, analyse the appropriateness of:	*Three* years at the latest after the entry into force of this Regulation, the Commission shall forward to the Council and the European Parliament a report on the application of the Regulation and proposals for amendments, where appropriate. The report shall, in particular, analyse *the impact of this Regulation on small and medium-sized enterprises, in particular any obstacles to their forming an SE, and* the appropriateness of:
(a) allowing the location of an SE's head office and registered office in different Member States;	(a) allowing the location of an SE's head office and registered office in different Member States;
(b) broadening the concept of merger in Article 17(2) in order to admit also other types of merger than those defined in Articles 3(1) and 4(1) of Directive 78/855/EEC;	(b) broadening the concept of merger in Article 17(2) in order to admit also other types of merger than those defined in Articles 3(1) and 4(1) of Directive 78/855/EEC;
(c) revising the jurisdiction clause in Article 8(12) in the light of any provision which may have been inserted in the 1968 Brussels Convention or in any text adopted by Member States or by the Council to replace such Convention;	(c) revising the jurisdiction clause in Article 8(12) in the light of any provision which may have been inserted in the 1968 Brussels Convention or in any text adopted by Member States or by the Council to replace such Convention;
(d) allowing provisions in the statutes of an SE adopted by a Member State in execution of authorisations given to the Member States by this Regulation or laws adopted to ensure the effective application of this Regulation in respect to the SE which deviate from or are complementary to these laws, even when such provisions would not be authorised in the statutes of a public limited-liability company having its registered office in the Member State.	(d) allowing provisions in the statutes of an SE adopted by a Member State in execution of authorisations given to the Member States by this Regulation or laws adopted to ensure the effective application of this Regulation in respect to the SE which deviate from or are complementary to these laws, even when such provisions would not be authorised in the statutes of a public limited-liability company having its registered office in the Member State;

Text proposed by the Council	Amendments by Parliament
	(e) establishing a common tax on all SEs, regardless of the Member State in which they are registered, with a view to preventing any restriction or distortion of competition.

Justification

3 years:
A shorter deadline is proposed for making an initial evaluation, in order to avoid shortcomings impeding for too long the proper functioning of the regulation.

Small and medium-sized companies:
The regulation currently takes too little account of SMEs, which provide a great deal of employment and are the driving force behind a large section of the European economy.

(e):
Only if there are coordinated tax systems applying to all SEs can SEs really function effectively within the whole of Europe. Without such coordination, free competition will continue to be impeded.

European Parliament legislative resolution on the Draft Council regulation on the Statute for a European Company (SE)

The European Parliament,
- having regard to the Draft Council regulation (14886/2000),
- having regard to the Commission proposal to the Council (COM(1989) 268)[21] amended in 1991 by COM(1991) 174,[22]
- having regard to its position at first reading of 24 January 1991[23] confirmed on 2 December 1993[24] and 27 October 1999,[25]
- having been consulted by the Council again under Article 308 of the EC Treaty (C5-0092/2001),
- having regard to Rule 67 and 71(2) of its Rules of Procedure,
- having regard to the report of the Committee on Legal Affairs and the Internal Market and the opinion of the Committee on Employment and Social Affairs (A5-0243/2001),

1. Approves the Council draft as amended;
2. Calls on the Commission to alter its proposal accordingly, pursuant to Article 250(2) of the EC Treaty;
3. Calls on the Council to notify Parliament should it intend to depart from the text approved by Parliament;
4. Asks to be consulted again if the Council intends to amend the draft regulation substantially;
5. Instructs its President to forward its position to the Council and Commission.

21.　　*O.J.*, C 263, 16 October 1989.
22.　　*O.J.*, C 138, 29 May 1991.
23.　　*O.J.*, C 48, 25 February 1991.
24.　　*O.J.*, C 342, 20 December 1993.
25.　　*O.J.*, C 154, 5 June 2000.

III.   REPORT ON THE DRAFT COUNCIL DIRECTIVE
       SUPPLEMENTING THE STATUTE FOR A EUROPEAN
       COMPANY WITH REGARD TO THE INVOLVEMENT OF
       EMPLOYEES (21 JUNE 2001)

Procedural page

On 30 June 1970 the European Commission submitted its initial proposal for a regulation on the European company. The proposal was amended in 1975. On 25 August 1989 the Commission submitted new proposals for a regulation on the Statute for a European company and a related directive concerning the involvement of employees in the European company (COM(1989) 268 – 1989/0218-0219(SYN)),[26] which were amended in 1991 (COM(1991) 174).[27]

The 1989 and 1991 proposals were based on Article 54 (current Article 44) of the EC Treaty, which provided for the cooperation procedure. Following the entry into force of the Maastricht Treaty, these proposals became subject to the codecision procedure.

At the sitting of 24 January 1991, Parliament adopted its position at first reading on these proposals, confirmed on 2 December 1993 and again on 27 October 1999.

Subsequently, the Council decided that the correct legal basis for the proposals was Article 308 of the EC Treaty which provided for consultation of Parliament.

By letter of 9 March 2001 the Council consulted Parliament again under Article 308 of the EC Treaty on the Draft Council directive supplementing the Statute for a European Company with regard to the involvement of employees (14732/2000 – 1989/0219 (CNS)).

At the sitting of 15 March 2001 the President of Parliament announced that she had referred this Council text to the Committee on Employment and Social Affairs as the committee responsible and the Committee on Legal Affairs and the Internal Market for its opinion (C5-0093/2001).

The Committee on Employment and Social Affairs appointed Winfried Menrad rapporteur at its meeting of 15 February 2001.

The committee considered the draft Council directive and draft report at its meetings of 20 March 2001, 29 May 2001 and 21 June 2001.

At the last meeting it adopted the draft legislative resolution unanimously.

The opinion of the Committee on Legal Affairs and the Internal Market including its position on the legal basis is attached.

---

26.   *O.J.*, C 263, 16 October 1989.
27.   *O.J.*, C 138, 14 May 1991.

Legislative proposal

Draft Council directive supplementing the Statute for a European Company with regard to the involvement of employees (14732/2000 – C5-0093/2001 – 1989/ 0219(CNS))

The proposal is amended as follows:

Text proposed by the Council[28]	Amendments by Parliament
Amendment 1 Citation 1	
Having regard to the Treaty establishing the European Community, and in particular *Article 308 thereof,*	Having regard to the Treaty establishing the European Community, and in particular *the third indent of Article 137(3),*

Justification

The correct legal basis is Article 137(3) (third indent), since the Directive concerns the representation and collective defence of the interests of workers and employees, including co-determination (participation of workers' representatives in the competent bodies of the company). Since the Treaty contains a specific legal basis, there is no need for recourse to the powers conferred on the Community by Article 308 of the Treaty.

Amendment 2
Recital 3 a (new)

> *(3a) The purpose of this Directive is to establish minimum requirements for the information, participation and consultation of employees in undertakings within the European Community.*

Justification

The conditions in those Member States which have additional social legislation should not be diluted.

Amendment 3
Recital 5a (new)

> *(5a) It is, however, appropriate to harmonise the national implementing provisions of the Member States, since acquired rights are not called into question,*

Justification

In order to prevent a situation in which there are 15 different national implementing provisions, the transposition of the Directive must be coordinated because otherwise the raison d'être of the SE would be lost.

Amendment 4
Recital 7a (new)

> *(7a) Member States should ensure through appropriate provisions that, in the case of substantial structural changes following the creation of an SE, there are negotiations on the future participation of workers.*

---

28.   Not yet published.

Text proposed by the Council	Amendments by Parliament

Justification
The right to negotiations on worker participation can not be limited to the period in which an SE is being created; if there are to be substantial structural changes (e.g. mergers, the integration of other undertakings and companies), there must be the possibility of fresh negotiations.

Amendment 5
Recital 12a (new)

> *(12a) Clear rules are required on management's obligation to provide information, specifying areas to which this obligation applies.*

Justification

The present text does not contain clear rules on management's obligation to provide information. It is essential, however, that the areas in respect of which there is an obligation to provide information are clearly described.

Amendment 6
Recital 17

(17) The Treaty *has not provided the necessary powers for the Community to adopt the proposed Directive, other than those provided for in Article 308.*

(17) The Treaty *provides the necessary legal basis in the form of Article 137(3) third indent.*

Justification

The correct legal basis is Article 137(3) (third indent) since the directive concerns the representation and collective defence of the interests of workers and employees, including co-determination (participation of workers' representatives in the competent bodies of the company). Since the Treaty contains a specific legal basis, there is no need for recourse to the powers conferred on the community by Article 308 of the Treaty.

Amendment 7
Article 2(k)

(k) "Participation" means the influence of the *body representative of the employees and/or the* employees' representatives in the affairs of a company *by way of:*
– the right to elect or appoint some of the members of the company's supervisory or administrative organ; or
– the right to recommend and/or oppose the appointment of some or all of the members of the company's supervisory or administrative organ.

(k) "Participation" means the influence of the employees' representatives *on the supervisory or administrative board* in the affairs of a company;

Justification

The tasks of the body representative of the employees involve questions of information and consultation, not participation. This institution is the special form of the European Works Council in SEs. Participation must be an ongoing task, rather than a one-off right such as recommending, nominating and rejecting employees' representatives in the supervisory organ. This Directive seeks to enshrine the right to broader consultation which could be described as participation. The Committee of Employment's report on the Commission's report on the application of the Directive on the establishment of a European works council (COM (2000/2214(COS))) suggests that decisions on information, consultation and participation should be taken in the Council of Ministers by majority voting and that only codetermination should require unanimity.

Amendment 8
Article 4(g)

(g) if, during negotiations, the parties decide to establish arrangements for participation, the substance of those arrangements including (if applicable) the number of members in the SE's administrative or supervisory body which the employees will be entitled to elect, appoint, recommend or oppose, the procedures as to how these members may be elected, appointed, recommended or opposed by the employees, and their rights;	(g) if, during negotiations, the parties decide to establish arrangements for participation, the substance of those arrangements including (if applicable) the number of members in the SE's administrative or supervisory body which the employees will be entitled to elect, appoint, recommend or oppose, the procedures as to how these members may be elected, appointed, recommended or opposed by the employees, and their rights. *Without prejudice to the arrangements decided on, the election or appointment of employees to the SE's administrative or supervisory body shall take place according to relevant national customs or legal provisions of the Member States governing the appointment of employees to the bodies of joint stock companies.*

Justification

The Council's proposal for a Directive omitted this point by an oversight, but it appeared in the original Commission proposal.

Amendment 9
Article 12(3) (new)

	The Commission shall chair an implementation group, comprising experts from the Member States, to facilitate and coordinate the transposition of this directive at national level into national law.

Justification

In order to avoid having 15 different sets of provisions for national implementation, the Commission needs to chair a delegation comprising officials from the Member States to coordinate the correct transposition of the directive.

Amendment 10
Annex, Part 3 (b), first paragraph

(b) In other cases of the establishing of an SE, the employees of the SE, its subsidiaries and establishments and/or their representative body shall have the right to elect, appoint, recommend or oppose the appointment of a number of members of the administrative or supervisory body of the SE equal to the highest proportion in force in the participating companies concerned before registration of the SE.	(b) In other cases of the establishing of an SE, the employees of the SE, its subsidiaries and establishments and/or their representative body shall have the right to elect, appoint, recommend or oppose the appointment of a number of members of the administrative or supervisory body of the SE equal to the highest proportion in force in the participating companies concerned before registration of the SE. *The election or appointment of employees to the SE's administrative or supervisory body shall take place according to relevant national customs or legal provisions of the Member States governing the appointment of employees to the bodies of joint stock companies.*

| Text proposed by the Council | Amendments by Parliament |

Justification

The Council's proposal for a Directive omitted this point by an oversight, but it appeared in the original Commission proposal.

Amendment 11
Annex, Part 3 (b), paragraph 3

The representative body shall decide on the allocation of seats within the administrative or supervisory *body* among the members representing the employees from the various Member States or on the way in which the SE's employees may recommend or oppose the appointment of the members of these bodies according to the proportion of the SE's employees in each Member State. If the employees of one or more Member States are not covered by this proportional criterion, the representative body shall appoint a member from one of those Member States, in particular the Member State of the SE's registered office where that is appropriate. Each Member State may determine the allocation of the seats it is given within the administrative or supervisory body.	The representative body shall decide on the allocation of seats within the administrative or supervisory *board* among the members representing the employees from the various Member States or on the way in which the SE's employees may recommend or oppose the appointment of the members of these bodies according to the proportion of the SE's employees in each Member State. If the employees of one or more Member States are not covered by this proportional criterion, the representative body shall appoint a member from one of those Member States, in particular the Member State of the SE's registered office where that is appropriate. Each Member State may determine the allocation of the seats it is given within the administrative or supervisory body.

Justification

(Translator's note: This amendment applies only in part to the English version. The justification does not relate to the part of the amendment applying to the English version).

Draft legislative resolution

European Parliament legislative resolution on the Draft Council directive supplementing the Statute for a European Company with regard to the involvement of employees (Consultation procedure – renewed consultation)

> The European Parliament,

- having regard to the draft Council directive (14732/2000[29]),
- having regard to the Commission proposal to the Council (COM(1989) 268)[30] amended in 1991 by COM(1991) 174[31]
- having regard to its position at first reading of 24 January 1991[32] confirmed on 2 December 1993[33] and 27 October 1999,[34]
- having been consulted by the Council again under Article 308 of the EC Treaty (C5-0093/2001),

---

29.   Not yet published.
30.   *O.J.*, C 263, 16 October 1989.
31.   *O.J.*, C 138, 29 May 1991.
32.   *O.J.*, C 48, 25 February 1991.
33.   *O.J.*, C 342, 20 December 1993.
34.   *O.J.*, C 154.

- having regard to Rule 67 and 71(2) of its Rules of Procedure,
- having regard to the report of the Committee on Employment and Social Affairs and the opinion of the Committee on Legal Affairs and the Internal Market including its position on the legal basis (A5-0231/2001),

1. Approves the Council draft as amended;
2. Calls on the Commission to alter its proposal accordingly, pursuant to Article 250(2) of the EC Treaty;
3. Calls on the Council to notify Parliament should it intend to depart from the text approved by Parliament;
4. Asks to be consulted again if the Council intends to amend the draft directive substantially;
5. Instructs its President to forward its position to the Council and Commission.

Explanatory statement

I. BACKGROUND

After thirty years of tough negotiations the Employment and Social Affairs Ministers managed to reach an agreement finally at their Council meeting on 20 December 2000 on a Statute for a European Company. The Council chose Article 308 TEC as the legal basis for the regulation and directive.

In 1970 the Commission had submitted its initial proposal for a regulation on the uniform establishment of the European company; this was submitted to Parliament at the end of the 1980s in the form of two separate proposals, the first a proposal for a regulation on a statute for a European company, based on Article 100 TEC (95 TEU), and the second a proposal for a directive complementing this statute with regard to the involvement of employees,[35] on the basis of Article 54 TEC (44 TEU). As in the fifth proposal for a directive, a choice was provided between a monolithic and a dual construction and between a number of different models of the participation of employees. The proposal for a regulation and the proposal for a directive thus formed an indissoluble whole, since a European company without participation in some form is unthinkable.

The core elements of both proposals were as follows:
- the optionally applicable, cross-border fiscally advantageous blueprint for a European company created either by the merger of national undertakings, or the establishment of a holding company or a common subsidiary;
- the option between a monolithic and dual structure;
- binding provisions concerning the participation of employees' representatives;

---

35. COM(89/268) of 16 October 1989. Parliament adopted its legislative proposal on 24 January 1991 and tabled amendments to both texts in the reports drawn up jointly by Mrs Oddy and Mr Rothley on behalf of the Committee on Legal Affairs and Citizens' Rights and Mr Suarez and Mr Brok, on behalf of the Committee on Social Affairs.

- information and consultation requirements, or the obligation of the administrative or supervisory board to obtain authorisation before implementing decisions such as:
  - shutting down or relocating establishments;
  - cutting back or expanding establishments;
  - changing establishments;
  - the establishment of subsidiaries or holding companies;
- election procedures and the working methods of employees' representatives should follow normal practice in the Member State concerned.

The proposals failed owing to the issue of worker participation. The European Parliament motion for a resolution adopted in January 1997 on the basis of a Commission communication on the information and consultation of employees attempted to give a fresh impulse to the legislative procedure to solve the question of worker participation in the SE. A group of experts was then set up, chaired by Etienne Davignon, to attempt to address this problem. It rapidly came to the conclusion that none of the existing Member State systems, if they had been taken as a point of reference, could be expected to command the necessary majority in the Council, so it proposed the following structure:

- negotiations must be held between the parties before the registration of the company. In the event of a breakdown, they should continue for a further three months. Under no circumstances may negotiations last longer than one year in total;
- if no agreement is reached by the end of that period, the rules on the information and consultation of workers and their participation (the reference rules) will apply;
- the application of the reference rules will ensure that "priority given to negotiations does not lead to legal insecurity or the possible blocking of the establishment of the European company".[36]

On the basis of the report of the Group of experts, the Luxembourgish Council Presidency submitted to the Council a new legislative proposal which, however, was unable to overcome the opposition of the United Kingdom, Ireland and Spain in particular. The same applies to the proposals submitted by Parliament (motions for resolutions of January 1997 and November 1997) in which it adopted a position on these documents. Parliament wished to avoid two dangers, namely:

- the imposition of a certain model for employee participation favoured by a small number of Member States on the other Member States (no "export of employee participation");
- circumvention of more far-reaching co-determination in certain countries by means of a European legal instrument (no "escape route from employee participation").

---

36.   Final report of the Davignon Group of May 1997 (C4-0455/97). Parliament adopted a report on this matter in November 1997. Rapporteur: W. Menrad.

Numerous rounds of negotiations and changes to the legislative proposal were needed before the Council was able to reach the present agreement on the European company on 20 December 2000 which managed to overcome the most serious misgivings. Spanish opposition could only be overcome at the Nice Summit by introducing an option: Member States are given the option not to transpose the rules on employee participation – restricted to a scenario where the European company is established by merger – into national law (opting-out clause).

II. MAIN OUTLINE OF THE REGULATION AND DIRECTIVE

Under the present proposal a European company may be established:
- by the merger of at least two companies which are subject to the law of different Member States;
- as a holding company of joint stock and limited liability companies from various Member States (the essential difference between this and establishment through merger is that the founding companies continue to exist);
- as a joint subsidiary of companies within the meaning of Article 48(2);
- through the transformation of a company established under the law of a Member State and which has had a subsidiary for at least two years which is subject to the law of another Member State.

The organs of the European company are the shareholders' general meeting and the supervisory and management body in the dual system or the administrative body in the monolithic system; the negotiating partners may opt for either system.

The directive supplementing the regulation governs both the information and consultation of workers' representatives on matters concerning the European company itself, its subsidiaries or establishments – essentially the provisions of the European Works Council have been taken over – and employee participation in the supervisory or administrative body of the European company.

The scale of employee participation will be decided through free negotiations between the companies concerned and the workers represented by a special negotiating body. In principle this negotiating body shall take decisions by an absolute majority of its members, provided that such a majority also represents an absolute majority of the employees. However, should the result of the negotiations lead to a reduction of participation rights, the majority required for a decision to approve such an agreement shall be the votes of two thirds of the members of the special negotiating body representing at least two thirds of the employees, including the votes of members representing employees employed in at least two Member States.

Reduction of participation rights means a proportion of employees' representatives of organs of the SE which is lower than the highest proportion existing within the participating companies. However, a qualified majority is only necessary where certain limit values are attained concerning the

proportion of employees with participation rights compared to the overall number of employees. These are:
- in the case of merger: 25%
- in the case of a holding company: 50%; and
- in the case of the formation of a subsidiary: 50%.

In the event of a breakdown of negotiations a safety clause is provided to protect participation rights and applies where:
- the parties agree on such a measure;
- no agreement has been reached within half a year or, in the case of an extension, one year and the negotiating body has not decided to allow national provisions to apply, providing the competent organ of each of the companies concerned has agreed to a continuation of the procedure. The same limit values also apply here, i.e. the minimum level of participation under the safety clause in the annex to the directive applies automatically when these values are attained.

The following provisions apply to employee participation:
- In the case of an SE established by transformation, if the rules of a Member State relating to employee participation in the administrative or supervisory body applied before registration, all aspects of employee participation shall continue to apply to the SE.
- In other cases of the establishing of an SE, the employees of the SE, its subsidiaries and establishments and/or their representative body shall have the right to elect, appoint, recommend or oppose the appointment of a number of members of the administrative or supervisory body of the SE equal to the highest appropriate proportion in force in the participating companies concerned before registration of the SE.

III.   AMENDMENTS TO THE DIRECTIVE

Taking into account the Commission proposal, the Davignon report, Parliament's opinion on these proposals and the results of the hearing of 25 April on the information, consultation and participation rights of workers, your rapporteur wishes to make the following critical remarks concerning the proposal for a Council Directive:

1.   Changing the legal basis

The Council has taken Article 308 TEC as the legal basis. Article 308 is to be used as the legal basis where:
- action by the Community should prove necessary to attain, in the course of the operation of the common market, one of the objectives of the Community and
- this Treaty has not provided the necessary powers for the legal acts in question.

The European Parliament's Legal Service has found that the Treaty does in fact provide a special legal basis, namely Article 137(3), which it believes should be implemented.

2. Tax problems

(a) Tax neutrality

In order to make the European company financially more attractive the tax merger directive adopted on 23 July 1990 should be applied to this legal form.

(b) Tax base

A European company will only be attractive to employers if it is no longer subject to national taxation in the Member State concerned.

(c) Uncovering undisclosed reserves

The final taxation of the previous company is a tax law problem which has not yet been solved.

3. Transposition of the directive

After the adoption of the SE, a three-year transitional period begins. Rules implementing the regulation and transposing the Directive must be uniformly applied throughout the Community so as to prevent a situation in which 15 different sets of rules apply, because otherwise this would remove the very raison d'être of a European company.

4. Election procedure

The Commission's original proposal provided that the procedure for electing employees' representatives should follow existing practice or legal provisions in individual Member States.

5. European works council – European company

Article 12 of the Directive states that the European company and its subsidiaries are not subject to the provisions of the European Works Council, and provision is made for a special employees' body. Measures must, however, be taken to ensure that the provisions on information and consultation rights in both directives are harmonised.

IV. OPINION OF THE COMMITTEE ON LEGAL AFFAIRS AND THE
     INTERNAL MARKET FOR THE COMMITTEE ON
     EMPLOYMENT AND SOCIAL AFFAIRS ON THE DRAFT
     COUNCIL DIRECTIVE SUPPLEMENTING THE STATUTE FOR A
     EUROPEAN COMPANY WITH REGARD TO THE
     INVOLVEMENT OF EMPLOYEES (20 JUNE 2001)

Procedure

The Committee on Legal Affairs and the Internal Market appointed Bill Miller draftsman at its meeting of 29 February 2000.

It considered the draft opinion at its meetings of 27 February, 5 March, 24 April, 25 May and 20 June 2001.

At the last meeting it adopted the following amendments unanimously.

Amendments

The Committee on Legal Affairs and the Internal Market calls on the Committee on Employment and Social Affairs, as the committee responsible, to incorporate the following amendments in its report:

Text proposed by the Council[37]	Amendments by Parliament
Amendment 1 Citation 1	
Having regard to the Treaty establishing the European Community, and in particular *Article 308 thereof*,	Having regard to the Treaty establishing the European Community, and in particular *the third indent of Article 137(3)*,

Justification

The correct legal basis is Article 137(3) (third indent), since the Directive concerns the representation and collective defence of the interests of workers and employees, including co-determination (participation of workers' representatives in the competent bodies of the company). Since the Treaty contains a specific legal basis, there is no need for recourse to the powers conferred on the Community by Article 308 of the Treaty.

Amendment 2 Recital 3 a (new)	*(3a) The purpose of this Directive is to establish minimum requirements for the information, participation and consultation of employees in undertakings within the European Community.*

Justification

The conditions in those Member States which have additional social legislation should not be diluted.

Amendment 3 Recital 6 a (new)	*(6a) For the purposes of this Directive, consultation is taken to mean dialogue and an exchange of views between employees' representatives and the competent body of the SE. The time, nature, means and content of that consultation must be such as to allow employees' representatives to communicate their position.*

---

37.   Not yet published.

Text proposed by the Council	Amendments by Parliament

Justification
Any consultation has to be meaningful.

Amendment 4
Recital 7 a (new)

(7a) For the purposes of this Directive, participation is taken to mean the possibility for representatives of the employees of an SE to exercise an influence on the undertaking in the future.

Justification
Any participation must be meaningful.

Amendment 5
Recital 8 a (new)

(8a) Under this proposed Directive, the information, participation and consultation shall be carried out by the employees' representatives and the competent body of the SE.

Justification
The representatives are chosen by the employees.

Amendment 6
Recital 17

(17) The Treaty *has not provided the necessary powers for the Community to adopt the proposed Directive, other than those provided for in Article 308.*

(17) The Treaty *provides the necessary legal basis in the form of Article 137(3), third indent.*

Justification
See justification for Amendment 1.

Involvement of employees in the Statute for a European company

European Parliament legislative resolution on the Draft Council directive supplementing the Statute for a European Company with regard to the involvement of (Consultation procedure – renewed consultation)
    The European Parliament,
–   having regard to the draft Council directive (14732/2000)
–   having regard to the Commission proposal to the Council (COM(1989) 268)[38] amended in 1991 by COM(1991) 174,[39]
–   having regard to its position at first reading of 24 January 1991[40] confirmed on 2 December 1993[41] and 27 October 1999,[42]

---

38.   *O.J.*, C 263, 16 October 1989.
39.   *O.J.*, C 138, 29 May 1991.
40.   *O.J.*, C 48, 25 February 1991.
41.   *O.J.*, C 342, 20 December 1993.
42.   *O.J.*, C 154, 5 June 2000.

- having been consulted by the Council again under Article 308 of the EC Treaty (C5-0093/2001),
- having regard to Rules 67 and 71(2) of its Rules of Procedure,
- having regard to the report of the Committee on Employment and Social Affairs and the opinion of the Committee on Legal Affairs and the Internal Market including its position on the legal basis (A5-0231/2001),

1. Approves the Council draft as amended;
2. Calls on the Commission to alter its proposal accordingly, pursuant to Article 250(2) of the EC Treaty;
3. Calls on the Council to notify Parliament should it intend to depart from the text approved by Parliament;
4. Asks to be consulted again if the Council intends to amend the draft directive substantially;
5. Instructs its President to forward its position to the Council and Commission.

Informing and consulting employees

Proposal for a Council Directive establishing a general framework for informing and consulting employees in the European Community
The proposal was approved with the following amendments:

(Amendment 1)
Recital 9

Text proposed by the Commission[43]
Whereas there is a need to strengthen dialogue and promote mutual trust within undertakings in order to improve risk anticipation, make work organisation more flexible and facilitate employee access to training within the undertaking while maintaining security, make employees aware of adaptation needs, increase employees' availability to undertake measures and activities to increase their employability, promote employee involvement in the operation and future of the undertaking and increase its competitiveness;

Amendments by Parliament
Whereas there is a need to strengthen dialogue and promote mutual trust within undertakings in order to improve risk anticipation, make work organisation more flexible and facilitate employee access to training within the undertaking while maintaining security, make employees aware of adaptation needs, increase employees' availability to undertake measures and activities to increase their employability, promote employee involvement in the operation and future of the undertaking and increase its competitiveness through the continuing acquisition of qualifications, the employment of workers in innovation and adherence to new forms of work organisation which are more creative and rewarding for both sides;

---

43.   *O.J.*, C 2, 5 January 1999.

(Amendment 2)
Recital 17

Whereas the purpose of this general framework is to establish minimum requirements applicable throughout the European Community while avoiding any administrative, financial or legal constraints which would hinder the creation and development of small and medium-sized undertakings; whereas, to this end, the scope of this Directive should be restricted to undertakings with at least 50 employees, without prejudice to any more favourable national or Community provisions whereas, in order to maintain the appropriate balance between the above-mentioned factors, this minimum may be raised to 100 employees in the case of the more innovative measures proposed herein on the information and consultation of employees on developments in the employment situation within the undertaking;

Whereas the purpose of this general framework is to establish minimum requirements applicable throughout the European Community while avoiding any administrative, financial or legal constraints which would hinder the creation and development of small and medium-sized undertakings; whereas, to this end, the scope of this Directive should be restricted to undertakings with at least 50 employees, without prejudice to any more favourable national or Community provisions

(Amendment 3)
Recital 19

Whereas the objectives of this Directive are to be achieved through the establishment of a general framework comprising the definitions and purpose of the information and consultation, which it will be up to the Member States to complete and adapt to their own national situation, ensuring, where appropriate, that the social partners have a leading role by allowing them to define freely the arrangements for informing and consulting employees which they consider to be best suited to their needs and wishes;

Whereas the objectives of this Directive are to be achieved through the establishment of a general framework comprising the definitions and purpose of the information and consultation, which it will be up to the Member States to complete and adapt to their own national situation, ensuring, where appropriate, that the social partners have a leading role by allowing them to define freely the arrangements for informing and consulting employees which they consider to be best suited to their needs and wishes.
Whereas existing provisions at national level may not be altered to the disadvantage of employees;

(Amendment 4)
Recital 20

Whereas care must be taken to avoid affecting some specific rules in the field of employees' information and consultation existing in some national laws, addressed to undertakings which pursue political, professional organisation, religious, charitable, educational, scientific or artistic aims, as well as aims involving information and the expression of opinions;

Deleted

(Amendment 37)
Recital 21

Whereas undertakings must be protected against public disclosure of certain particularly sensitive information;

Whereas undertakings must be protected against public disclosure of certain particularly sensitive information, though such protection must not entail any restriction of the right to information and consultation;

(Amendment 5)
Recital 25

Whereas other employee information and consultation rights, including those arising from Council Directive 94/45/EC of 22 September 1994 on the establishment of a European Works Council or a procedure in Community-scale undertakings and Community-scale groups of undertakings for the purposes of informing and consulting employees, must not be affected by this Directive;

Whereas other employee information and consultation rights, including those arising from Council Directive 94/45/EC of 22 September 1994 on the establishment of a European Works Council or a procedure in Community-scale undertakings and Community-scale groups of undertakings for the purposes of informing and consulting employees, must not be affected by this Directive, provided that they are more favourable to employees;

(Amendment 6)
Recital 25a (new)

Whereas the implementation of the provisions of this Directive shall under no circumstances constitute sufficient reason to justify a lowering of the general level of protection for employees in the field covered by it;

(Amendment 7)
Article 1(1)

1. The purpose of this Directive is to establish a general framework for informing and consulting employees in undertakings within the European Community.

1. The purpose of this Directive is to establish minimum requirements for the information and consultation of employees in undertakings within the European Community.

(Amendment 8)
Article 1(2)

2. When defining or implementing information and consultation procedures, the employer and the employees' representatives shall work in a spirit of co-operation and with due regard for their reciprocal rights and obligations, taking into account the interests both of the undertaking and of the employees;

2. Member States shall ensure that the employer and the employees' representatives, when defining or implementing information and consultation procedures, respect these minimum requirements and work together in good faith and with due respect for their reciprocal rights and obligations, taking into account the interests both of the undertaking and of the employees.

(Amendment 9)
Article 2(1)(a)

(a) "undertakings" means public or private undertakings carrying out an economic activity, whether or not operating for gain, which are located within the territory of the Member States of the European Community and have at least 50 employees, without prejudice to the provisions of Article 4(3);

(a) "undertakings" means public or private undertakings carrying out an economic activity, whether or not operating for gain, which are located within the territory of the Member States of the European Community and have at least 50 employees;

(Amendment 10)
Article 2(1)(b)

(b) "employer" means the natural or legal person party to employment contracts or employment relationships with employees;

(b) "employer" means the natural or legal person party to employment contracts or employment relationships with employees pursuant to national law and/or practice;

(Amendment 11)
Article 2(1)(c)

(c) "employees' representatives" means the
employees' representatives provided for by
national laws and/or practices;

(c) "employees' representatives" means the
permanent, stable and independent employees'
representatives provided for by national law
and/or practice;

(Amendment 41)
Article 2(1)(ca) (new)

(ca) "social partners" means the competent
representative organisation of the trade unions,
the employee representatives of the
undertaking, as provided by law, the employers'
organisation or the employer;

(Amendment 13)
Article 2(1)(e)

(e) "consultation" means the organisation of a
dialogue and exchange of views between the
employer and the employees' representatives on
the subjects set out in Article 4(1)(b) and (c),
– ensuring that the timing, method and content
are such that this step is effective

– at the appropriate level of management and
representation, depending on the subject under
discussion;
– on the basis of the relevant information to be
supplied by the employer and the opinion which
the employees' representatives are entitled to
formulate
– including the employees' representatives' right
to meet with the employer and obtain a
response, and the reasons for that response, to
any opinion they may formulate
– including, in the case of decisions within the
scope of the employer's management powers,
an attempt to seek prior agreement on the
decisions referred to in Article 4(1)(c).

(e) "consultation" means dialogue and
exchange of views between the employer and
the employees' representatives on the subjects
set out in Article 4(1),
– during the planning stage, so as to ensure that
this step is effective and that an influence can be
exerted
– at the appropriate level of management and
representation, depending on the subject under
discussion
– on the basis of information in accordance
with subparagraph (d) and the opinion which
the employees' representatives are entitled to
formulate
– including the employees' representatives' right
to meet with the employer and obtain a
response, and the reasons for that response, to
any opinion they may formulate
– including, in the case of decisions within the
scope of the employer's management powers,
an attempt to seek prior agreement.

(Amendment 15)
Article 2(2)

2. In conformity with the principles and
objectives of this Directive, Member States may
lay down particular provisions applicable to
undertakings which pursue directly and
essentially political, professional organisation,
religious, charitable, educational, scientific or
artistic aims, as well as aims involving
information and the expression of opinions, on
condition that, at the date of adoption of this
Directive, such particular provisions already
exist in national legislation.

Deleted

(Amendment 16)
Article 2(2a) (new)

2a. The Member States shall determine the levels (plant, undertaking or group of undertakings at national level) which, depending on the subject dealt with, guarantee full compliance with the objectives of this Directive.

(Amendment 17)
Article 2(2b) (new)

2b. The Member States, without prejudice to existing national provisions or practice, shall create mechanisms designed to foster and promote social dialogue also in small and medium-sized enterprises, which do not come within the field of application of this Directive, in order to extend to them the achievement of the general objectives contained in it.

(Amendment 43)
Article 3(1)

1. Member States may authorise the social partners at the appropriate level, including at undertaking level, to define freely and at any time through negotiated agreement the procedures for implementing the employee information and consultation requirements referred to in Articles 1, 2 and 4 of this Directive.

1. Member States may authorise the social partners at the appropriate level, including at undertaking level, to define freely and at any time through negotiated agreement the procedures for implementing the employee information and consultation requirements referred to in Articles 1, 2 and 4 of this Directive, provided that the minimum standards laid down at national level are upheld.

(Amendment 20)
Article 3(2)

2. The agreements referred to in paragraph 1 may establish, while respecting the general objectives laid down by the Directive and subject to conditions and limitations laid down by the Member States, arrangements which are different to those referred to in Article 2(1)(d) and (e) and Article 4 of the present Directive.

2. The social partners may conclude agreements which, while respecting the general objectives laid down by the Directive and subject to generally applicable conditions laid down by the Member States, provide for rules and arrangements which are more favourable for employees than those laid down by this Directive.

(Amendment 21)
Article 4(1)(a)

(a) information on the recent as well as the reasonably foreseeable development of the undertaking's activities and its economic and financial situation;

(a) information and consultation on the recent as well as the reasonably foreseeable development of the undertaking's activities and its economic and financial situation, in particular as regards investment, production, sales and structure;

(Amendment 22)
Article 4(1)(c)

(c) information and consultation on decisions likely to lead to substantial changes in work organisation or in contractual relations, including those covered by the Community provisions referred to in Article 8(1).	(c) information and consultation on decisions likely to lead to substantial changes in work organisation or in contractual relations, including those covered by the Community provisions referred to in Article 8(1), such as the introduction of new production processes, transfers of production, relocation, mergers, reductions in capacity or the closure of the undertaking, of plants or of substantial parts thereof.

(Amendment 23)
Article 4(1)(ca) (new)

(ca) information and consultation on training and continuing training, equal opportunities and health and safety at the workplace (in accordance with the provisions of framework Directive 89/391/EEC).

(Amendment 24)
Article 4(2a) (new)

2a. Member States shall ensure that, where a decision to be implemented will have considerable adverse consequences for employees, the final decision may be postponed for an appropriate period at the request of the employees' representatives so that consultations may continue with the aim of avoiding or mitigating such adverse consequences.

(Amendment 25)
Article 4(3)

3. Member States may exclude from the information and consultation obligations referred to in paragraph 1(b) of this Article undertakings with fewer than 100 employees.	Deleted

(Amendment 26)
Article 4a (new)

Article 4a
Experts
Employees' representatives may, if they so wish, request the assistance of experts specified by them.

(Amendment 27)
Article 5(2)

2. Member States shall provide, in specific cases and within the conditions and limits laid down by national legislation, that the employer is not obliged to communicate information or undertake consultation when the nature of that information or consultation is such that, according to objective criteria, it would seriously harm the functioning of the undertaking or would be prejudicial to it.	Deleted

(Amendment 28)
Article 6

Employees' representatives shall, when carrying out their functions, enjoy adequate protection and guarantees to enable them to perform properly the duties which have been assigned to them.

Employees' representatives shall, when carrying out their functions, enjoy adequate protection and guarantees to enable them to perform the duties which have been assigned to them.

In particular, employees' representatives must be entitled to
(a) legal protection against dismissal or disadvantage with regard to career, wage and training during their term of office and for six months thereafter (they may not be dismissed during that period except with the consent of their representative organisation), and
(b) appropriate and continuing training, including paid training leave, the organisation of periodic meetings among themselves and with all the employees and the use of the firm's internal computer networks.

(Amendment 29)
Article 7(3)(b)

(b) the withholding of important information or provision of false information rendering ineffective the exercise of the right to information and consultation.

(b) the withholding of information or provision of incomplete or false information with the intention of rendering ineffective the exercise of the right to information and consultation.

(Amendment 31)
Article 8(3)

3. This Directive shall be without prejudice to other rights of employees to information, consultation and participation under national law.

3. This Directive shall be without prejudice to other existing rights to information, consultation and participation under national law which are more favourable to employees

(Amendment 32)
Article 8(3a) (new)

3a. Implementation of the provisions of this Directive shall under no circumstances constitute sufficient reason to justify a lowering of existing standards in the Member States or the general level of protection for employees in the field covered by it.

(Amendment 33)
Article 8a (new)

Article 8a
Public sector
1. This Directive shall also apply to the public sector, including the civil service and public services.
2. The Member States shall ensure that the social partners introduce the necessary provisions by means of agreements, or that the laws, regulations or administrative provisions needed to comply with this Article are adopted.

(Amendment 34)
Article 9(1)

1. Member States shall adopt the laws, regulations and administrative provisions necessary to comply with this Directive no later than ... (two years after adoption) or shall ensure that the social partners introduce the required provisions by way of agreement, the Member States being obliged to take all necessary steps enabling them to guarantee the results imposed by this Directive at all times. They shall forthwith inform the Commission thereof.	1. After consulting the social partners, in accordance with current legislation and practice in the Member States, Member States shall adopt the laws, regulations and administrative provisions necessary to comply with this Directive no later than ... (two years after adoption) or shall ensure that the social partners introduce the required provisions by way of agreement, the Member States being obliged to take all necessary steps enabling them to guarantee the results imposed by this Directive at all times. They shall forthwith inform the Commission thereof.

(Amendment 35)
Article 10

Not later than ... (five years after adoption), the Commission shall, in consultation with the Member States and the social partners at Community level, review the application of this Directive with a view to proposing to the Council any necessary amendments.	Not later than ... (five years after adoption), the Commission shall, in consultation with the Member States and the social partners at Community level, review the application of this Directive, and in particular the validity of the ceilings on staff numbers, with a view to proposing to the Council any necessary amendments

Informing and consulting employees

Legislative resolution embodying Parliament's opinion on the proposal for a Council Directive establishing a general framework for informing and consulting employees in the European Community (Cooperation procedure: first reading)

The European Parliament,

- having regard to the Commission proposal to the Council (COM(98)0612-98/0315(SYN)),[44]
- having been consulted by the Council pursuant to Article 189c of the EC Treaty and to Article 2(2) of the Agreement on Social Policy attached to Protocol No 14 on Social Policy annexed to the EC Treaty (C4-0706/98),
- having regard to Rule 58 of its Rules of Procedure,
- having regard to the report of the Committee on Employment and Social Affairs and the opinion of the Committee on Legal Affairs and Citizens' Rights (A4-0186/1999),

1. Approves the Commission proposal, subject to Parliament's amendments;
2. Calls on the Commission to alter its proposal accordingly, pursuant to Article 189a(2) of the EC Treaty;
3. Calls on the Council to incorporate Parliament's amendments in the common position that it adopts in accordance with Article 189c(a) of the EC Treaty;

4. Calls for the conciliation procedure to be opened should the Council intend to depart from the text approved by Parliament;
5. Instructs its President to forward this opinion to the Council and Commission.

PART III

A GENERAL FRAMEWORK FOR INFORMING AND CONSULTING EMPLOYEES IN THE EUROPEAN COMMUNITY

PART III

A GENERAL FRAMEWORK FOR INFORMING AND CONSULTING EMPLOYEES IN THE EUROPEAN COMMUNITY

1. Analysis

I. GENESIS OF THE PROPOSAL

On 11 November 1998 the European Commission issued a proposal[1] for a Directive "establishing a general framework for informing and consulting employees in the European Community". The move followed the refusal of UNICE to enter into negotiations over a European agreement on the subject. The draft Directive provides for rules on the information and consultation of workers at national level – based on agreement or legislation – applying to undertakings with 50 or more employees. The ETUC welcomed the draft Directive, but considers that it does not go far enough on a number of issues. UNICE rejected European legislation in this area as unnecessary.

The possibility of the introduction of an EU-level framework for employee information and consultation was first raised in the European Commission's 1995 medium-term Social Action Programme. Calls for EU legislative action in this area became louder after the crisis sparked off by the closure of the Renault plant at Vilvoorde in Belgium, which was seen by many to have demonstrated the inadequacies of current EU legislation in this area. In June 1997, the Commission initiated a first round of consultations of the European-level social partners on the advisability of legislation in this area.

In November 1997, the Commission opened a second round of consultations on the content of possible EU legislation on this issue. The social partners had an opportunity at this stage – within a six-week deadline – to decide to attempt to negotiate a framework agreement, thus forestalling a Directive.

At the second stage of consultations, the Commission expressed a clear preference for a social partner initiative to reach a European agreement on this topic. However, while ETUC and CEEP indicated their willingness to negotiate on this basis, UNICE remained opposed and in March 1998 rejected joining such talks. UNICE said that member federations were virtually unanimous in their conviction that the European Union should not intervene in such a matter, which has no transnational implications.

ETUC maintained its position that the objective of a framework agreement in this area would not be to replace well-functioning systems for information and consultation at national level, but to set minimum standards for this basic right. National provisions that are more advantageous should take precedence over those laid down in a European agreement.

---

1.   COM/98/0612 final-SYN 98/0315, *O.J.*, C 5.1.1999.

R. Blanpain (ed.), Involvement of Employees in the European Union, 217–226.
© 2002 *Kluwer Law International. Printed in Great Britain.*

The draft Directive offers a substantial degree of flexibility in relation to the exact shape and scope of information and consultation arrangements to be instituted.

The draft was amended by the EP, the ESC and the Committee of the Regions.

The Comission justifies the proposal as follows:

"The existence of legal frameworks at national and Community level intended to ensure that workers are involved in the affairs of the undertaking employing them and in decisions which affect them has not always prevented serious decisions affecting workers from being taken and made public without adequate procedures having been put in place beforehand to inform and consult them;

There is a need to strengthen dialogue and promote mutual trust within undertakings in order to improve risk anticipation, make work organisation more flexible and facilitate employee access to training within the undertaking while maintaining security, make employees aware of adaptation needs, increase employees' availability to undertake measures and activities to increase their employability, promote employee involvement in the operation and future of the undertaking and increase its competitiveness;

In particular, there is a need to promote and strengthen information and consultation on the situation and probable development of employment within the undertaking and, where it ensues from the evaluation carried out by the employer that employment within the undertaking is likely to come under threat, on any anticipatory measures envisaged, in particular in terms of training and enhancing employees' skills, with a view to offsetting negative developments or their consequences and improving the employability and adaptability of the employees likely to be affected;

Timely information and consultation is a prerequisite for the success of restructuring and adaptation of undertakings to the new conditions created by globalisation of the economy, particularly via the development of new forms of work organisation";

. . .

"The existing legal frameworks for employee information and consultation at Community and national level tend to adopt an excessively a posteriori approach to the process of change, neglect the economic aspects of decisions taken and do not contribute to genuine anticipation of employment developments within the undertaking or to risk prevention";

. . .

"In accordance with the principles of subsidiarity and proportionality as set out in Article 5 of the Treaty, the objectives of the proposed action, as outlined above, cannot be adequately achieved by the Member States, in that the object is to establish a framework for employee information and consultation appropriate for the new European context described above; however, in view of the scale and impact of the proposed action, these objectives can be better achieved at Community level by the introduction of minimum regulations applicable to the entire European Community; the present Directive constitutes no more than the minimum necessary to achieve these objectives."

II.   OBJECT AND PRINCIPLES

The purpose of this Directive is to establish a general framework laying down minimum requirements concerning employees' rights to information and consultation in undertakings within the European Community. The Directive indicates that information and consultation procedures shall be established and implemented so as to ensure their effectiveness and underlines that the employer and the employees' representatives shall work in a spirit of co-operation and with due regard for their reciprocal rights and obligations, taking into account the interests both of the undertaking and of the employees (Article 1).

III.   DEFINITIONS

For the purposes of this Directive:
(a)   "undertakings" means public or private undertakings carrying out an economic activity, whether or not operating for gain, which are located within the territory of the Member States of the European Community;
(b)   "establishment" means a place of business with no legal personality, which is part of an undertaking and where a non-transitory economic activity is carried out with human means and goods;
(c)   "employer" means the natural or legal person party to employment contracts or employment relationships with employees, in accordance with national legislation and practice;
(d)   "employee" means any person who, in the Member State concerned, is protected as an employee under national labour legislation and in accordance with national practice;
(e)   "employees' representatives" means the employees' representatives provided for by national laws and/or practices;
(f)   "information" means transmission of details by the employer to the employees' representatives so that they can take note of and consider the subject in question;
(g)   "consultation" means the exchange of views and establishing of a dialogue between the employees' representatives and the employer (Article 2).

IV.   SCOPE

This Directive shall apply, at the Member States' choice, to:
−   undertakings with at least 50 employees in a Member State, or
−   establishments with at least 20 employees in a Member State.

The Member States shall establish the manner in which the number of employees is calculated.

The Member States may make provision for specific arrangements applicable to undertakings pursuing political, professional organisation, religious, charitable, educational, scientific or artistic aims, as well as aims involving information and the expression of opinions, provided such specific arrangements already exist in national law on the date on which this Directive is adopted (Article 3).

V. PROCEDURES FOR INFORMATION AND CONSULTATION

The Member States shall establish the procedures under which employees can exercise the right to information and consultation at the appropriate level.

Information and consultation shall cover:

(a)   information on the recent as well as the probable development of the undertaking's activities and its economic and financial situation;

(b)   information and consultation on the situation, structure and probable development of employment within the undertaking and on any anticipatory measures envisaged, especially in the event of a threat to employment;

(c)   information and consultation on decisions likely to lead to significant changes in work organisation or in contractual relations, including those covered by the provisions concerning collective redundancies and transfer of enterprises.

Appropriate information shall be provided at the appropriate time and in the appropriate manner, so as to allow the employees' representatives to examine the matter properly and, where appropriate, to prepare for consultation.

Appropriate consultation shall take place:

–   at an appropriate time and using appropriate means;

–   at the relevant management and representation level, depending on the subject;

–   on the basis of relevant information provided by the employer and the opinion which the employees' representatives are entitled to formulate;

–   in a manner which allows the employees' representatives to meet the employer and obtain a reasoned response to any opinion they have formulated;

–   with a view to reaching an agreement on the decisions regarding changes in work organisation, contractual relations, collective redundancies and transfer of enterprises, which come under the employer's prerogative (Article 4).

VI. INFORMATION AND CONSULTATION UNDER AN AGREEMENT

The Member States may allow the social partners at the appropriate level, including undertaking or establishment level, to define freely and at any time, through negotiated agreements, the procedures for informing and consulting employees (Article 5).

VII. CONFIDENTIAL INFORMATION

The employees' representatives and any experts who may assist them are not authorised to disclose, except to employees bound by a confidentiality obligation, any information which has expressly been provided to them in confidence, if this is in the legitimate interest of the undertaking. This obligation shall continue to apply irrespective of where the said representatives or experts are, even after expiry of their term of office.

Member States shall provide, in specific cases, that the employer is not obliged to communicate information or undertake consultation when the nature of that information or consultation is such that, according to objective criteria, it would seriously harm the functioning of the undertaking or would be prejudicial to it. Member States shall make provision for administrative or judicial appeal procedures should the employer claim confidentiality or fail to provide information in accordance with the above paragraphs. They may also make provision for procedures to safeguard the confidentiality of the information in question (Article 6).

VIII. PROTECTION OF EMPLOYEES' REPRESENTATIVES

Employees' representatives, when carrying out their functions, enjoy adequate protection and guarantees to enable them to perform properly the duties which have been assigned to them (Article 7).

IX. PROTECTION OF RIGHTS

Member States shall provide
- for appropriate measures in the event of non-compliance with this Directive by the employer or the employees' representatives; in particular, they shall ensure that adequate administrative or judicial procedures are available to enable the obligations deriving from this Directive to be enforced;
- for adequate penalties to be applicable in the event of infringement of this Directive by the employer or the employees' representatives. These penalties must be effective, proportionate and dissuasive;

– that in the case of serious breach by the employer of the information and consultation obligations in respect of decisions, which would have direct and immediate consequences in terms of substantial change or termination of the employment contracts or employment relations, these decisions shall have no legal effect on the employment contracts or employment relationships of the employees affected. The non-production of legal effects will continue until such time as the employer has fulfilled his obligations or, if this is no longer possible, adequate redress has been established, in accordance with the arrangements and procedures to be determined by the Member States.

Serious breaches are:
(a) the total absence of information and/or consultation of the employees' representatives prior to a decision being taken or the public announcement of that decision; or
(b) the withholding of important information or provision of false information rendering ineffective the exercise of the right to information and consultation (Article 8).

X. LINK BETWEEN THIS DIRECTIVE AND OTHER COMMUNITY AND NATIONAL PROVISIONS

This Directive constitutes the general framework for employee information and consultation in undertakings in the European Community. It is also applicable to the information and consultation procedures in case of collective redundancies and transfer of enterprises (Article 9).

XI. POLITICAL AGREEMENT OF JUNE 2001

On 11 June 2001, the EU Employment and Social Policy Council of Ministers reached political agreement on a common position on the proposed Directive. Formal adoption of the common position will take place following legal and linguistic finalisation of the text. Thereafter, the draft Directive will be submitted to the European Parliament (EP) for a second reading in accordance with the co-decision procedure.

Key provisions of the common position

The purpose of the draft Directive is "to establish a general framework setting out minimum requirements for the right to information and consultation of employees in undertakings or establishments within the European Community". Its requirements will apply, according to the choice made by Member States, to:
– undertakings employing at least 50 employees in any one Member State; or
– establishments employing at least 20 employees in any one Member State.

The right to information and consultation covers:

- information on the recent and probable development of the undertaking's or the establishment's activities and economic situation;
- information and consultation on the situation, structure and probable development of employment within the undertaking and on any anticipatory measures envisaged, in particular where there is a threat to employment; and
- information and consultation on decisions likely to lead to substantial changes in work organisation or in contractual relations.

The information should be given at such time, in such fashion and with such content as are appropriate to enable employees' representatives (as provided for by national laws and/or practices) to conduct an adequate study and, where necessary, prepare for consultation.

Consultation shall take place:

- while ensuring that the timing, method and content are appropriate;
- at the relevant level of management and representation;
- on the basis of relevant information to be supplied by the employer and the opinion which the employees' representatives are entitled to formulate;
- in such a way as to enable employees' representatives to meet with the employer and obtain a response, and the reasons for that response, to any opinion they might formulate; and
- with a view to reaching an agreement on decisions within the scope of the employer's powers likely to lead to substantial changes in work organisation or in contractual relations.

The practical arrangements for information and consultation are to be defined and implemented by Member States in accordance with national law and industrial relations practice. Member States can also entrust management and labour with defining such arrangements freely and at any time through negotiated agreements, including at undertaking or establishment level. These may differ from those set out by the Directive.

As regards confidentiality, Member States must ensure that employee representatives and any experts who assist them should not disclose any expressly confidential information provided to them, though Member States may authorise its disclosure to employees and third parties bound by an obligation of confidentiality.

Member States must also ensure, in specific cases and within the limits laid down by national legislation, that employers are not obliged to communicate any information or undertake any consultation which would seriously harm the functioning of the undertaking or would be prejudicial to it. Member States must provide for administrative or judicial review procedures where employers require confidentiality or withhold prejudicial information.

Member States will have to provide for appropriate measures in the event of non-compliance by employers or employees' representatives with the provisions of the Directive, and ensure that adequate administrative or judicial procedures are available to enable the obligations deriving from the Directive to be enforced.

Member States must also provide for adequate penalties to be applicable in the event of infringement of the Directive. These must be "effective, proportionate and dissuasive".

Member States will have three years from the date of final adoption of the Directive to comply with its provisions. Under the transitional provisions introduced to accommodate the UK and Ireland, Member States in which there is, at the date of adoption of the Directive, no "general, permanent and statutory system" of information and consultation nor of employee representation at the workplace, will be able to apply the Directive in three phases:

- undertakings with at least 150 employees (or establishments with at least 100 employees) would be covered as from the three-year implementation deadline;
- undertakings with at least 100 employees (or establishments with at least 50 employees) would be covered two years later; and
- full application of the Directive (i.e. to undertakings with at least 50 employees or establishments with at least 20 employees) would become obligatory four years after the normal implementation deadline.

2. Legislation

I. PROPOSAL FOR A COUNCIL DIRECTIVE ESTABLISHING A
GENERAL FRAMEWORK FOR INFORMING AND
CONSULTING EMPLOYEES IN THE EUROPEAN COMMUNITY
(1999/C 2/03) (TEXT WITH EEA RELEVANCE) COM(1998) 612
FINAL-98/0315(SYN) (SUBMITTED BY THE COMMISSION ON
17 NOVEMBER 1998) OFFICIAL JOURNAL C 002, 05/01/1999)
(11 NOVEMBER 1998)

The Council of the European Union,

Having regard to the Agreement on Social Policy attached to the Protocol (No 14) on Social Policy annexed to the Treaty establishing the European Community, and in particular Article 2(2) thereof,

Having regard to the proposal from the Commission,

Having regard to the opinion of the Economic and Social Committee,

Acting in accordance with the procedure referred to in Article 189c,

Whereas, on the basis of the Protocol on Social Policy annexed to the Treaty establishing the European Community, and with the exception of the United Kingdom of Great Britain and Northern Ireland, the Member States of the European Community, hereinafter referred to as the "Member States", desirous of implementing the Social Charter of 1989, have adopted an Agreement on Social Policy;

Whereas Article 2(2) of the said Agreement authorises the Council to adopt minimum requirements by means of directives;

Whereas, pursuant to Article 1 of the Agreement, a particular objective of the Community and the Member States is to promote social dialogue between management and labour;

Whereas point 17 of the Community Charter of Fundamental Social Rights of Workers provides, inter alia, that "information, consultation and participation for workers must be developed among appropriate lines, taking account of the practices in force in different Member States";

Whereas the Commission, pursuant to Article 3(2) of the Agreement on Social Policy, has consulted management and labour at Community level on the possible direction of Community action on the information and consultation of workers in undertakings within the European Union;

R. Blanpain (ed.), Involvement of Employees in the European Union, 227–302.
© 2002 *Kluwer Law International. Printed in Great Britain.*

Whereas the Commission, considering after this consultation that Community action was advisable, has again consulted the social partners on the content of the planned proposal, pursuant to Article 3(3) of the said Agreement, and the social partners have presented their opinions to the Commission;

Whereas, having completed this second stage of consultation, the social partners have not informed the Commission of their wish to initiate the process potentially leading to the conclusion of an agreement, as provided for in Article 4 of the said Agreement;

Whereas the existence of legal frameworks at national and Community level intended to ensure that workers are involved in the affairs of the undertaking employing them and in decisions which affect them has not always prevented serious decisions affecting workers from being taken and made public without adequate procedures having been implemented beforehand to inform and consult them;

Whereas there is a need to strengthen dialogue and promote mutual trust within undertakings in order to improve risk anticipation, make work organisation more flexible and facilitate employee access to training within the undertaking while maintaining security, make employees aware of adaptation needs, increase employees' availability to undertake measures and activities to increase their employability, promote employee involvement in the operation and future of the undertaking and increase its competitiveness;

Whereas timely information and consultation is a prerequisite for the success of restructuring and adaptation of undertakings to the new conditions created by globalisation of the economy, particularly via the development of new forms of work organisation;

Whereas the European Community has drawn up and implemented an employment strategy based on the concepts of "anticipation", "prevention" and "employability", which are to be incorporated as key elements into all public policies likely to benefit employment, including the policies of individual undertakings, by strengthening the social dialogue with a view to promoting change compatible with preserving the priority objective of employment;

Whereas further development of the Internal Market must be properly balanced, maintaining the essential values on which our societies are based and ensuring that all citizens benefit from economic development;

Whereas the third stage of economic and monetary union will extend and accelerate the competitive pressures at European level; whereas this will mean that more supportive measures are needed at national level;

Whereas the existing legal frameworks for employee information and consultation at Community and national level tend to adopt an excessively *a posteriori* approach to the process of change, neglect the economic aspects of decisions taken and do not contribute to genuine anticipation of employment developments within the undertaking or to risk prevention;

Whereas, as a result of all these political, economic, social and legal developments, action is needed at Community level to make the essential changes to the existing legal framework;

Whereas, in accordance with the principles of subsidiarity and proportionality as set out in Article 3b of the Treaty, the objectives of the proposed action, as outlined above, cannot be adequately achieved by the Member States, in that the object is to establish a framework for employee information and consultation appropriate for the new European context described above; but whereas, in view of the scale and impact of the proposed action, these objectives can be better achieved at Community level by the introduction of minimum regulations applicable to the entire European Community, and whereas the present Directive constitutes no more than minimum necessary to achieve these objectives;

Whereas the purpose of this general framework is to establish minimum requirements applicable throughout the European Community while avoiding any administrative, financial or legal constraints which would hinder the creation and development of small and medium-sized undertakings; whereas, to this end, the scope of this Directive should be restricted to undertakings with at least 50 employees, without prejudice to any more favourable national or Community provisions; whereas, in order to maintain the appropriate balance between the abovementioned factors, this minimum may be raised to 100 employees in the case of the more innovative measures proposed herein on the information and consultation of employees on developments in the employment situation within the undertaking;

Whereas a Community framework for informing and consulting employees must keep to a minimum the burden on businesses while ensuring the effective exercise by employees of their rights;

Whereas the objectives of this Directive are to be achieved through the establishment of a general framework comprising the definitions and purpose of the information and consultation, which it will be up to the Member States to complete and adapt to their own national situation, ensuring, where appropriate, that the social partners have a leading role by allowing them to define freely the arrangements for informing and consulting employees which they consider to be best suited to their needs and wishes;

Whereas care must be taken to avoid affecting some specific rules in the field of employees' information and consultation existing in some national laws, addressed to undertakings which pursue political, professional organisation, religious, charitable, educational, scientific or artistic aims, as well as aims involving information and the expression of opinions;

Whereas undertakings must be protected against public disclosure of certain particularly sensitive information;

Whereas modernisation of work implies both rights and obligations for the two social partners at undertaking level;

Whereas a reinforced and dissuasive sanction, applicable in the case of decisions taken in serious breach of the obligations under this Directive must be established at Community level, without prejudice to the general obligations of Member States in this respect;

Whereas this Directive also applies to the subjects covered by Council Directive 98/59/EC of 20 July 1998 on the approximation of the laws of the Member States relating to collective redundancies[1] and Council Directive 77/187/EEC of 14 February 1998 on the approximation of the laws of the Member States relating to the safeguarding of employees' rights in the event of transfers of undertakings, businesses or parts of businesses, amended by the Council Directive 98/50/EC of 29 June 1998;[2]

Whereas other employee information and consultation rights, including those arising from Council Directive 94/45/EEC of 22 September 1994 on the establishment of a European Works Council or a procedure in Community-scale undertakings and Community-scale groups of undertakings for the purposes of informing and consulting employees,[3] must not be affected by this Directive,

HAS ADOPTED THIS DIRECTIVE:

Article 1
Object and principles

1. The purpose of this Directive is to establish a general framework for informing and consulting employees in undertakings within the European Community.
2. When defining or implementing information and consultation procedures, the employer and the employees' representatives shall work in a spirit of cooperation and with due regard for their reciprocal rights and obligations, taking into account the interests both of the undertaking and of the employees.

Article 2
Definitions and scope

1. For the purposes of this Directive:
(a) "undertakings" means public or private undertakings carrying out an economic activity, whether or not operating for gain, which are located within the territory of the Member States of the European Community and have at least 50 employees, without prejudice to the provisions of Article 4(3);
(b) "employer" means the natural or legal person party to employment contracts or employment relationships with employees;

---

1.   *O.J.*, L 225, 12.8.1998.
2.   *O.J.*, L 61, 5.3.1977. *O.J.*, L 201, 17.7.1998.
3.   *O.J.*, L 254, 30.9.1994.

(c) "employees' representatives" means the employees' representatives provided for by national laws and/or practices;

(d) "information" means transmission by the employer to the employees' representatives of information containing all relevant facts on the subjects set down in Article 4(1), ensuring that the timing, means of communication and content of the information are such as to ensure its effectiveness, particularly in enabling the employees' representatives to examine the information thoroughly and, where appropriate, prepare consultations;

(e) "consultation" means the organisation of a dialogue and exchange of views between the employer and the employees' representatives on the subjects set out in Article 4(1)(b) and (c),

– ensuring that the timing, method and content are such that this step is effective;

– at the appropriate level of management and representation, depending on the subject under discussion;

– on the basis of the relevant information to be supplied by the employer and the opinion which the employees' representatives are entitled to formulate;

– including the employees' representatives' right to meet with the employer and obtain a response, and the reasons for that response, to any opinion they may formulate;

– including, in the case of decisions within the scope of the employer's management powers, an attempt to seek prior agreement on the decisions referred to in Article 4(1)(c).

2. In conformity with the principles and objectives of this Directive, Member States may lay down particular provisions applicable to undertakings which pursue directly and essentially political, professional organisation, religious, charitable, education, scientific or artistic aims, as well as aims involving information and the expression of opinions, on condition that, at the date of adoption of this Directive, such particular provisions already exist in national legislation.

Article 3
Information and consultation procedures deriving from an agreement

1. Member States may authorise the social partners at the appropriate level, including at undertaking level, to define freely and at any time through negotiated agreement the procedures for implementing the employee information and consultation requirements referred to in Articles 1, 2 and 4 of this Directive.

2. The agreements referred to in paragraph 1 may establish, while respecting the general objectives laid down by the Directive and subject to conditions and limitations laid down by the Member States, arrangements which are different to those referred to in Article 2(1)(d) and (e)

and Article 4 of the present Directive.

Article 4
Content of, and procedures for, information and consultation

1. Without prejudice to any provisions and/or practices more favourable to employees in force in the Member States, employee information and consultation shall, if there is no agreement between the social partners as envisaged in Article 3, cover:

(a) information on the recent as well as the reasonably foreseeable development of the undertaking's activities and its economic and financial situation;

(b) information and consultation on the situation, structure and reasonably foreseeable developments of employment within the undertaking and, where the employer's evaluation suggests that employment within the undertaking may be under threat, the anticipatory measures envisaged, in particular for employee training and skill development, with a view to offsetting the potential negative developments or their consequences and increasing the employability of the employees likely to be affected;

(c) information and consultation on decisions likely to lead to substantial changes in work organisation or in contractual relations, including those covered by the Community provisions referred to in Article 8(1).

2. The Member States shall ensure that information and consultation are effective and useful within the meaning of Article 1 and Article 2(1)(d) and (e). To this end, they shall determine the information and consultation procedures for the subjects listed in paragraph 1.

3. Member States may exclude from the information and consultation obligations referred to in paragraph 1(b) of this Article undertakings with fewer than 100 employees.

Article 5
Confidential information

1. Member States shall provide that the employees' representatives and any experts who assist them are not authorised to disclose any information which has expressly been provided to them in confidence. This obligation shall continue to apply irrespective of where the said representatives or experts are, even after expiry of their term of office.

2. Member States shall provide, in specific cases and within the conditions and limits laid down by national legislation, that the employer is not obliged to communicate information or undertake consultation when the nature of that information or consultation is such that, according to

objective criteria, it would seriously harm the functioning of the undertaking or would be prejudicial to it.

Article 6
Protection of employees' representatives

Employees' representatives shall, when carrying out their functions, enjoy adequate protection and guarantees to enable them to perform properly the duties which have been assigned to them.

Article 7
Protection of rights

1. Member States shall provide for appropriate measures in the event of non-compliance with this Directive by the employer or the employees' representatives; in particular, they shall ensure that adequate administrative or judicial procedures are available to enable the obligations deriving from this Directive to be enforced, including procedures which may be instituted by the employer or the employees' representatives where either party considers that the other party is in breach of the obligations provided for in Article 5.
2. Member States shall provide for adequate penalties to be applicable in the event of infringement of this Directive by the employer or the employees' representatives. These penalties must be effective, proportionate and dissuasive.
3. Member States shall provide that in case of serious breach by the employer of the information and consultation obligations in respect of the decisions referred to in Article 4(1)(c) of this Directive, where such decisions would have direct and immediate consequences in terms of substantial change or termination of the employment contracts or employment relations, these decisions shall have no legal effect on the employment contracts or employment relationships of the employees affected. The non production of legal effects will continue until such time as the employer has fulfilled his obligations or, if this is no longer possible, adequate redress has been established, in accordance with the arrangements and procedures to be determined by the Member States.

   The provision of the previous paragraph also applies to corresponding obligations under the agreements referred to in Article 3.
   Within the meaning of the previous paragraphs, serious breaches are:
(a) the total absence of information and/or consultation of the employees' representatives prior to a decision being taken or the public announcement of that decision; or

(b)   the withholding of important information or provision of false information rendering ineffective the exercise of the right to information and consultation.

Article 8
Link between this Directive and other Community and national provisions

1.   This Directive constitutes the general framework for employee information and consultation in undertakings in the European Community. It is also applicable to the information and consultation procedures set out in Article 2 of Council Directive 98/59/EC and Article 6 of Directive 77/187/EC.
2.   This Directive does not prejudice the provisions adopted in accordance with Council Directive 94/45/EC of 24 September 1994 on the establishment of a European Works Council or a procedure in Community-scale undertakings and Community-scale groups of undertakings for the purposes of informing and consulting employees.
3.   This Directive shall be without prejudice to other rights of employees to information, consultation and participation under national law.

Article 9
Transposition of the Directive

1.   Member States shall adopt the laws, regulations and administrative provisions necessary to comply with this Directive no later than ... (two years after adoption) or shall ensure that the social partners introduce the required provisions by way of agreement, the Member States being obliged to take all necessary steps enabling them to guarantee the results imposed by this Directive at all times. They shall forthwith inform the Commission thereof.
2.   Where Member States adopt these provisions, they shall contain a reference to this Directive or shall be accompanied by such reference on the occasion of their official publication. The methods of making such reference shall be laid down by the Member States.

Article 10
Review by the Commission

Not later than ... (five years after adoption), the Commission shall, in consultation with the Member States and the social partners at Community level, review the application of this Directive with a view to proposing to the Council any necessary amendments.

Article 11

This Directive is addressed to the Member States.

II. AMENDED PROPOSAL FOR A DIRECTIVE OF THE EUROPEAN
     PARLIAMENT AND OF THE COUNCIL ESTABLISHING A
     GENERAL FRAMEWORK FOR IMPROVING INFORMATION
     AND CONSULTATION RIGHTS OF EMPLOYEES IN THE
     EUROPEAN COMMUNITY (PRESENTED BY THE COMMISSION
     PURSUANT TO ARTICLE 250(2) OF THE EC TREATY) (23 MAY
     2001)

Explanatory Memorandum

1. Introduction

On 11 November 1998, the Commission adopted a proposal for a Council
Directive establishing a general framework for informing and consulting
employees in the European Community.[4] This proposal was forwarded to the
European Parliament and the Council on 17 November 1998.

   The European Parliament delivered its opinion at first reading on 14
April 1999.[5]

   Following entry into force of the Treaty of Amsterdam, the legal basis
for the Commission's proposal (Article 2(2) of the Agreement on Social Policy
appended to the Protocol on Social Policy annexed to the Treaty establishing
the European Community) was changed, and the proposal now comes under
Article 137(2) of the Treaty establishing the European Community. On 16
September 1999, under the codecision procedure, the European Parliament
confirmed its opinion adopted at first reading on 14 April 1999.

   On 7 July 1999, the Economic and Social Committee delivered its
opinion on the Commission's proposal.[6] The Committee of the Regions
delivered its opinion on 13 December 2000.

   The various Council bodies started to discuss the Commission's
proposal, and the amendments proposed by the European Parliament at first
reading, in June 2000.

2. Amendments

The Commission's amended proposal contains three types of amendment:
those resulting automatically from the change in the legal basis, those designed
to incorporate into the text a number of European Parliament amendments
which the Commission regards as relevant, and, finally, those resulting from

4.   COM(1998) 612, *O.J.*, C 2, 5.1.1999.
5.   *O.J.*, C 219, 30.7.1999.
6.   *O.J.*, C 258, 10.9.1999.

the debates within the Council to the extent that the Commission agrees with the changes put forward.

Amendments resulting from the change in the legal basis:

The various references to Article 2(2) of the Agreement on Social Policy appended to the Protocol on Social Policy annexed to the Treaty establishing the European Community have been replaced by references to Article 137(2) of the Treaty establishing the European Community. Other changes which follow automatically from this change have been made.

Amendments proposed by the European Parliament:

The Commission is able to accept all of the following amendments, which it feels help to improve its initial text whilst preserving its political viability, taking account of the positions already expressed by the Member States to the Council:

Amendments 2, 9 and 25 (removal of the specific threshold of 100 employees with regard to information and consultation of employees on the development of the employment situation within the undertaking): see recital 19 and Articles 3 and 4;

- amendments 3, 6 and 32 (non-regression clause): see Article 9(4);
- amendment 7 (reference to minimum requirements): see Article 1(1);
- amendment 10 (reference to national law and/or practice concerning the definition of "employer"): see Article 2(c);
- amendment 13, first paragraph (definition of "consultation"): see Article 2(g);
- amendment 16, in part (determination by the Member States of the level at which information and consultation must be provided): see Articles 3(1) and 4(1).

A number of other amendments seem to be consistent with the spirit of the text and therefore do not necessarily require an explicit reference in the Directive. This is the case with the following amendments:

- amendment 1 (reference to the continuing acquisition of qualifications, innovation and adherence by employees to new forms of work organisation);
- amendment 37 (limits to the right of employers to claim confidentiality or withhold particularly sensitive information);
- amendment 5 (reference to provisions that are more favourable to employees);
- amendments 8 and 43 (obligation to respect the minimum requirements laid down by the proposed Directive);
- amendment 11 (permanent, stable and independent nature of employees' representatives);
- amendment 13, third paragraph (details concerning the instrumental nature of information with regard to consultation);
- amendments 22 and 23 (non-exhaustive list of decisions that have to be the subject of information and consultation);
- amendment 26 (employees' right to request the assistance of experts);

- amendment 28 (details concerning the protection of employees' representatives);
- amendment 35 (inclusion of ceilings among the subjects to be covered by the review of the Directive).

By contrast, the Commission is unable at this stage to accept the other amendments proposed by Parliament, which it feels could make it difficult to reach agreement or obtain a sufficient majority within the Council. The Commission's stance reflects its awareness of its codecision procedure role as the intermediary between the two branches of Community legislative power. The following amendments are concerned:

- amendments 4 and 15 ("Tendenzschutz");
- amendment 41 (definition of "social partners");
- amendment 13, second and fourth paragraphs (reference to the planning stage in the context of defining "consultation" and to the obligation to seek agreement on all issues which are the subject of information and consultation);
- amendment 17 (promotion of the social dialogue in small and medium-sized enterprises);
- amendments 20 and 43 (limit on the autonomy of parties in the context of agreements);
- amendment 21 (consultation on the development of the undertaking's economic and financial situation);
- amendment 24 (continuation of consultations in particularly serious cases);
- amendment 27 (removal of the employer's right to withhold particularly sensitive information);
- amendment 29 (extension of the concept of serious violation of information and consultation obligations);
- amendment 33 (application of the Directive in the civil service);
- amendment 34 (obligation on the Member States to consult the social partners in connection with transposition of the Directive).

Amendments resulting from the debates within the Council:
The latest text for examination by the Council contains a number of changes compared with the initial proposal and the Parliament's amendments which the Commission is prepared to accept at the moment. Most of these amendments seem compatible with Parliament's wish to see appropriate and effective information and consultation of the employees of a company in the European Community promoted through this new Community legal instrument. Furthermore, a number of the amendments respond to concerns expressed by Member States with reference to their particular national practices and do not call into question the central objective of the proposed Directive.

The Commission has therefore decided to include most of these amendments in its amended proposal.

However, there is one important exception to this desire to accommodate the Council: at this stage the Commission is unable to accept that

Article 7(3) of its initial proposal (sanctions in the event of a serious breach of information and consultation obligations) should simply be deleted. It therefore maintains its initial proposal on this matter (see Article 8(3)).

Amended proposal for a

DIRECTIVE OF THE EUROPEAN PARLIAMENT AND OF THE COUNCIL ESTABLISHING A GENERAL FRAMEWORK FOR IMPROVING INFORMATION AND CONSULTATION RIGHTS OF EMPLOYEES IN THE EUROPEAN COMMUNITY

THE EUROPEAN PARLIAMENT AND THE COUNCIL OF THE EUROPEAN UNION,

Having regard to the Agreement on Social Policy attached to the Protocol (No 14) on Social Policy annexed to the Treaty establishing the European Community, and in particular Article 2(2) thereof;

Having regard to the Treaty establishing the European Community, and in particular Article 137(2) thereof,

Having regard to the proposal from the Commission;[7]

Having regard to the opinion of the Economic and Social Committee;[8]

Having regard to the opinion of the Committee of the Regions;[9]

Acting in accordance with the procedure referred to in Article 251.[10]

Whereas, on the basis of the Protocol on Social Policy annexed to the Treaty establishing the European Community, and with the exception of the United Kingdom of Great Britain and Northern Ireland, the Member States of the European Community, hereinafter referred to as the "Member States", desirous of implementing the Social Charter of 1989, have adopted an Agreement on Social Policy;

Whereas Article 2(2) of the said Agreement authorises the Council to adopt minimum requirements by means of directives;

1. Whereas, pursuant to Article 136 of the Treaty, a particular objective of the Community and the Member States is to promote social dialogue between management and labour;

2. Whereas point 17 of the Community Charter of Fundamental Social Rights of Workers provides, inter alia, that "information, consultation and participation for workers must be developed among appropriate lines, taking account of the practices in force in different Member States";

3. Whereas the Commission, has consulted management and labour at Community level on the possible direction of Community action on the information and consultation of workers in undertakings within the European Union;

4. Whereas the Commission, considering after this consultation that Community action was advisable, has again consulted the social partners

---

7.   *O.J.*, C 2, 5.1.1999, p. 3.
8.   *O.J.*, C 258, 10.9.1999, p. 24.
9.   14.12.2000
10.   The opinion of the European Parliament was published in *O.J.*, C 219, 30.7.1999, p. 223.

on the content of the planned proposal, and the social partners have presented their opinions to the Commission;

5. Whereas, having completed this second stage of consultation, the social partners have not informed the Commission of their wish to initiate the process potentially leading to the conclusion of an agreement;

6. The existence of legal frameworks at national and Community level intended to ensure that workers are involved in the affairs of the undertaking employing them and in decisions which affect them has not always prevented serious decisions affecting workers from being taken and made public without adequate procedures having been put in place beforehand to inform and consult them;

7. There is a need to strengthen dialogue and promote mutual trust within undertakings in order to improve risk anticipation, make work organisation more flexible and facilitate employee access to training within the undertaking while maintaining security, make employees aware of adaptation needs, increase employees' availability to undertake measures and activities to increase their employability, promote employee involvement in the operation and future of the undertaking and increase its competitiveness;

8. In particular, there is a need to promote and strengthen information and consultation on the situation and probable development of employment within the undertaking and, where it ensues from the evaluation carried out by the employer that employment within the undertaking is likely to come under threat, on any anticipatory measures envisaged, in particular in terms of training and enhancing employees' skills, with a view to offsetting negative developments or their consequences and improving the employability and adaptability of the employees likely to be affected;

9. Timely information and consultation is a prerequisite for the success of restructuring and adaptation of undertakings to the new conditions created by globalisation of the economy, particularly via the development of new forms of work organisation;

10. The European Community has drawn up and implemented an employment strategy based on the concepts of "anticipation", "prevention" and "employability", which must constitute key elements of all public policies likely to benefit employment, including enterprise policies, by strengthening the social dialogue with a view to promoting change compatible with preserving the priority objective of employment;

11. Further development of the internal market must be properly balanced, maintaining the essential values on which our societies are based and ensuring that all citizens benefit from economic development;

12. The third stage of economic and monetary union will extend and accelerate the competitive pressures at European level; this will mean that more supportive measures are needed at national level;

13. The existing legal frameworks for employee information and consultation at Community and national level tend to adopt an excessively

a posteriori approach to the process of change, neglect the economic aspects of decisions taken and do not contribute to genuine anticipation of employment developments within the undertaking or to risk prevention;

14. As a result of all these political, economic, social and legal developments, action is needed at Community level to make the essential changes to the existing legal framework in the form of legal and practical instruments allowing the right of information and consultation to be exercised;

15. This Directive does not prejudice national systems under which the concrete exercising of this right implies a collective expression of will on the part of the entitled parties;

16. This Directive does not prejudice systems providing for the direct involvement of employees, provided the latter are always free to exercise their right to information and consultation via their representatives;

17. In accordance with the principles of subsidiarity and proportionality as set out in Article 5 of the Treaty, the objectives of the proposed action, as outlined above, cannot be adequately achieved by the Member States, in that the object is to establish a framework for employee information and consultation appropriate for the new European context described above; however, in view of the scale and impact of the proposed action, these objectives can be better achieved at Community level by the introduction of minimum regulations applicable to the entire European Community; the present Directive constitutes no more than the minimum necessary to achieve these objectives;

18. The purpose of this general framework is to establish minimum requirements applicable throughout the European Community. while avoiding any administrative, financial or legal constraints which would hinder the creation and development of small and medium-sized undertakings; whereas, to this end, the scope of this Directive should be restricted to undertakings with at least 50 employees, without prejudice to any more favourable national or Community provisions; whereas, in order to maintain the appropriate balance between the abovementioned factors, this minimum may be raised to 100 employees in the case of the more innovative measures proposed herein on the information and consultation of employees on developments in the employment situation within the undertaking. It does not prevent Member States from adopting provisions that are more favourable to employees;

19. It is also the purpose of this general framework to avoid any administrative, financial or legal constraints which would hinder the creation and development of small and medium-sized undertakings; it would appear appropriate, to this end, to restrict the scope of this Directive to undertakings with at least 50 employees or establishments with at least 20 employees, at the choice of the Member States;

20. The Community framework for informing and consulting employees must keep to a minimum the burden on businesses while ensuring the effective exercise by employees of their rights;

21. The objective of this Directive will be achieved by establishing a general framework comprising the definitions and purpose of the information and consultation, which it will be up to the Member States to complete and adapt to their own national situation, ensuring, where appropriate, that the social partners have a leading role by allowing them to define freely the arrangements for informing and consulting employees which they consider to be best suited to their needs and wishes setting out the principles, definitions and procedures for information and consultation which Member States will have to comply with and adapt to their own national situation, ensuring where appropriate that the social partners have a leading role by allowing them to define freely, through agreements, the procedures for informing and consulting employees which they consider to be best suited to their needs and wishes;

22. Care must be taken to avoid affecting some specific rules in the field of employees' information and consultation existing in some national laws, addressed to undertakings which pursue political, professional organisation, religious, charitable, educational, scientific or artistic aims, as well as aims involving information and the expression of opinions;

23. Undertakings must be protected against public disclosure of certain particularly sensitive information;

24. Employers must be entitled not to inform or consult employees where this would be seriously prejudicial to the undertaking or where they have to comply immediately with an injunction issued by a monitoring or surveillance authority;

25. Information and consultation are both rights and obligations of the social partners at undertaking level;

26. A reinforced and dissuasive sanction, applicable in the case of decisions taken in serious breach of the obligations under this Directive must be established at Community level, without prejudice to the general obligations of Member States in this respect;

27. This Directive also applies to the subjects covered by Council Directive 98/59/EC of 20 July 1998 on the approximation of the laws of the Member States relating to collective redundancies[11] and Council Directive 2001/23/EC of 12 March 2001 on the approximation of the laws of the Member. This Directive consolidates Council Directive 75/129/EC of 17 February 1975 (*O.J.*, L 48, 22.2.1975, p. 29) and Council Directive 92/56/EC of 24 June 1992 (*O.J.*, L 245, 26.8.1992, p. 3). States relating to the safeguarding of employees' rights in the event of transfers of undertakings, businesses or parts of businesses;

28. This Directive must not prejudice other employee information and consultation rights, including those arising from Council Directive 94/45/EEC of 22 September 1994 on the establishment of a European Works Council or a procedure in Community-scale undertakings and Community-scale groups of undertakings for the purposes of informing and

---

11. *O.J.*, L 225, 12.8.1998.

consulting employees[12] and Council Directive 97/74/EC of 15 December 1997 extending this Directive[13] to the United Kingdom;

29. Application of the provisions of this Directive must not constitute grounds for reducing the general level of employee protection within the scope of the Directive,

HAVE ADOPTED THIS DIRECTIVE:

Article 1
Object and principles

1. The purpose of this Directive is to establish a general framework laying down minimum requirements concerning employees' rights to information and consultation for informing and consulting employees in undertakings within the European Community.
2. Information and consultation procedures shall be established and implemented so as to ensure their effectiveness.
3. When defining or implementing information and consultation procedures, the employer and the employees' representatives shall work in a spirit of co-operation and with due regard for their reciprocal rights and obligations, taking into account the interests both of the undertaking and of the employees.

Article 2
Definitions

For the purposes of this Directive:
(a) "undertakings" means public or private undertakings carrying out an economic activity, whether or not operating for gain, which are located within the territory of the Member States of the European Community;
(b) "establishment" means a place of business with no legal personality, which is part of an undertaking and where a non-transitory economic activity is carried out with human means and goods;
(c) "employer" means the natural or legal person party to employment contracts or employment relationships with employees, in accordance with national legislation and practice;
(d) "employee" means any person who, in the Member State concerned, is protected as an employee under national labour legislation and in accordance with national practice;
(e) "employees' representatives" means the employees' representatives provided for by national laws and/or practices;

---

12.   *O.J.*, L 254, 30.9.1994, p. 64.
13.   *O.J.*, L 10, 16.1.1998, p. 23.

(f) "information" means transmission of details by the employer to the employees' representatives so that they can take note of and consider the subject in question;

(g) "consultation" means the exchange of views and establishing of a dialogue between the employees' representatives and the employer.

Article 3
Scope

1. This Directive shall apply, at the Member States' choice, to:
   - undertakings with at least 50 employees in a Member State, or
   - establishments with at least 20 employees in a Member State.
   The Member States shall establish the manner in which the number of employees is calculated.
2. In line with the principles and objectives laid down in this Directive, the Member States may make provision for specific arrangements applicable to undertakings pursuing political, professional organisation, religious, charitable, educational, scientific or artistic aims, as well as aims involving information and the expression of opinions, provided such specific arrangements already exist in national law on the date on which this Directive is adopted.

Article 4
Procedures for information and consultation

1. Acting in compliance with the principles set out in Article 1, and without prejudice to current provisions and/or practices which are more favourable to employees, the Member States shall establish the procedures under which employees can exercise the right to information and consultation at the appropriate level, in accordance with paragraphs 2, 3 and 4 below.
2. Information and consultation shall cover:
(a) information on the recent as well as the probable development of the undertaking's activities and its economic and financial situation;
(b) information and consultation on the situation, structure and probable development of employment within the undertaking and, on any anticipatory measures envisaged, especially in the event of a threat to employment;
(c) information and consultation on decisions likely to lead to significant changes in work organisation or in contractual relations, including those covered by the provisions referred to in Article 9(1).
3. Appropriate information shall be provided at the appropriate time and in the appropriate manner, so as to allow the employees' representatives to

examine the matter properly and, where appropriate, to prepare for consultation.
4. Appropriate consultation shall take place:
– at an appropriate time and using appropriate means;
– at the relevant management and representation level, depending on the subject;
– on the basis of relevant information provided by the employer and the opinion which the employees' representatives are entitled to formulate;
– in a manner which allows the employees' representatives to meet the employer and obtain a reasoned response to any opinion they have formulated;
– with a view to reaching an agreement on the decisions referred to in paragraph 2(c) which come under the employer's prerogative.

Article 5
Information and consultation under an agreement

The Member States may allow the social partners at the appropriate level, including undertaking or establishment level, to define freely and at any time, through negotiated agreements, the procedures for informing and consulting employees. Provided they comply with the principles set out in Article 1, and subject to conditions and limits laid down by the Member States, such agreements may make provision for procedures which differ from those set out in Article 4.

Article 6
Confidential information

1. 1. Member States shall provide, subject to conditions and limits laid down in national legislation, that the employees' representatives and any experts who may assist them are not authorised to disclose, except to employees bound by a confidentiality obligation, any information which has expressly been provided to them in confidence, if this is in the legitimate interest of the undertaking. This obligation shall continue to apply irrespective of where the said representatives or experts are, even after expiry of their term of office.
2. Member States shall provide, in specific cases and within the conditions and limits laid down by national legislation, that the employer is not obliged to communicate information or undertake consultation when the nature of that information or consultation is such that, according to objective criteria, it would seriously harm the functioning of the undertaking or would be prejudicial to it.
3. Without prejudice to existing national procedures, Member States shall make provision for administrative or judicial appeal procedures should

the employer claim confidentiality or fail to provide information in accordance with the above paragraphs. They may also make provision for procedures to safeguard the confidentiality of the information in question.

Article 7
Protection of employees' representatives

Employees' representatives shall, when carrying out their functions, enjoy adequate protection and guarantees to enable them to perform properly the duties which have been assigned to them.

Article 8
Protection of rights

1. Member States shall provide for appropriate measures in the event of non-compliance with this Directive by the employer or the employees' representatives; in particular, they shall ensure that adequate administrative or judicial procedures are available to enable the obligations deriving from this Directive to be enforced.
2. Member States shall provide for adequate penalties to be applicable in the event of infringement of this Directive by the employer or the employees' representatives. These penalties must be effective, proportionate and dissuasive.
3. Member States shall provide that in case of serious breach by the employer of the information and consultation obligations in respect of the decisions referred to in Article 4(2)(c) of this Directive, where such decisions would have direct and immediate consequences in terms of substantial change or termination of the employment contracts or employment relations, these decisions shall have no legal effect on the employment contracts or employment relationships of the employees affected. The non-production of legal effects will continue until such time as the employer has fulfilled his obligations or, if this is no longer possible, adequate redress has been established, in accordance with the arrangements and procedures to be determined by the Member States.

The provision of the previous paragraph also applies to corresponding obligations under the agreements referred to in Article 5,
Within the meaning of the previous paragraphs, serious breaches are:
(a) the total absence of information and/or consultation of the employees' representatives prior to a decision being taken or the public announcement of that decision; or
(b) the withholding of important information or provision of false information rendering ineffective the exercise of the right to information and consultation.

Article 9
Link between this Directive and other Community and national provisions

1. This Directive constitutes the general framework for employee information and consultation in undertakings in the European Community. It is also applicable to the information and consultation procedures set out in Article 2 of Council Directive 98/59/EC and Article 7 of Council Directive 2001/23/EC.
2. This Directive does not prejudice the provisions adopted in accordance with Council Directive 94/45/EC of 24 September 1994 on the establishment of a European Works Council or a procedure in Community-scale undertakings and Community-scale groups of undertakings for the purposes of informing and consulting employees or Council Directive 97/74/EC of 15 December 1997 extending this Directive to the United Kingdom.
3. This Directive shall be without prejudice to other rights of employees to information, consultation and participation under national law.
4. Application of the provisions of this Directive shall not constitute grounds for any regression in relation to the situation which already exists in the Member States in respect of the general level of employee protection within the scope of the Directive.

Article 10
Transposition of the Directive

1. Member States shall adopt the laws, regulations and administrative provisions necessary to comply with this Directive no later than ... ... (three years after adoption) or shall ensure that the social partners introduce the required provisions by way of agreement, the Member States being obliged to take all necessary steps enabling them to guarantee the results imposed by this Directive at all times. They shall forthwith inform the Commission thereof.
2. Where Member States adopt these provisions, they shall contain a reference to this Directive or shall be accompanied by such reference on the occasion of their official publication. The methods of making such reference shall be laid down by the Member States.

Article 11
Review by the Commission

Not later than ... (five years after adoption), the Commission shall, in consultation with the Member States and the social partners at Community level, review the application of this Directive with a view to proposing to the Council any necessary amendments.

Article 12

This Directive is addressed to the Member States.
Done at Brussels,

III. COMMON POSITION (EC) NO 33/2001 OF 23 JULY 2001
     ADOPTED BY THE COUNCIL, ACTING IN ACCORDANCE
     WITH THE PROCEDURE REFERRED TO IN ARTICLE 251 OF
     THE TREATY ESTABLISHING THE EUROPEAN COMMUNITY,
     WITH A VIEW TO ADOPTING A DIRECTIVE OF THE
     EUROPEAN PARLIAMENT AND OF THE COUNCIL
     ESTABLISHING A GENERAL FRAMEWORK FOR INFORMING
     AND CONSULTING EMPLOYEES IN THE EUROPEAN
     COMMUNITY (2001/C 307/03) (*OFFICIAL JOURNAL* C 307,
     31/10/2001)

The European Parliament and the Council of the European Union,
     Having regard to the Treaty establishing the European Community, and
in particular
     Article 137(2) thereof,
     Having regard to the proposal from the Commission,[14]
     Having regard to the opinion of the Economic and Social Committee,[15]
     Having regard to the opinion of the Committee of the Regions,[16]
     Acting in accordance with the procedure referred to in Article 251 of the
Treaty,[17]
     Whereas:
  1. Pursuant to Article 136 of the Treaty, a particular objective of the
     Community and the Member States is to promote social dialogue between
     management and labour.
  2. Point 17 of the Community Charter of Fundamental Social Rights of
     Workers provides, inter alia, that information, consultation and
     participation for workers must be developed along appropriate lines,
     taking account of the practices in force in different Member States.

---

14.   OJ C 2, 5.1.1999, p. 3.
15.   OJ C 258, 10.9.1999, p. 24.
16.   OJ C 144, 16.5.2001, p. 58.
17.   Opinion of the European Parliament of 14 April 1999 (OJ C 219, 30.7.1999, p. 223),
       confirmed on 16 September 1999 (OJ C 54, 25.2.2000, p. 55), Council Common Position of
       23 July 2001 and Decision of the European Parliament of ... (not yet published in the
       Official Journal).

3. The Commission consulted management and labour at Community level on the possible direction of Community action on the information and consultation of employees in undertakings within the Community.

4. Following this consultation, the Commission considered that Community action was advisable and again consulted management and labour on the contents of the planned proposal; management and labour have presented their opinions to the Commission.

5. Having completed this second stage of consultation, management and labour have not informed the Commission of their wish to initiate the process potentially leading to the conclusion of an agreement.

6. The existence of legal frameworks at national and Community level intended to ensure that employees are involved in the affairs of the undertaking employing them and in decisions which affect them has not always prevented serious decisions affecting employees from being taken and made public without adequate procedures having been implemented beforehand to inform and consult them.

7. There is a need to strengthen dialogue and promote mutual trust within undertakings in order to improve risk anticipation, make work organisation more flexible and facilitate employee access to training within the undertaking while maintaining security, make employees aware of adaptation needs, increase employees' availability to undertake measures and activities to increase their employability, promote employee involvement in the operation and future of the undertaking and increase its competitiveness.

8. There is a need, in particular, to promote and enhance information and consultation on the situation and likely development of employment within the undertaking and, where the employer's evaluation suggests that employment within the undertaking may be under threat, the possible anticipatory measures envisaged, in particular in terms of employee training and skill development, with a view to offsetting the negative developments or their consequences and increasing the employability and adaptability of the employees likely to be affected.

9. Timely information and consultation is a prerequisite for the success of the restructuring and adaptation of undertakings to the new conditions created by globalisation of the economy, particularly through the development of new forms of organisation of work.

10. The Community has drawn up and implemented an employment strategy based on the concepts of "anticipation", "prevention" and "employability", which are to be incorporated as key elements into all public policies likely to benefit employment, including the policies of individual undertakings, by strengthening the social dialogue with a view to promoting change compatible with preserving the priority objective of employment.

11. Further development of the internal market must be properly balanced, maintaining the essential values on which our societies are based and ensuring that all citizens benefit from economic development.

12.   Entry into the third stage of economic and monetary union has extended and accelerated the competitive pressures at European level. This means that more supportive measures are needed at national level.

13.   The existing legal frameworks for employee information and consultation at Community and national level tend to adopt an excessively a posteriori approach to the process of change, neglect the economic aspects of decisions taken and do not contribute either to genuine anticipation of employment developments within the undertaking or to risk prevention.

14.   All of these political, economic, social and legal developments call for changes to the existing legal framework providing for the legal and practical instruments enabling the right to be informed and consulted to be exercised.

15.   This Directive is without prejudice to national systems regarding the exercise of this right in practice where those entitled to exercise it are required to indicate their wishes collectively.

16.   This Directive is without prejudice to those systems which provide for the direct involvement of employees, as long as they are always free to exercise the right to be informed and consulted through their representatives.

17.   Since the objectives of the proposed action, as outlined above, cannot be adequately achieved by the Member States, in that the object is to establish a framework for employee information and consultation appropriate for the new European context described above, and can therefore, in view of the scale and impact of the proposed action, be better achieved at Community level, the Community may adopt measures in accordance with the principle of subsidiarity as set out in Article 5 of the Treaty. In accordance with the principle of proportionality, as set out in that Article, this Directive does not go beyond what is necessary in order to achieve these objectives.

18.   The purpose of this general framework is to establish minimum requirements applicable throughout the Community while not preventing Member States from laying down provisions more favourable to employees.

19.   The purpose of this general framework is also to avoid any administrative, financial or legal constraints which would hinder the creation and development of small and medium-sized undertakings. To this end, the scope of this Directive should be restricted, according to the choice made by Member States, to undertakings with at least 50 employees or establishments employing at least 20 employees.

20.   However, on a transitional basis Member States in which there is no established statutory system of information and consultation of employees or employee representation should have the possibility of further restricting the scope of the Directive as regards the numbers of employees.

21.   A Community framework for informing and consulting employees should keep to a minimum the burden on undertakings or establishments while ensuring the effective exercise of the rights granted.

22.   The objective of this Directive is to be achieved through the establishment of a general framework comprising the principles, definitions and arrangements for information and consultation, which it will be for the Member States to comply with and adapt to their own national situation, ensuring, where appropriate, that management and labour have a leading role by allowing them to define freely, by agreement, the arrangements for informing and consulting employees which they consider to be best suited to their needs and wishes.

23.   Care should be taken to avoid affecting some specific rules in the field of employee information and consultation existing in some national laws, addressed to undertakings or establishments which pursue political, professional, organisational, religious, charitable, educational, scientific or artistic aims, as well as aims involving information and the expression of opinions.

24.   Undertakings and establishments should be protected against disclosure of certain particularly sensitive information.

25.   The employer should be allowed not to inform and consult where this would seriously damage the undertaking or the establishment or where he has to comply immediately with an order issued to him by a regulatory or supervisory body.

26.   Information and consultation imply both rights and obligations for management and labour at undertaking or establishment level.

27.   This Directive should not affect the provisions, where these are more specific, of Council Directive 98/59/EC of 20 July 1998 on the approximation of the laws of the Member States relating to collective redundancies[18] and of Council Directive 2001/23/EC of 12 March 2001 on the approximation of the laws of the Member States relating to the safeguarding of employees' rights in the event of transfers of undertakings, businesses or parts of undertakings or businesses.[19]

28.   Other rights of information and consultation, including those arising from Council Directive 94/45/EC of 22 September 1994 on the establishment of a European Works Council or a procedure in Community-scale undertakings and Community-scale groups of undertakings for the purposes of informing and consulting employees,[20] should not be affected by this Directive.

29.   Implementation of this Directive should not be sufficient grounds for a reduction in the general level of protection of workers in the areas to which it applies,

HAVE ADOPTED THIS DIRECTIVE:

---

18.   OJ L 225, 12.8.1998, p. 16.
19.   OJ L 82, 22.3.2001, p. 16.
20.   OJ L 254, 30.9.1994, p. 64. Directive as amended by Directive 97/74/EC (OJ L 10, 16.1.1998, p. 22).

Article 1
Object and principles

1. The purpose of this Directive is to establish a general framework setting out minimum requirements for the right to information and consultation of employees in undertakings or establishments within the Community.
2. The practical arrangements for information and consultation shall be defined and implemented in accordance with national law and industrial relations practices in individual Member States in such a way as to ensure their effectiveness.
3. When defining or implementing practical arrangements for information and consultation, the employer and the employees' representatives shall work in a spirit of cooperation and with due regard for their reciprocal rights and obligations, taking into account the interests both of the undertaking or establishment and of the employees.

Article 2
Definitions

For the purposes of this Directive:
(a) "undertaking" means a public or private undertaking carrying out an economic activity, whether or not operating for gain, which is located within the territory of the Member States;
(b) "establishment" means a unit of business defined in accordance with national law and practice, and located within the territory of a Member State, where an economic activity is carried out on an ongoing basis with human and material resources;
(c) "employer" means the natural or legal person party to employment contracts or employment relationships with employees, in accordance with national law and practice;
(d) "employee" means any person who, in the Member State concerned, is protected as an employee under national employment law and in accordance with national practice;
(e) "employees' representatives" means the employees' representatives provided for by national laws and/or practices;
(f) "information" means transmission by the employer to the employees' representatives of data in order to enable them to acquaint themselves with the subject-matter and to examine it;
(g) "consultation" means the exchange of views and establishment of dialogue between the employees' representatives and the employer.

Article 3
Scope

1. This Directive shall apply, according to the choice made by Member States, to:
(a) undertakings employing at least 50 employees in any one Member State, or
(b) establishments employing at least 20 employees in any one Member State. Member States shall determine the method for calculating the thresholds of employees employed.
2. In conformity with the principles and objectives of this Directive, Member States may lay down particular provisions applicable to undertakings or establishments which pursue directly and essentially political, professional organisational, religious, charitable, educational, scientific or artistic aims, as well as aims involving information and the expression of opinions, on condition that, at the date of entry into force of this Directive, provisions of that nature already exist in national legislation.
3. Member States may derogate from this Directive through particular provisions applicable to the crews of vessels plying the high seas.

Article 4
Practical arrangements for information and consultation

1. In accordance with the principles set out in Article 1 and without prejudice to any provisions and/or practices in force more favourable to employees, the Member States shall determine the practical arrangements for exercising the right to information and consultation at the appropriate level in accordance with this Article.
2. Information and consultation shall cover:
(a) information on the recent and probable development of the undertaking's or the establishment's activities and economic situation;
(b) information and consultation on the situation, structure and probable development of employment within the undertaking or establishment and on any anticipatory measures envisaged, in particular where there is a threat to employment;
(c) information and consultation on decisions likely to lead to substantial changes in work organisation or in contractual relations, including those covered by the Community provisions referred to in Article 9(1).
3. Information shall be given at such time, in such fashion and with such content as is appropriate to enable, in particular, employees' representatives to conduct an adequate study and, where necessary, prepare for consultation.
4. Consultation shall take place:

(a)   while ensuring that the timing, method and content thereof are appropriate;
(b)   at the relevant level of management and representation, depending on the subject under discussion;
(c)   on the basis of relevant information to be supplied by the employer and of the opinion which the employees' representatives are entitled to formulate;
(d)   in such a way as to enable employees' representatives to meet the employer and obtain a response, and the reasons for that response, to any opinion they might formulate;
(e)   with a view to reaching an agreement on decisions within the scope of the employer's powers referred to in paragraph 2(c).

Article 5
Information and consultation deriving from an agreement

Member States may entrust management and labour at the appropriate level, including at undertaking or establishment level, with defining freely and at any time through negotiated agreement the practical arrangements for informing and consulting employees. These agreements, and agreements existing on the date laid down in Article 11, as well as any subsequent renewals of such agreements, may establish, while respecting the principles set out in Article 1 and subject to conditions and limitations laid down by the Member States, provisions which are different from those referred to in Article 4.

Article 6
Confidential information

1.   Member States shall provide that, within the conditions and limits laid down by national legislation, the employees' representatives, and any experts who assist them, are not authorised to reveal to employees or to third parties, any information which, in the legitimate interest of the undertaking or establishment, has expressly been provided to them in confidence. This obligation shall continue to apply, wherever the said representatives or experts are, even after expiry of their terms of office. However, a Member State may authorise the employees' representatives and anyone assisting them to pass on confidential information to employees and to third parties bound by an obligation of confidentiality.
2.   Member States shall provide, in specific cases and within the conditions and limits laid down by national legislation, that the employer is not obliged to communicate information or undertake consultation when the nature of that information or consultation is such that, according to objective criteria, it would seriously harm the functioning of the undertaking or establishment or would be prejudicial to it.

3. Without prejudice to existing national procedures, Member States shall provide for administrative or judicial review procedures when the employer requires confidentiality or does not provide the information in accordance with paragraphs 1 and 2. They may also provide for procedures intended to safeguard the confidentiality of the information in question.

Article 7
Protection of employees' representatives

Member States shall ensure that employees' representatives, when carrying out their functions, enjoy adequate protection and guarantees to enable them to perform properly the duties which have been assigned to them.

Article 8
Protection of rights

1. Member States shall provide for appropriate measures in the event of non-compliance with this Directive by the employer or the employees' representatives. In particular, they shall ensure that adequate administrative or judicial procedures are available to enable the obligations deriving from this Directive to be enforced.
2. Member States shall provide for adequate penalties to be applicable in the event of infringement of this Directive by the employer or the employees' representatives.

    These penalties must be effective, proportionate and dissuasive.

Article 9
Link between this Directive and other Community and national provisions

1. This Directive shall be without prejudice to the specific information and consultation procedures set out in Article 2 of Directive 98/59/EC and Article 7 of Directive 2001/23/EC.
2. This Directive shall be without prejudice to provisions adopted in accordance with Directives 94/45/EC and 97/74/EC.
3. This Directive shall be without prejudice to other rights to information, consultation and participation under national law.
4. Implementation of this Directive shall not be sufficient grounds for any regression in relation to the situation which already prevails in each Member State and in relation to the general level of protection of workers in the areas to which it applies.

Article 10
Transitional provisions

Notwithstanding Article 3, a Member State in which there is, at the date of entry into force of this Directive, no general, permanent and statutory system of information and consultation of employees, nor a general, permanent and statutory system of employee representation at the workplace allowing employees to be represented for that purpose, may limit the application of the national provisions implementing this Directive to:
(a) undertakings employing at least 150 employees or establishments employing at least 100 employees until ... ,[21] and
(b) undertakings employing at least 100 employees or establishments employing at least 50 employees during the two years following the date in point (a).

Article 11
Transposition

1. Member States shall adopt the laws, regulations and administrative provisions necessary to comply with this Directive not later than ... [22] or shall ensure that management and labour introduce by that date the required provisions by way of agreement, the Member States being obliged to take all necessary steps enabling them to guarantee the results imposed by this Directive at all times. They shall forthwith inform the Commission thereof.
2. Where Member States adopt these measures, they shall contain a reference to this Directive or shall be accompanied by such reference on the occasion of their official publication. The methods of making such reference shall be laid down by the Member States.

Article 12
Review by the Commission

Not later than ... ,[23] the Commission shall, in consultation with the Member States and the social partners at Community level, review the application of this Directive with a view to proposing any necessary amendments.

---

21. Five years after the date of entry into force of this Directive.
22. Three years after the date of entry into force of this Directive.
23. Five years after the date of entry into force of this Directive.

Article 13
Entry into force

This Directive shall enter into force on the day of its publication in the Official Journal of the European Communities.

Article 14
Addresses

This Directive is addressed to the Member States.

STATEMENT OF THE COUNCIL'S REASONS

I.   Introduction

The Commission's proposal for a Directive of the European Parliament and of the Council establishing a general framework for informing and consulting employees in the Community was submitted to the Council on 17 November 1998. It was based on Article 137(2) of the Treaty.

The European Parliament, the Economic and Social Committee, and the Committee of the Regions delivered their opinions on 14 April 1999, 7 July 1999, and 13 and 14 December 2000 respectively.

The Commission submitted an amended proposal on 23 May 2001.

The Council adopted a Common Position on 23 July 2001, in accordance with the procedure laid down in Article 251 of the Treaty.

II.   Aim of the proposal

The purpose of the Commission proposal is to lay down a general framework setting minimum requirements for the right of employees to be informed and consulted, applicable at national level to undertakings in the Member States. Its aim is also to supplement the existing Directives on collective redundancies and transfers of undertakings, as well as the Directive on a European Works Council applying to undertakings situated in two or more Member States.

III.   Analysis of the common position

1.   General observations

According to Article 136 of the Treaty, the Community and the Member States "shall have as their objectives (...) improved living and working conditions (...), dialogue between management and labour (...)", etc. To this end Article 137(2) of the Treaty states that the Council "may adopt, by means of directives, minimum requirements for gradual implementation, having regard to the conditions and technical rules obtaining in each of the Member States".

The Council Common Position is in accordance with the objectives of Article 137(2) of the Treaty in the area covered, since it is designed to introduce minimum requirements for the information and consultation of employees in undertakings or establishments in the European Union. Furthermore, the Common Position largely respects the objectives put forward by the Commission and supported by Parliament.

The Directive is to apply to undertakings employing at least 50 employees or to establishments employing at least 20 employees within a Member State, in accordance with the choice made by the Member State.

However, Member States in which there is currently no general, permanent and statutory system of information and consultation of employees, nor of employee representation at the workplace, may apply an additional transitional period. They may, during the first five years after the entry into force of the Directive, limit the application of the national provisions implementing the Directive to undertakings employing at least 150 employees or to establishments employing at least 100 employees and, for a further two years, to undertakings employing at least 100 employees or establishments employing at least 50 employees. The reason for this derogation being included in the text of the Directive was the need to provide an adequate timetable for small and medium-sized undertakings to adjust to the Directive's requirements where such undertakings at present have no formal information and consultation obligations at all.

Member States should define and implement the practical arrangements for information and consultation at the appropriate level, in accordance with national law and industrial relations practices.

This includes entrusting management and labour at the appropriate national level with defining freely and at any time through negotiated agreement the practical arrangements for informing and consulting employees. These agreements may establish provisions which are different from those referred to in Article 4 of the Directive.

The key element is the right of the employees to be informed on the recent and probable development of central aspects of the undertaking's activities and economic and employment situation, and to be consulted on these as well as on anticipatory measures regarding the employment situation, and on decisions likely to lead to substantial changes in work organisation or in contractual relations. Consultation includes an exchange of views and a dialogue between the employer and the representatives of the employees, enabling them to express their opinions to the employer and to obtain a reasoned response, with a view to reaching agreement on decisions to be taken by the employer.

The Directive contains provisions enabling the employer to provide certain information in confidence to the employees' representatives, where this is in the legitimate interest of the employer. It also authorises the employer not to communicate information or undertake consultation where this would seriously harm the functioning of the undertaking or establishment.

The Directive requires effective, proportionate and dissuasive penalties to be applicable in the event of infringement of the Directive by the employer or the employees' representatives.

2. The European Parliament's amendments on first reading

2.1. European Parliament amendments adopted by the Council

2.1.1. The following 10 amendments were taken up in their entirety, both in the Commission's amended proposal and in the Council's Common Position, either word for word, or at least in spirit and substance: 2, 3, 6, 7, 9, 10, 13 (introductory sentence) 16, 25 and 32.

2.1.2. The following 24 amendments were neither taken up in the Commission's amended proposal nor, for the following reasons, in the Council's Common Position:

— amendment 1: this was regarded as consistent with recitals 7 and 8, but at the same time unnecessarily detailed,

— amendments 4 and 15: the recital and the article on "Tendenzschutz" were considered necessary, in line with the "European Works Council Directive",

— amendment 37: this was considered too inflexible in respect of the employer's right to withhold particularly sensitive information, in line with the Council's position on amendment 27; furthermore, recitals should not contain wording which has the nature of a binding provision,

— amendment 5 and 31: these were considered unnecessary, as they were already covered by the provisions of Article 9(3),

— amendment 8: although this was considered to be consistent with the spirit of Article 1(3), it was also considered to put demands on the Member States which these would not be able to meet,

— amendment 11: this was regarded as being too resctrictive for matters which should be left to national law and practice, including the social partners,

— amendment 41: this was considered too detailed and unnecessary, and incompatible with the situation in some Member States,

— amendment 13 (first and third indents): this was considered unnecessarily detailed, since consultation could, in any case, only take place on the basis of information given,

— amendment 17: this was regarded as potentially burdensome for small and medium-sized enterprises, and as not entirely appropriate as a legal provision,

— amendment 43: although this was considered to be consistent with the spirit of Article 5, it was regarded as an unnecessary restriction of the freedom of negotiation of the social partners,

- amendment 20: this was regarded as too restrictive for the freedom of the social partners to conclude agreements,
- amendment 21: this was considered to be too detailed and to cover areas which were not suitable for consultation,
- amendments 22 and 23: these were considered to be in line with the spirit of the Directive, but at the same time unnecessarily detailed,
- amendment 24: this was considered too far-reaching in the light of national legislation in most Member States, which did not give the employees' representatives such a right to a suspensive veto,
- amendment 26: this was regarded as unnecessary in the light of Article 6(1) which already mentions "any experts who assist" the employees' representatives, and also too vague in respect of the rights and role of such experts,
- amendment 27: the employer's right not to communicate information and undertake consultation when this would seriously harm the undertaking was considered necessary,
- amendment 28: this was considered too detailed and alien to the situation existing in many Member States,
- amendment 29: this was considered to present problems of legal enforcement, given that the intention of the employer would be very difficult to establish; in fact the Council rejected the whole paragraph to which the amendment was related,
- amendment 33: this amendment, which aimed to extend the scope of the Directive to the whole of the public sector, was not considered appropriate, given that publicly-owned undertakings would in any event be covered; the Directive was not, however, adapted to the nature, activities, and types of decisions taken by other public sector bodies,
- amendment 34: this was considered to interfere unduly with the legislative process in the Member States, which in any case normally includes the consultation of the social partners,
- amendment 35: this was considered unnecessary because it singled out one particular aspect of the Directive, which is likely to be included in the review in any case.

3.   *The common position in relation to the Commission's amended proposal*

3.1. Article 3(3), which allows Member States to derogate from the Directive in respect of the crews of vessels plying the high seas, was not included in the Commission's amended proposal, but was considered necessary by the Council because of the practical difficulties of consulting seafarers absent on lengthy voyages, and was subsequently accepted by the Commission.

3.2. The Commission's amended proposal (and its initial proposal) contained a provision (Article 8(3)) on specific sanctions in case of serious breach by the employer of his/her information and consultation obligations. However, although the Council recognised the need for sanctions in such a

case, it considered that Article 8(2) provided a sufficient basis for introducing effective, proportionate and dissuasive penalties into national legislation. The Council could therefore not accept paragraph 3, the following specific reasons also being mentioned by several Member States:
- the provision included the notion of the "non-production of legal effects" of certain decisions by the employer, which was alien to most national legal systems,
- the provision could lead to legal uncertainty because of lengthy judicial procedures, with serious financial consequences for the undertaking and its ability to safeguard its present level of employment, and for its relations with its business partners, and – the provision could lead to legal uncertainty in respect of information and consultation in situations covered by the existing Directives on collective redundancies and transfers of undertakings.

3.3. Article 10, which provides for transitional periods in respect of the thresholds laid down in Article 3 for the application of the Directive, was not included in the Commission's amended proposal; it was proposed by the Commission at the meeting of the Council on 11 June 2001, and was accepted by the Council.

IV.   Conclusion

The Council considers that, as a whole, the Common Position is well in line with the objectives of the amended Commission proposal. It also considers that it has basically taken account of the main objectives pursued by the European Parliament in its proposed amendments.

IV.   REPORT ON THE PROPOSAL FOR A COUNCIL DIRECTIVE
      ESTABLISHING A GENERAL FRAMEWORK FOR INFORMING
      AND CONSULTING EMPLOYEES IN THE EUROPEAN
      COMMUNITY (COM(98)0612 – C4-0706/98 – 98/0315(SYN))
      (31 MARCH 1999)

A.   Legislative proposal

Proposal for a Council Directive establishing a general framework for informing and consulting employees in the European Community (COM(98)0612 – C4-0706/98 – 98/0315(SYN))
The proposal is approved with the following amendments:

Text proposed by the Commission[24]	Amendments by Parliament

(Amendment 1)
Recital 9

| Whereas there is a need to strengthen dialogue and promote mutual trust within undertakings in order to improve risk anticipation, make work organisation more flexible and facilitate employee access to training within the undertaking while maintaining security, make employees aware of adaptation needs, increase employees' availability to undertake measures and activities to increase their employability, promote employee involvement in the operation and future of the undertaking and increase its competitiveness; | Whereas there is a need to strengthen dialogue and promote mutual trust within undertakings in order to improve risk anticipation, make work organisation more flexible and facilitate employee access to training within the undertaking while maintaining security, make employees aware of adaptation needs, increase employees' availability to undertake measures and activities to increase their employability, promote employee involvement in the operation and future of the undertaking and increase its competitiveness in the interests of the continuing acquisition of qualifications, the employment of workers in innovation and adherence to new forms of work organisation which are more creative and rewarding for both sides; |

(Amendment 2)
Recital 17

| Whereas the purpose of this general framework is to establish minimum requirements applicable throughout the European Community while avoiding any administrative, financial or legal constraints which would hinder the creation and development of small and medium-sized undertakings; whereas, to this end, the scope of this Directive should be restricted to undertakings with at least 50 employees, without prejudice to any more favourable national or Community provisions whereas, in order to maintain the appropriate balance between the above-mentioned factors, this minimum may be raised to 100 employees in the case of the more innovative measures proposed herein on the information and consultation of employees on developments in the employment situation within the undertaking; | Whereas the purpose of this general framework is to establish minimum requirements applicable throughout the European Community while avoiding any administrative, financial or legal constraints which would hinder the creation and development of small and medium-sized undertakings; whereas, to this end, the scope of this Directive should be restricted to undertakings with at least 50 employees, without prejudice to any more favourable national or Community provisions; |

---

24.   *O.J.*, C 2, 5.1.1999, p. 3.

Text proposed by the Commission	Amendments by Parliament

(Amendment 3)
Recital 19

Whereas the objectives of this Directive are to be achieved through the establishment of a general framework comprising the definitions and purpose of the information and consultation, which it will be up to the Member States to complete and adapt to their own national situation, ensuring, where appropriate, that the social partners have a leading role by allowing them to define freely the arrangements for informing and consulting employees which they consider to be best suited to their needs and wishes;

Whereas the objectives of this Directive are to be achieved through the establishment of a general framework comprising the definitions and purpose of the information and consultation, which it will be up to the Member States to complete and adapt to their own national situation, ensuring, where appropriate, that the social partners have a leading role by allowing them to define freely the arrangements for informing and consulting employees which they consider to be best suited to their needs and wishes. Existing legal provision at national level may not be altered to the disadvantage of employees;

(Amendment 4)
Recital 20

Whereas care must be taken to avoid affecting some specific rules in the field of employees' information and consultation existing in some national laws, addressed to undertakings which pursue political, professional organisation, religious, charitable, educational, scientific or artistic aims, as well as aims involving information and the expression of opinions;

Deleted

(Amendment 5)
Recital 25

Whereas other employee information and consultation rights, including those arising from Council Directive 94/45/EEC of 22 September 1994 on the establishment of a European Works Council or a procedure in Community-scale undertakings and Community-scale groups of undertakings for the purposes of informing and consulting employees, must not be affected by this Directive,

Whereas other employee information and consultation rights, including those arising from Council Directive 94/45/EEC of 22 September 1994 on the establishment of a European Works Council or a procedure in Community-scale undertakings and Community-scale groups of undertakings for the purposes of informing and consulting employees, must not be affected by this Directive, provided that they are more favourable to employees

(Amendment 6)
Recital 26 (new)

Whereas the implementation of the provisions of this Directive shall under no circumstances constitute a sufficient reason to justify a lowering of the general level of protection for employees in the field covered by it;

Text proposed by the Commission	Amendments by Parliament

(Amendment 7)
Article 1, para. 1

1. The purpose of this Directive is to establish a general framework for informing and consulting employees in undertakings within the European Community;

1. The purpose of this Directive is to establish minimum requirements for the information and consultation of employees in undertakings within the European Community;

(Amendment 8)
Article 1, para. 2

2. When defining or implementing information and consultation procedures, the employer and the employees' representatives shall work in a spirit of co-operation and with due regard for their reciprocal rights and obligations, taking into account the interests both of the undertaking and of the employees;

2. Member States shall ensure that the employer and the employees' representatives when defining or implementing information and consultation procedures, shall respect these minimum requirements and shall work together in good faith and with due respect for their reciprocal rights and obligations, taking into account the interests both of the undertaking and of the employees;

(Amendment 9)
Article 2(1)(a)

1. For the purposes of this Directive: (a) "undertakings" means public or private undertakings carrying out an economic activity, whether or not operating for gain, which are located within the territory of the Member States of the European Community and have at least 50 employees, without prejudice to the provisions of Article 4(3);

1. For the purposes of this Directive: (a) "undertakings" means public or private undertakings carrying out an economic activity, whether or not operating for gain, which are located within the territory of the Member States of the European Community and have at least 50 employees;

(Amendment 10)
Article 2(1)(b)

"employer" means the natural or legal person party to employment contracts or employment relationships with employees;

"employer" means the natural or legal person party to employment contracts or employment relationships with employees pursuant to national law and/or practice.;

(Amendment 11)
Article 2(1)(c)

(c) "employees' representatives" means the employees' representatives provided for by national laws and/or practices;

(c) "employees' representatives" means the permanent, stable and independent employees' representatives provided for by national laws and/or practices;

(Amendment 12)
Article 2 (1)(c)(2) (new)

(ca) "social partners" means the competent representative organisation of trade unions and organisations of employers or employer

Text proposed by the Commission	Amendments by Parliament

(Amendment 13)
Article 2(1)(d)

(e) "consultation" means the organisation of a dialogue and exchange of views between the employer and the employees' representatives on the subjects set out in Article 4(1)(b) and (c), – ensuring that the timing, method and content are such that this step is effective; – at the appropriate level of management and representation, depending on the subject under discussion; – on the basis of the relevant information to be supplied by the employer and the opinion which the employees' representatives are entitled to formulate; – including the employees' representatives' right to meet with the employer and obtain a response, and the reasons for that response, to any opinion they may formulate; – including, in the case of decisions within the scope of the employer's management powers, an attempt to seek prior agreement on the decisions referred to in Article 4(1)c.	(e) "consultation" means dialogue and exchange of views between the employer and the employees' representatives on the subjects set out in Article 4(1), – during the planning stage, so as to ensure the effectiveness of the step; – at the appropriate level of management and representation, depending on the subject under discussion; – on the basis of information in accordance with letter (d) of this Article and the opinion which the employees' representatives are entitled to formulate; – including the employees' representatives' right to meet with the employer and obtain a response, and the reasons for that response, to any opinion they may formulate; – including, in the case of decisions within the scope of the employer's management powers, an attempt to seek prior agreement.

(Amendment 14)
Article 2(1)(e), first indent

– ensuring that the timing, method and content are such that this step is effective;	– ensuring that the timing, method and content are such that this step is effective and that an influence can be exerted;

(Amendment 15)
Article 1(2)

2. In conformity with the principles and objectives of this Directive, Member States may lay down particular provisions applicable to undertakings which pursue directly and essentially political, professional organisation, religious, charitable, educational, scientific or artistic aims, as well as aims involving information and the expression of opinions, on condition that, at the date of adoption of this Directive, such particular provisions already exist in national legislation.	Deleted

(Amendment 16)
Article 2(3) (new)

	3. The Member States shall determine the levels (plant, undertaking or group of undertakings at national level) which, depending on the subject dealt with, guarantee full compliance with the objectives of this Directive.

Text proposed by the Commission	Amendments by Parliament
(Amendment 17) Article 2(4) (new)	
	4. The Member States, without prejudice to existing national provisions or practice, shall create mechanisms designed to foster and promote social dialogue also in small and medium-sized enterprises, which do not come within the field of application of this Directive, in order to extend to them the achievement of the general objectives contained in it.
(Amendment 18) Article 3(1)	
Member States may authorise the social partners at the appropriate level, including at undertaking level, to define freely and at any time through negotiated agreement the procedures for implementing the employee information and consultation requirements referred to in Articles 1, 2 and 4 of this Directive.	Member States may authorise the social partners at the appropriate level, including at undertaking level, to define freely and at any time through negotiated agreement the procedures for implementing the employee information and consultation requirements referred to in Articles 1, 2 and 4 of this Directive, provided that under the agreement the minimum standards laid down at national level are upheld;
(Amendment 19) Article 3(1)	
Member States may authorise the social partners at the appropriate level, including at undertaking level, to define freely and at any time through negotiated agreement the procedures for implementing the employee information and consultation requirements referred to in Articles 1, 2 and 4 of this Directive.	Member States may leave the social partners at the appropriate level, including at undertaking level, to define freely and at any time through negotiated agreement the procedures for implementing the employee information and consultation requirements referred to in Articles 1, 2 and 4 of this Directive.
(Amendment 20) Article 3(2)	
The agreements referred to in paragraph 1 may establish, while respecting the general objectives laid down by the Directive and subject to conditions and limitations laid down by the Member States, arrangements which are different to those referred to in Article 2(1)(d) and (e) and Article 4 of the present Directive.	The social partners may conclude agreements which, while respecting the general objectives laid down by the Directive and subject to generally applicable conditions laid down by the Member States, provide for rules and arrangements which are more favourable for employees than those laid down by this Directive.
(Amendment 21) Article 4(1)(a)	
(a) information on the recent as well as the reasonably foreseeable development of the undertaking's activities and its economic and financial situation;	(a) information and consultation on the recent as well as the reasonably foreseeable development of the undertaking's activities and its economic and financial situation, in particular as regards investment, production, sales and structure;

Text proposed by the Commission	Amendments by Parliament

(Amendment 22)
Article 4(1)(c)

(c) information and consultation on decisions likely to lead to substantial changes in work organisation or in contractual relations, including those covered by the Community provisions referred to in Article 8(1).

(c) information and consultation on decisions likely to lead to substantial changes in work organisation or in contractual relations, including those covered by the Community provisions referred to in Article 8(1), such as the introduction of new production processes, transfers of production, relocation, mergers, reductions in capacity or the closure of the undertaking, of plants or of substantial parts thereof.

(Amendment 23)
Article 4(1)(d) (new)

(d) information and consultation on training and further training, equal opportunities and health and safety at the workplace (in accordance with the provisions of framework Directive 89/391/EEC).

(Amendment 24)
Article 4(2)(a) (new)

Member States shall ensure that, where a decision to be implemented will have considerable adverse consequences for employees, the final decision may be postponed for an appropriate period at the request of the employees' representatives so that consultations may continue with the aim of avoiding or mitigating such adverse consequences.

(Amendment 25)
Article 4(3)

3. Member States may exclude from the information and consultation obligations referred to in paragraph 1(b) of this Article undertakings with fewer than 100 employees.

Deleted

(Amendment 26)
Article 4(a) (new) (experts)

Employees' representatives may, if they so wish, request the assistance of experts specified by them.

Text proposed by the Commission	Amendments by Parliament

(Amendment 27)
Article 5(2)

2. Member States shall provide, in specific cases and within the conditions and limits laid down by national legislation, that the employer is not obliged to communicate information or undertake consultation when the nature of that information or consultation is such that, according to objective criteria, it would seriously harm the functioning of the undertaking or would be prejudicial to it.	Deleted

(Amendment 28)
Article 6

Employees' representatives shall, when carrying out their functions, enjoy adequate protection and guarantees to enable them to perform properly the duties which have been assigned to them.	Employees' representatives shall, when carrying out their functions, enjoy adequate protection and guarantees to enable them to perform (one word deleted) the duties which have been assigned to them. In particular, employees' representatives must be entitled to a) legal protection against dismissal or disadvantage with regard to career, wage and training during their term of office and for six months thereafter and they may not be dismissed during that period except with the consent of the employees representative, and b) appropriate and continuous training, including paid training leave, the organisation of periodic meetings between them and all the employees and the use of the firm's internal computer networks.

(Amendment 29)
Article 7(3)(b)

(b) the withholding of important information or provision of false information rendering ineffective the exercise of the right to information and consultation.	(b) the withholding of information or provision of incomplete or false information rendering ineffective the exercise of the right to information and consultation.

(Amendment 30)
Article 7(3)(b)

the withholding of important information or provision of false information rendering ineffective the exercise of the right to information and consultation.	the withholding of important information or provision of false information with the intention of rendering ineffective the exercise of the right to information and consultation.

(Amendment 31)
Article 8(3)

3. This Directive shall be without prejudice to other rights of employees to information, consultation and participation under national law.	3. This Directive shall be without prejudice to other rights to information, consultation and participation under national law which are more favourable to employees.

Text proposed by the Commission	Amendments by Parliament

(Amendment 32)
Article 8(4) (new)

4. Implementation of the provisions of this Directive shall under no circumstances constitute sufficient reason to justify a lowering of existing standards in the Member States or the general level of protection for employees in the field covered by it.

(Amendment 33)
Article 8(a) (new)

Public sector
1. This Directive shall also apply to the public sector, including the Civil Service and public services.
2. The Member States shall ensure that the social partners introduce the necessary provisions by means of agreements, or that the laws, regulations or administrative provisions needed to comply with this Article are adopted.

(Amendment 34)
Article 9(1)

1. Member States shall adopt the laws, regulations and administrative provisions necessary to comply with this Directive no later than ... (two years after adoption) or shall ensure that the social partners introduce the required provisions by way of agreement, the Member States being obliged to take all necessary steps enabling them to guarantee the results imposed by this Directive at all times. They shall forthwith inform the Commission thereof.

1. After consulting the social partners, in accordance with current legislation and practice in the Member States, Member States shall adopt the laws, regulations and administrative provisions necessary to comply with this Directive no later than ... (two years after adoption) or shall ensure that the social partners introduce the required provisions by way of agreement, the Member States being obliged to take all necessary steps enabling them to guarantee the results imposed by this Directive at all times. They shall forthwith inform the Commission thereof.

(Amendment 35)
Article 10

Review by the Commission Not later than ... (five years after adoption), the Commission shall, in consultation with the Member States and the social partners at Community level, review the application of this Directive with a view to proposing to the Council any necessary amendments.

Review by the Commission Not later than ... (five years after adoption), the Commission shall, in consultation with the Member States and the social partners at Community level, review the application of this Directive and – in particular – the validity of the limits on staff numbers with a view to proposing to the Council any necessary amendments.

Draft legislative resolution

Legislative resolution embodying Parliament's opinion on the proposal for a Council Directive establishing a general framework for informing and consulting employees in the European Community (COM(98)0612 – C4-0706/98 – 98/0315(SYN)

(Cooperation procedure: first reading)

The European Parliament,

- having regard to the Commission proposal to the Council (COM(98)0612–98/0315(SYN),[25]
- having been consulted by the Council pursuant to Article 189c of the EC Treaty and to Article 2, par. 2 of the Agreement on Social Policy attached to Protocol (No 14) on Social Policy annexed to the Treaty EC (C4-0706/98),
- having regard to Rule 58 of its Rules of Procedure,
- having regard to the report of the Committee on Social Affairs and Employment and the opinion of the Committee on Legal Affairs and Citizens Right (A4-0186/99),

1. Approves the Commission proposal, subject to Parliament's amendments;
2. Calls on the Commission to alter its proposal accordingly, pursuant to Article 189a(2) of the EC Treaty;
3. Calls on the Council to incorporate Parliament's amendments in the common position that it adopts in accordance with Article 189c(a) of the EC Treaty;
4. Calls for the conciliation procedure to be opened should the Council intend to depart from the text approved by Parliament;
5. Instructs its President to forward this opinion to the Council and Commission.

B.   Explanatory statement

1.   Legal basis

The legal basis for the proposed Directive is Article 2(1) and (2) of the Agreement on Social Policy appended to the Protocol on Social Policy annexed to the Treaty establishing the European Community.

2.   Introduction

The information, consultation and participation of workers has been a key theme in European debate since the first social action programme was adopted by the Council in 1974. Since then several initiatives have been launched by the Commission. These have often, however, encountered resistance in the Council

---

25.   *O.J.*, L 48. 22.2. 1975. This Directive was amended by Council Directive 92/56/EC of 24 June 1992 (*O.J.*, L 245, 26.8.1992). The two Community acts have been consolidated by Council Directive 98/59/EC of 20 July 1998 (*O.J.*, L 225, 12.8.1998).

and a number of proposals have therefore not yet been adopted. This should be seen in the light of the fact that Community legal acts in this field could only be adopted by a unanimous vote until the adoption of the Treaty on European Union.

Council Directive 94/45/EC of September 1995 on the introduction of European Works Councils is the major existing piece of EU legislation in this area. The adoption of this directive was an innovation in that unlike previously adopted directives in this field, it does not address specific situations. General rules are instead laid down to ensure that workers in big multinational companies and consortia are informed and consulted. It is also the first directive adopted under the Agreement on Social Policy.

The other important Community provision on information and consultation is found in the Framework Directive on the working environment, 89/391/EEC.

Other proposals have long been pending in the Council without it being possible to reach a decision.

Unlike the directives that have been adopted, most of these proposals are based on a model which goes beyond information and consultation procedures and contains rules on worker participation on company boards or management. They are: the proposals for Council regulations on a European company statute (COM(91)0174/I and II), a European association, European cooperatives and a European mutual society, together with the associated proposals for Council directives containing supplementary provisions on the position of workers (COM(93)0252); the proposal for a fifth directive on company law, as amended by a third proposal (COM(91)0372), containing a number of alternative models for participation in decision-making applicable to companies employing more than 1,000 workers.

It has however become clear that, even where information and consultation provisions exist, they are not effective, as they tend to be either ritual in nature or only effective a posteriori.

Parliament has adopted several resolutions calling for workers to have the right to be involved in company decision-making (e.g. the resolutions of 13 September 1990, 3 May 1994 and 19 January 1995). Parliament's position is that workers should not only be entitled to be informed and consulted but that they should also have the right to participate in decision-making. This right should apply in multinational and national companies and the right should apply to all companies irrespective of legal status.

3.   *Background to the Commission's proposal*

In the modern working environment with constant change, increased transborder activities etc. the current state of affairs with its limitations and flaws has proven not to give workers sufficient information and possibilities to be consulted on matters that really matter for the decisions of the undertaking. Although legislation on information and consultation exists in all Member

States and at EU level in some limited fields, it has been proven (Supplement 3/96 "Social Europe"), that these social rights are not always respected in practice and are often not effective, particularly in cases involving cross-border situations. As a response to mounting criticism from the public and at the direct request of the European Parliament the Commission launched a new initiative.

On 14 November 1995, the Commission's Communication on worker information and consultation encouraged the social partners to identify the arrangements for a general framework for the information and consultation of employees in the European Community. The Commission subsequently initiated the procedures provided for in the Protocol on Social Policy.

Parliament expressed in its resolution of 16 January 1996 (A4-0311/95) its satisfaction that the Commission in its "Communication on worker information and consultation" (COM(95)0547) encouraged the social partners to identify the arrangements for a general framework for the information and consultation of employees in the European Union.

The second stage of consultations started on 5 November 1997. In accordance with its well established practice, the Commission was in favour of the social partners establishing these rules themselves. However, while some of them, particularly the ETUC and CEEP, indicated their willingness to enter into Community-level negotiations on the subject, UNICE declined to do so, giving as its reasons the non-conformity of such a move with the principle of subsidiarity, the existence of adequate legal frameworks at national level, the lack of any link between employee information and consultation and job security, the view that labour management should be the exclusive preserve of the company's internal organisation and management, and the risks inherent in a measure which would prejudice the company's own management prerogatives.

In the absence of consensus between the social partners, the Commission felt duty-bound to present its proposal for a Directive with a view to establishing a general framework for employee information and consultation in the European Community.

4.   The principles of the Commission's proposal

The proposed framework is aimed at remedying the gaps and countering the shortcomings of existing national and Community legislation currently in force. The objectives are:

i.   to ensure existence of the right to regular information and consultation of employees on economic and strategic developments in the undertaking and on the decisions which affect them in all Member States of the European Community;

ii.   to consolidate the social dialogue and relations of trust within the undertaking in order to assist risk anticipation, develop the flexibility of work organisation within a framework of security, enhance employees' awareness of the need to adapt, encourage them to participate in measures and operations designed to boost their employability, promote employee involvement in the operation and future of the undertaking, and make the undertaking more competitive;

iii.   to include the situation and anticipated development of employment within the undertaking among the subjects of information and consultation;

iv.   to ensure that workers are informed and consulted prior to decisions which are likely to lead to substantial changes in work organisation or in contractual relations;

v.   ensure the effectiveness of these procedures by introducing specific penalties for those who seriously violate their obligations in this field.

5. Comments on the main amendments proposed by the rapporteur

The rapporteur very much welcomes the Commission's initiative. There is no doubt that, with a single currency and a single large-scale market, increasingly interdependent economies and fiscal policies which, albeit belatedly, are beginning to be coordinated, social policies are bound to become increasingly supranational in scale, so as to preserve and further promote our social model, which is recognised by a large number of authoritative sources as one of the decisive factors in our competitiveness.

    In particular, the proposal under consideration will ensure minimum standards for information and consultation to be applied throughout the Community, by harmonising the fundamental rights of employees and helping to strengthen the European social dimension.

    The proposal also aims, most appropriately, to reinforce European and national legislation concerning sanctions, which your rapporteur considers to be the most significant part of the proposal, not least in the light of recent dramatic events, the most well known (but not the sole) example of which was the closure of the Renault plant at Vilvoorde.

    Your rapporteur deplores the fact that the negotiations between the social partners at European level for an agreement in accordance with Article 4(2) of the Social Protocol have failed, in particular because of one of the side's total unwillingness to negotiate, but at the same time congratulates the Commission for having swiftly submitted the proposal for a directive under consideration, thereby fully exercising its right of initiative as sanctioned by the Treaty.

    Your rapporteur wishes to propose a number of amendments, aimed in particular at specifying practicalities and defining information and consultation, extending the Directive's field of application and ensuring that it contains minimum provisions at Community level, derogations from which may be allowed only if they are more favourable to employees.

Article 2

Your rapporteur considers that the proposal should be extended to a larger number of undertakings.

If the purpose of the directive is to anticipate change and help to promote our social model, it is unacceptable that the provisions under consideration should concern only 3% of the undertakings in the EU. There are many arguments in favour of this approach, ranging from the importance attributed to information and consultation in various contexts (for example in the conclusions of the final report of the high level group on the economic and social implications of industrial change), to the need to bring certain social provisions in the Member States closer together. It should also be added that the overwhelming majority of the Member States have lower thresholds.

Your rapporteur therefore proposes a threshold of 20 employees, and adds a new paragraph 3, aimed at encouraging dialogue in SMEs, which are excluded from the field of application of this proposal, so as to promote the extension of its objectives on a voluntary basis.

It also seems appropriate to clarify, in the definition of employees' representatives, the need for them to be stable and independent.

Your rapporteur also proposes a number of amendments to the definition of information and consultation, in particular as regards the moment at which the information should be transmitted (the Commission's definition is too vague, information must be supplied at the planning stage, so as to allow employees to "anticipate change"), and the content of the information itself, which must be as complete as possible.

She also proposes deleting the "ideological clause" (paragraph 2); it is unclear why the undertakings mentioned in it should be exempted from promoting proper social dialogue. She is nevertheless aware that some Member States whose legal systems make provision for such a clause will probably request that it be reinstated.

The proposal does not specify at what levels of the undertaking information and consultation should be ensured. For this reason she proposes that the Member States should establish at what level the aim of the Directive can best be pursued, depending on the subject being dealt with.

Articles 3 and 8

Article 3 authorises the social partners to depart from the provisions on information and consultation.

Your rapporteur would point out that the Directive establishes a general reference framework containing minimum provisions, from which no derogations must be allowed except in the event of provisions more favourable to employees being adopted. The Directive must also not interfere with other rights to information and consultation currently in force at national level, provided that they are more favourable to employees. In any event, the general level of protection for employees in the Member States at the time when the directive is adopted must not under any circumstances be lowered (Article 8).

Article 4

The content of information and consultation should be specified more precisely in certain cases, not least in the light of the recent progress made in the negotiations on the arrangements for the participation of employees in the statute of the European company, which is still being considered by the Council. The content of "economic" information should be extended, in particular, to investment, a fundamental factor for the future of a company and employment, and also be the subject of consultation; there is no reason why workers should not be entitled to express their opinion on strategic matters which have an important impact on present and future employment. The area of decisions likely to have an impact on contracts and the organisation of work must also be more precisely defined.

Your rapporteur considers that the content of information and consultation should be extended to other subjects which directly involve the rights of employees and their future, such as continuing training, measures linked to equal opportunities for men and women and health and safety at the workplace (the last in accordance with European legislation on the matter).

Article 4a (new)

Your rapporteur considers that the right of employees' representatives to be assisted by experts, in accordance with procedures and in a form to be established at national level, should be included in the Directive.

Article 5

Your rapporteur has no objections to the content of paragraph 1, but she does not see the need to maintain paragraph 2. Apart from the fact that the wording is unclear, it is hard to understand why the obligation of secrecy laid down in paragraph 1 should not be sufficient to ensure the necessary confidentiality of specific information on the undertaking's economic activity or any of its management decisions which may be sensitive. We therefore propose that paragraph 2 be deleted.

Article 6

The protection and guarantees covered in this article need to be more precisely defined, not least in the light of recent developments in other areas to which we referred above.

Article 8a

Your rapporteur does not consider that there are any valid reasons for not including the public sector in the field of application of this directive, whilst leaving it up to the Member States and the social partners to establish the provisions needed to ensure compliance with the general objectives of the directive.

Article 10

Your rapporteur proposes using the wording already used to revise Directive 94/45/EC on European Works Councils regarding the need to review, in particular, the threshold for application of the directive, extending it in future to firms with fewer than 20 employees (as in the amendment).

OPINION FOR THE COMMITTEE ON EMPLOYMENT AND SOCIAL AFFAIRS ON THE PROPOSAL FOR A COUNCIL DIRECTIVE ESTABLISHING A GENERAL FRAMEWORK FOR INFORMING AND CONSULTING EMPLOYEES IN THE EUROPEAN COMMUNITY (PRESENTED BY THE COMMISSION) (COM(98)0612 – C4-0706/98 – 98/0315(SYN)) (RAPPORT GHILARDOTTI) (18 MARCH 1999)

1. General remarks

The proposed directive establishing a general framework for informing and consulting employees in the European Community is another important plank in an ambitious plan stretching since the mid 1970s to extend the rights of workers to be informed and consulted in European companies. Although the European Company Statute is still under negotiation which involves an element of workers information and consultation five directives have been successfully concluded and operate in this field namely collective redundancies, amending directive to the collective redundancies, transfer of undertakings, amending directive to the transfer of undertaking and European Works Council.[26]

---

26.   *O.J.*, L 61, 5.3.197. This Directive was amended by Council Directive 98/50/EC of 29 June 1998 (*O.J.*, L 201, 17.7.1998) *O.J.*, L 254 30.9.1994.

The philosophy behind the directives is that the European firm operates differently from the American and Japanese firm and works best when there is a consensus of the workforce created by informing and consulting representatives of the workers. The topic has taken on greater significance since the European Union recognised the need to emphasise job creation and employment as a community objective and as an integral part of the employment strategy adopted by the European Council in Luxembourg. It is generally accepted that a weakness of the European economy is a relatively low job creation rate. There is also concern about European competitiveness in the world economy and a potential need to restructure European firms to render them more competitive. It is generally felt that a firm's attempt to restructure to become more competitive will be more successful if the workforce is taken into management's confidence and is informed of the strategy. It is this belief which underpins the Commission's proposal in this area and is to be welcomed because it strengthens links between management and workers' representatives and fosters harmonious workplace relations.

The precursor of this directive was the "Communication on worker information and consultation" which led to consultation with the social partners commencing 5 November 1995. Although the ETUC and CEEP were willing to enter into negotiations, UNICE were disinclined to do so because of concerns over the principle of subsidiarity. However, these concerns over subsidiarity are probably misplaced for the following reasons:

The proposal is based on Article 2 of the Agreement on Social Policy attached to the Protocol (NE 14) on Social Policy annexed to the Treaty establishing the European Community (Treaty of Maastricht).

Pursuant to Article 1 of the Agreement the Community and the Member States shall have as their objectives i.a. the "dialogue between management and labour".

With a view to achieving the objectives of Article 1, the Community shall, according to Article 2 of the Agreement "support and complement the activities of the Member States" i.a. in the field of "information and consultation of workers".

Article 2 paragraph 2 finally stipulates that "to this end, the Council may adopt, by means of directives, minimum requirements for gradual implementation, having regard to the conditions and technical rules obtaining in each of the Member States ... ".

This paragraph clearly gives an exclusive competence to the Member States of the Agreement because the "objectives of the proposed action", in the wording of Article 3b EC ("subsidiarity principle"), which is to fix minimum requirements in the field of workers information and consultation binding on the Member States, can not, by nature and by no means, "be sufficiently achieved by the Member States" themselves (Article 3b EC).

The argument of subsidiarity is therefore in this context not relevant. The debate should focus on the quality of the proposal in terms of the degree of harmonisation and legislative technique.

2. Explanation of amendments

Amendment 1 corresponds with amendment 2 and removes the misleading expression "general framework".

A "framework" has to be flashed out in order to be applicable whereas the aim and the content of this proposal is to establish minimum requirements which only have to be transposed into national labour law.

Amendment 3 corresponds with amendment 7. It isn't clear why the information and consultation on the development of employment should not be necessary in an undertaking with for example 99 workers.

3. Conclusions

The Committee on Legal Affairs and Citizens' Rights calls on the Committee on Employment and Social Affairs, as the committee responsible, to incorporate the following amendments in its report:

Text proposed by the Commission	Amendments by Parliament
(Amendment 1) Article 1, para. 1	
1. The purpose of this Directive is to establish a general framework for informing and consulting employees in undertakings within the European Community;	1. The purpose of this Directive is to establish minimum requirements for the information and consultation of employees in undertakings within the European Community;
(Amendment 2) Article 1, para. 2	
2. When defining or implementing information and consultation procedures, the employer and the employees' representatives shall work in a spirit of co-operation and with due regard for their reciprocal rights and obligations, taking into account the interests both of the undertaking and of the employees;	2. Member States shall ensure that the employer and the employees' representatives when defining or implementing information and consultation procedures, shall respect these minimum requirements and shall work together in good faith and with due respect for their reciprocal rights and obligations, taking into account the interests both of the undertaking and of the employees;
(Amendment 3) Article 2, para. 1. lit.a	
(a) "undertakings" means public or private undertakings carrying out an economic activity, whether or not operating for gain, which are located within the territory of the Member States of the European Community and have at least 50 employees, without prejudice to the provisions of Article 4 (3);	(a) "undertakings" means public or private undertakings carrying out an economic activity, whether or not operating for gain, which are located within the territory of the Member States of the European Community and have at least 50 employees;

Text proposed by the Commission	Amendments by Parliament

(Amendment 4)
Article 2, para. 2

2. In conformity with the principles and objectives of this Directive, Member States may lay down particular provisions applicable to undertakings which pursue directly and essentially political, professional organisation, religious, charitable, educational, scientific or artistic aims, as well as aims involving information and the expression of opinions, on condition that, at the date of adoption of this Directive, such particular provisions already exist in national legislation;

(delete)

(Amendment 5)
Article 3, para. 1

1. Member States may authorise the social partners at the appropriate level, including at undertaking level, to define freely and at any time through negotiated agreement the procedures for implementing the employee information and consultation requirements referred to in Articles 1, 2 and 4 of this Directive;

1. Member States may authorise the social partners at the appropriate level, including at undertaking level, to define through agreement alternative procedures for the employee information and consultation which meet the requirements referred to in Articles 1, 2 and 4 of this Directive;

(Amendment 6)
Article 3, para. 2

2. The agreements referred to in paragraph 1 may establish, while respecting the general objectives laid down by the Directive and subject to conditions and limitations laid down by the Member States, arrangements which are different to those referred to in Article 2(1)(d) and (e) and Article 4 of the present Directive;

(delete)

(Amendment 7)
Article 4, para. 3

3. Member States may exclude from the information and consultation obligations referred to in paragraph 1 b) of this Article undertakings with fewer than 100 employees;
(Amendment 8)
Article 5

(delete)

Confidential information 1. Member States shall provide that the employees' representatives and any experts who assist them are not authorised to disclose any information which has expressly been provided to them in confidence. This obligation shall continue to apply irrespective of where the said representatives or experts are, even after expiry of their term of office.

Confidential information 1. Members States shall ensure that Agreements are entered between employers, employees and their representatives on the method of handling "confidential information".

Text proposed by the Commission	Amendments by Parliament
2. Member States shall provide, in specific cases and within the conditions and limits laid down by national legislation, that the employer is not obliged to communicate information or undertake consultation when the nature of that information or consultation is such that, according to objective criteria, it would seriously harm the functioning of the undertaking or would be prejudicial to it. (Amendment 9) Article 5, para. 2 (new)	Deleted 2. Each Member State may lay down particular provisions for undertakings in its territory which pursue directly and essentially the aim of ideological guidance with respect to information and the expression of opinions, on condition that, at the date of adoption of this Directive such particular provisions already exist in the national legislation;

V. PROPOSAL FOR A COUNCIL DIRECTIVE ESTABLISHING A GENERAL FRAMEWORK FOR INFORMING AND CONSULTING EMPLOYEES IN THE EUROPEAN COMMUNITY (COM(98)0612 – C4-0706/98 – 98/0315(SYN)) (14 APRIL 1999)

The proposal was approved with the following amendments:

Text proposed by the Commission[27]	Amendments by Parliament
(Amendment 1) Recital 9 Whereas there is a need to strengthen dialogue and promote mutual trust within undertakings in order to improve risk anticipation, make work organisation more flexible and facilitate employee access to training within the undertaking while maintaining security, make employees aware of adaptation needs, increase employees' availability to undertake measures and activities to increase their employability, promote employee involvement in the operation and future of the undertaking and increase its competitiveness;	Whereas there is a need to strengthen dialogue and promote mutual trust within undertakings in order to improve risk anticipation, make work organisation more flexible and facilitate employee access to training within the undertaking while maintaining security, make employees aware of adaptation needs, increase employees' availability to undertake measures and activities to increase their employability, promote employee involvement in the operation and future of the undertaking and increase its competitiveness through the continuing acquisition of qualifications, the employment of workers in innovation and adherence to new forms of work organisation which are more creative and rewarding for both sides;

27. *O.J.*, C 2, 5.1.1999.

Text proposed by the Commission	Amendments by Parliament

(Amendment 2)
Recital 17

Whereas the purpose of this general framework is to establish minimum requirements applicable throughout the European Community while avoiding any administrative, financial or legal constraints which would hinder the creation and development of small and medium-sized undertakings; whereas, to this end, the scope of this Directive should be restricted to undertakings with at least 50 employees, without prejudice to any more favourable national or Community provisions whereas, in order to maintain the appropriate balance between the above-mentioned factors, this minimum may be raised to 100 employees in the case of the more innovative measures proposed herein on the information and consultation of employees on developments in the employment situation within the undertaking;

Whereas the purpose of this general framework is to establish minimum requirements applicable throughout the European Community while avoiding any administrative, financial or legal constraints which would hinder the creation and development of small and medium-sized undertakings; whereas, to this end, the scope of this Directive should be restricted to undertakings with at least 50 employees, without prejudice to any more favourable national or Community provisions

(Amendment 3)
Recital 19

Whereas the objectives of this Directive are to be achieved through the establishment of a general framework comprising the definitions and purpose of the information and consultation, which it will be up to the Member States to complete and adapt to their own national situation, ensuring, where appropriate, that the social partners have a leading role by allowing them to define freely the arrangements for informing and consulting employees which they consider to be best suited to their needs and wishes;

Whereas the objectives of this Directive are to be achieved through the establishment of a general framework comprising the definitions and purpose of the information and consultation, which it will be up to the Member States to complete and adapt to their own national situation, ensuring, where appropriate, that the social partners have a leading role by allowing them to define freely the arrangements for informing and consulting employees which they consider to be best suited to their needs and wishes.
Whereas existing provisions at national level may not be altered to the disadvantage of employees;

(Amendment 4)
Recital 20

Whereas care must be taken to avoid affecting some specific rules in the field of employees' information and consultation existing in some national laws, addressed to undertakings which pursue political, professional organisation, religious, charitable, educational, scientific or artistic aims, as well as aims involving information and the expression of opinions;

Deleted

280

Text proposed by the Commission	Amendments by Parliament

(Amendment 37)
Recital 21

Whereas undertakings must be protected against public disclosure of certain particularly sensitive information;	Whereas undertakings must be protected against public disclosure of certain particularly sensitive information, though such protection must not entail any restriction of the right to information and consultation;

(Amendment 5)
Recital 25

Whereas other employee information and consultation rights, including those arising from Council Directive 94/45/EC of 22 September 1994 on the establishment of a European Works Council or a procedure in Community-scale undertakings and Community-scale groups of undertakings for the purposes of informing and consulting employees, must not be affected by this Directive;	Whereas other employee information and consultation rights, including those arising from Council Directive 94/45/EC of 22 September 1994 on the establishment of a European Works Council or a procedure in Community-scale undertakings and Community-scale groups of undertakings for the purposes of informing and consulting employees, must not be affected by this Directive, provided that they are more favourable to employees;

(Amendment 6)
Recital 25a (new)

	Whereas the implementation of the provisions of this Directive shall under no circumstances constitute sufficient reason to justify a lowering of the general level of protection for employees in the field covered by it;

(Amendment 7)
Article 1(1)

1. The purpose of this Directive is to establish a general framework for informing and consulting employees in undertakings within the European Community.	1. The purpose of this Directive is to establish minimum requirements for the information and consultation of employees in undertakings within the European Community.

(Amendment 8)
Article 1(2)

2. When defining or implementing information and consultation procedures, the employer and the employees' representatives shall work in a spirit of co-operation and with due regard for their reciprocal rights and obligations, taking into account the interests both of the undertaking and of the employees;	2. Member States shall ensure that the employer and the employees' representatives, when defining or implementing information and consultation procedures, respect these minimum requirements and work together in good faith and with due respect for their reciprocal rights and obligations, taking into account the interests both of the undertaking and of the employees.

Text proposed by the Commission	Amendments by Parliament

(Amendment 9)
Article 2(1)(a)

(a) "undertakings" means public or private undertakings carrying out an economic activity, whether or not operating for gain, which are located within the territory of the Member States of the European Community and have at least 50 employees, without prejudice to the provisions of Article 4(3);	(a) "undertakings" means public or private undertakings carrying out an economic activity, whether or not operating for gain, which are located within the territory of the Member States of the European Community and have at least 50 employees;

(Amendment 10)
Article 2(1)(b)

(b) "employer" means the natural or legal person party to employment contracts or employment relationships with employees;	(b) "employer" means the natural or legal person party to employment contracts or employment relationships with employees pursuant to national law and/or practice;

(Amendment 11)
Article 2(1)(c)

(c) "employees' representatives" means the employees' representatives provided for by national laws and/or practices;	(c) "employees' representatives" means the permanent, stable and independent employees' representatives provided for by national law and/or practice;

(Amendment 41)
Article 2(1)(ca) (new)

	(ca) "social partners" means the competent representative organisation of the trade unions, the employee representatives of the undertaking, as provided by law, the employers' organisation or the employer;

(Amendment 13)
Article 2(1)(e)

(e) "consultation" means the organisation of a dialogue and exchange of views between the employer and the employees' representatives on the subjects set out in Article 4(1)(b) and (c), – ensuring that the timing, method and content are such that this step is effective;	(e) "consultation" means dialogue and exchange of views between the employer and the employees' representatives on the subjects set out in Article 4(1), – during the planning stage, so as to ensure that this step is effective and that an influence can be exerted;
– at the appropriate level of management and representation, depending on the subject under discussion; – on the basis of the relevant information to be supplied by the employer and the opinion which the employees' representatives are entitled to formulate; – including the employees' representatives' right to meet with the employer and obtain a response, and the reasons for that response, to any opinion they may formulate;	– at the appropriate level of management and representation, depending on the subject under discussion; – on the basis of information in accordance with subparagraph (d) and the opinion which the employees' representatives are entitled to formulate; – including the employees' representatives' right to meet with the employer and obtain a response, and the reasons for that response, to any opinion they may formulate;

Text proposed by the Commission	Amendments by Parliament
– including, in the case of decisions within the scope of the employer's management powers, an attempt to seek prior agreement on the decisions referred to in Article 4(1)(c).	– including, in the case of decisions within the scope of the employer's management powers, an attempt to seek prior agreement.

(Amendment 15)
Article 2(2)

2. In conformity with the principles and objectives of this Directive, Member States may lay down particular provisions applicable to undertakings which pursue directly and essentially political, professional organisation, religious, charitable, educational, scientific or artistic aims, as well as aims involving information and the expression of opinions, on condition that, at the date of adoption of this Directive, such particular provisions already exist in national legislation.	Deleted

(Amendment 16)
Article 2(2a) (new)

	2a. The Member States shall determine the levels (plant, undertaking or group of undertakings at national level) which, depending on the subject dealt with, guarantee full compliance with the objectives of this Directive.

(Amendment 17)
Article 2(2b) (new)

	2b. The Member States, without prejudice to existing national provisions or practice, shall create mechanisms designed to foster and promote social dialogue also in small and medium-sized enterprises, which do not come within the field of application of this Directive, in order to extend to them the achievement of the general objectives contained in it.

(Amendment 43)
Article 3(1)

1. Member States may authorise the social partners at the appropriate level, including at undertaking level, to define freely and at any time through negotiated agreement the procedures for implementing the employee information and consultation requirements referred to in Articles 1, 2 and 4 of this Directive.	1. Member States may authorise the social partners at the appropriate level, including at undertaking level, to define freely and at any time through negotiated agreement the procedures for implementing the employee information and consultation requirements referred to in Articles 1, 2 and 4 of this Directive, provided that the minimum standards laid down at national level are upheld.

Text proposed by the Commission	Amendments by Parliament

(Amendment 20)
Article 3(2)

2. The agreements referred to in paragraph 1 may establish, while respecting the general objectives laid down by the Directive and subject to conditions and limitations laid down by the Member States, arrangements which are different to those referred to in Article 2(1)(d) and (e) and Article 4 of the present Directive.

2. The social partners may conclude agreements which, while respecting the general objectives laid down by the Directive and subject to generally applicable conditions laid down by the Member States, provide for rules and arrangements which are more favourable for employees than those laid down by this Directive.

(Amendment 21)
Article 4(1)(a)

(a) information on the recent as well as the reasonably foreseeable development of the undertaking's activities and its economic and financial situation;

(a) information and consultation on the recent as well as the reasonably foreseeable development of the undertaking's activities and its economic and financial situation, in particular as regards investment, production, sales and structure;

(Amendment 22)
Article 4(1)(c)

(c) information and consultation on decisions likely to lead to substantial changes in work organisation or in contractual relations, including those covered by the Community provisions referred to in Article 8(1).

(c) information and consultation on decisions likely to lead to substantial changes in work organisation or in contractual relations, including those covered by the Community provisions referred to in Article 8(1), such as the introduction of new production processes, transfers of production, relocation, mergers, reductions in capacity or the closure of the undertaking, of plants or of substantial parts thereof.

(Amendment 23)
Article 4(1)(ca) (new)

(ca) information and consultation on training and continuing training, equal opportunities and health and safety at the workplace (in accordance with the provisions of framework Directive 89/391/EEC).

(Amendment 24)
Article 4(2a) (new)

2a. Member States shall ensure that, where a decision to be implemented will have considerable adverse consequences for employees, the final decision may be postponed for an appropriate period at the request of the employees' representatives so that consultations may continue with the aim of avoiding or mitigating such adverse consequences.

Text proposed by the Commission	Amendments by Parliament

(Amendment 25)
Article 4(3)

3. Member States may exclude from the information and consultation obligations referred to in paragraph 1(b) of this Article undertakings with fewer than 100 employees.

Deleted

(Amendment 26)
Article 4a (new)

Experts
Employees' representatives may, if they so wish, request the assistance of experts specified by them.

(Amendment 27)
Article 5(2)

2. Member States shall provide, in specific cases and within the conditions and limits laid down by national legislation, that the employer is not obliged to communicate information or undertake consultation when the nature of that information or consultation is such that, according to objective criteria, it would seriously harm the functioning of the undertaking or would be prejudicial to it.

Deleted

(Amendment 28)
Article 6

Employees' representatives shall, when carrying out their functions, enjoy adequate protection and guarantees to enable them to perform properly the duties which have been assigned to them.

Employees' representatives shall, when carrying out their functions, enjoy adequate protection and guarantees to enable them to perform the duties which have been assigned to them.

In particular, employees' representatives must be entitled to
(a) legal protection against dismissal or disadvantage with regard to career, wage and training during their term of office and for six months thereafter (they may not be dismissed during that period except with the consent of their representative organisation), and
(b) appropriate and continuing training, including paid training leave, the organisation of periodic meetings among themselves and with all the employees and the use of the firm's internal computer networks.

(Amendment 29)
Article 7(3)(b)

(b) the withholding of important information or provision of false information rendering ineffective the exercise of the right to information and consultation.

(b) the withholding of information or provision of incomplete or false information with the intention of rendering ineffective the exercise of the right to information and consultation.

Text proposed by the Commission	Amendments by Parliament

(Amendment 31)
Article 8(3)

3. This Directive shall be without prejudice to other rights of employees to information, consultation and participation under national law.

3. This Directive shall be without prejudice to other existing rights to information, consultation and participation under national law which are more favourable to employees.

(Amendment 32)
Article 8(3a) (new)

3a. Implementation of the provisions of this Directive shall under no circumstances constitute sufficient reason to justify a lowering of existing standards in the Member States or the general level of protection for employees in the field covered by it.

(Amendment 33)
Article 8a (new)

Public sector
1. This Directive shall also apply to the public sector, including the civil service and public services.
2. The Member States shall ensure that the social partners introduce the necessary provisions by means of agreements, or that the laws, regulations or administrative provisions needed to comply with this Article are adopted.

(Amendment 34)
Article 9(1)

1. Member States shall adopt the laws, regulations and administrative provisions necessary to comply with this Directive no later than ... (two years after adoption) or shall ensure that the social partners introduce the required provisions by way of agreement, the Member States being obliged to take all necessary steps enabling them to guarantee the results imposed by this Directive at all times. They shall forthwith inform the Commission thereof.

1. After consulting the social partners, in accordance with current legislation and practice in the Member States, Member States shall adopt the laws, regulations and administrative provisions necessary to comply with this Directive no later than ... (two years after adoption) or shall ensure that the social partners introduce the required provisions by way of agreement, the Member States being obliged to take all necessary steps enabling them to guarantee the results imposed by this Directive at all times. They shall forthwith inform the Commission thereof.

(Amendment 35)
Article 10

Not later than ... (five years after adoption), the Commission shall, in consultation with the Member States and the social partners at Community level, review the application of this Directive with a view to proposing to the Council any necessary amendments.

Not later than ... (five years after adoption), the Commission shall, in consultation with the Member States and the social partners at Community level, review the application of this Directive, and in particular the validity of the ceilings on staff numbers, with a view to proposing to the Council any necessary amendments.

VI. RECOMMENDATION FOR SECOND READING ON THE
     COUNCIL COMMON POSITION FOR ADOPTING A EUROPEAN
     PARLIAMENT AND COUNCIL DIRECTIVE ON ESTABLISHING
     A GENERAL FRAMEWORK FOR IMPROVING INFORMATION
     AND CONSULTATION RIGHTS OF EMPLOYEES IN THE
     EUROPEAN COMMUNITY (9919/1/01 – C5-0388/2001 – 1998/
     0315(COD)) (10 OCTOBER 2001)

Committee on Employment and Social Affairs
Rapporteur: Fiorella Ghilardotti

Procedural page

At the sitting of 16 September 1999 Parliament confirmed as its first reading
under the codecision procedure its vote of 14 April 1999 on the proposal for a
European Parliament and Council directive on establishing a general framework for improving information and consultation rights of employees in the
European Community (COM(1998) 612–1998/0315 (COD)).

At the sitting of 5 September 2001 the President of Parliament
announced that the common position had been received and referred to the
Committee on Employment and Social Affairs (9919/1/01 – C5-0388/2001).

The committee had appointed Fiorella Ghilardotti rapporteur at its
meeting of 27 July 1999. It considered the common position and draft
recommendation for second reading at its meetings of 20 September and 8/9
October 2001.

At the latter meeting it adopted the draft legislative resolution by 36
votes to 6, with 3 abstentions.

The recommendation for second reading was tabled on 10 October 2001.

Drat legislation resolution

European Parliament legislative resolution on the Council common position
for adopting a European Parliament and Council directive on establishing a
general framework for improving information and consultation rights of
employees in the European Community (9919/1/01 – C5-0388/2001 – 1998/
0315(COD))

(Codecision procedure: second reading)

The European Parliament,
– having regard to the Council common position (9919/1/01 – C5-0388/2001),
– having regard to its position at first reading[28] on the Commission proposal
  to Parliament and the Council (COM(1998) 612),[29]

---

28.   *O.J.*, C 219, 30.7.1999, p. 174.
29.   *O.J.*, C 2, 5.1.1999, p. 3.

- having regard to the Commission's amended proposal (COM(2001) 296),[30]
- having regard to Article 251(2) of the EC Treaty,
- having regard to Rule 80 of its Rules of Procedure,
- having regard to the recommendation for second reading of the Committee on Employment and Social Affairs (A5-0325/2001),

1. Amends the common position as follows;
2. Instructs its President to forward its position to the Council and Commission.

Council common position	Amendments by Parliament
Amendment 1 Recital 22a (new)	*(22a) Member States should take measures to guarantee that employee representatives are elected by employees or designated by employees' organizations only and have a minimum term of office with possibilities to be re-appointed.*

Justification

The amendment proposes a new formulation of the amendment adopted in the first reading. It is aimed to ensure the independence of employees' representatives.

| Amendment 2
Recital 26a (new) | *(26a) Reinforced and dissuasive sanctions and specific judicial procedures applicable in the case of decisions taken in serious breach of the obligations under this Directive must be established.* |

Justification

The amendment is aimed at finding a compromise between Parliament's and the Commission's position and the Council's position on the sanctions.

| Amendment 3
Article 2(ea) (new) | *2(ea) "social partners" means the competent representative organisation of the trade unions, the employee representatives of the undertaking, as provided by law, the employers' organization or the employer.* |

Justification

It is appropriate to give a definition of "social partners".

---

30.   *O.J.*, C 240, 28.8.2001, p. 133.

Council common position	Amendments by Parliament

Amendment 4
Article 2(f)

(f) "information" means transmission by the employer to the employees' representatives of *data* in order to enable them to acquaint themselves with the subject-matter and to examine it;

(f) "information" means transmission by the employer to the employees' representatives *and/ or employees of information containing all relevant facts on the subjects set down in Article 4,* in order to enable them to acquaint themselves with the subject-matter and to examine it, *before the decision is taken*;

Justification

The content of the information must be as complete as possible, according with the provision laid down in the Directive.

Amendment 5
Article 2, point (g)

(g) "consultation" means the exchange of views and establishment of dialogue between the employees' representatives and the employer.

(g) "onsultation" means the exchange of views and establishment of dialogue between the employees' representatives and the employer *during the planning stage in order to ensure the effectiveness of the procedure and make it possible to exert influence.*

Justification

Defining the term "consultation" makes sense only where consultation is carried out before the company has taken the decision.

Amendment 6
Article 3(3a) (new)

3(3a) The Member States, without prejudice to existing national provisions or practice, shall foster and promote social dialogue also in small and medium-sized enterprises, which do not come within the field of application of this Directive.

Justification

The new paragraph is aimed at encouraging social dialogue in SMEs, which are excluded from the field of this proposal.

Amendment 7
Article 4, point 2 (a)

2. Information and consultation shall cover:
(a) information on the recent and probable development of the undertaking's or the establishment's activities and economic situation;

(a) information on the recent and probable development of the undertaking's or the establishment's activities and *its* economic *and financial* situation, *in particular as regards investment, production, sales and structure as well as strategic plans including changes to organisational structures and market developments*;

Council common position	Amendments by Parliament

Justification

The content of information should be specified more precisely, particularly about "economic" information which should include investment, production, sales and infrastructure, fundamental factors for the future of a company and employment such as organisational structures and development, i.e. not only sales but also market developments.

Amendment 8
Article 4(4)

4. Consultation shall take place:
(a) while ensuring that the timing, method and content thereof are appropriate;
(b) at the relevant level of management and representation, depending on the subject under discussion;
(c) on the basis of *relevant* information to be supplied by the employer and *of* the opinion which the employees' representatives are entitled to formulate;

Justification

The area of information and consultation and the moment in which they take place should be specified more precisely.

Amendment 9
Article 4(4a) (new)

4. Consultation shall take place:
(a) while ensuring that the timing, method and content thereof are appropriate;
(b) at the relevant level of management and representation, depending on the subject under discussion;
(c) on the basis of information *in accordance with Article 2(f)* to be supplied by the employer and the opinion which the employees' representatives are entitled to formulate;

4(4a) Member States shall ensure that, where a decision to be implemented will have considerable adverse consequences for employees, the final decision may be postponed for an appropriate period at the request of the employees' representatives so that consultations may continue with the aim of avoiding or mitigating such adverse consequences.
(4b) Member States shall ensure that, where a decision to be implemented will have considerable adverse consequences for employees, in particular, transfers, relocations, closure of establishments or undertakings or large-scale redundancies, existing bodies representing employees may in the event of failure to reach agreement, where appropriate, meet once again with the relevant bodies of the undertaking.

Justification

It is necessary to guarantee the consultation of employees' representatives before implementing a final decision which will have an impact on future of employees.

Council common position	Amendments by Parliament

Amendment 10
Article 5

Member States may entrust management and labour at the appropriate level, *including at undertaking or establishment level,* with defining freely and at any time through negotiated agreement the practical arrangements for informing and consulting employees. *These agreements, and agreements existing on the date laid down in Article 11, as well as any subsequent renewals of such agreements, may establish, while respecting the principles set out in Article 1 and subject to conditions and limitations laid down by the Member States, provisions which are different from those referred to in Article 4.*

Member States may entrust management and labour at the appropriate level, with defining freely and at any time through negotiated agreement the practical arrangements for informing and consulting employees. *The social partners may conclude agreements respecting the general objectives laid down by the Directive and subject to generally applicable conditions laid down by the Member States. The existing legislative arrangements and/or statutory minimum standards for employees' representatives and/or employees at national level may not be diminished by such agreement. Where legislative arrangements and/or statutory minimum standards at national level do not exist, such agreements shall contain rules and arrangements which provide for fuller rights for information and consultation than those laid down by this Directive.*

Justification

The aim of the amendment is to ensure that the level of protection for employees in the Member States at the time when the directive is adopted must not under any circumstances be lowered, even by agreements.

Amendment 11
Article 7

Member States shall ensure that employees' representatives, when carrying out their functions, enjoy adequate protection and guarantees to enable them to perform properly the duties which have been assigned to them

Employees' representatives shall, when carrying out their functions, enjoy adequate protection and guarantees to enable them to perform properly the duties which have been assigned to them. *In particular, employees' representatives must be entitled to:*
(a) legal protection against disadvantage with regard to career, wage and training during their term of office and for six months thereafter, and
(b) appropriate and continuing training, including paid training leave, the organisation of periodic meetings among themselves and with all the employees and the use of the firm's internal computer networks.

Justification

The protection and guarantees covered in this Article need to be more precisely defined.

Council common position	Amendments by Parliament

Amendment 12
Article 8(2a) (new)

(2a) Member States shall provide more stringent sanctions in case of serious breach by the employer of the information and consultation obligations in respect of decisions which may lead to the termination of the employment contracts or employment relations.

Member States shall also provide for specific procedures allowing employees' representatives to obtain the suspension of decisions which may lead to the termination of the employment contracts or employment relations, when these decisions have been taken in serious breach by the employer of the information and consultation obligations. The suspension period shall last until such time as effective information and consultation would be carried on.

Within the meaning of the previous paragraphs, serious breaches are:

(a) the total absence of information and/or consultation of the employees' representatives prior to a decision being taken or the public announcement of that decision; or

(b) the withholding of important information or provision of false information rendering ineffective the exercise of the right to information and consultation.

Justification

The amendment is aimed at finding a compromise between Parliament's and the Commission's position and the Council's position on the sanctions.

Amendment 13
Article 9(a) (new)

Article 9(a)
Public administration
Member States shall examine in cooperation with the social partners appropriate ways in which the principles laid down in this Directive can be implemented in public administrations.

Justification

The Member States and the social partners should establish the provisions needed to ensure the implementation of the principles laid down in the Directive to public administration.

Council common position	Amendments by Parliament

Amendment 14
Article 9(b) (new)

Article 9 b
Avoidance
Member States shall take appropriate measures in conformity with Community law with a view to preventing a reduction in the number of employees in undertakings or establishments or the break-up of undertakings or establishments into groups of undertakings or establishments for the purpose of depriving employees of the rights to information and consultation laid down in this directive.

Justification

This amendment aims at avoiding changes in company structure designed solely to elude the field of application of the directive.

Amendment 15
Article 10

Notwithstanding Article 3, a Member State in which there is, at the date of entry into force of this Directive, no general, permanent and statutory system of information and consultation of employees, nor a general, permanent and statutory system of employee representation at the workplace allowing employees to be represented for that purpose, may limit the application of the national provisions implementing this Directive to:
(a) undertakings employing at least 150 employees or establishments employing at least 100 employees until . . . .,[31] and
(b) undertakings employing at least 100 employees or establishments employing at least 50 employees during the two years following the date in point (a).
Justification
The transition periods in the Member States in which there is no general system of information and consultation of employees seem no appropriate. The implementation period seems sufficient to guarantee the transposition of the Directive in such situation.

Deleted

---

31.   5 years after the entry into force of this Directive.

Council common position	Amendments by Parliament

Amendment 16
Article 11(1)

| 1. Member States shall adopt the laws, regulations and administrative provisions necessary to comply with this Directive not later than . . . .[32] or shall ensure that management and labour introduce by that date the required provisions by way of agreement, the Member States being obliged to take all necessary steps enabling them to guarantee the results imposed by this Directive at all times. They shall forthwith inform the Commission thereof. | 1. Member States shall adopt the laws, regulations and administrative provisions necessary to comply with this Directive not later than . . . .[33] or shall ensure that management and labour introduce by that date the required provisions by way of agreement, the Member States being obliged to take all necessary steps enabling them to guarantee the results imposed by this Directive at all times. They shall forthwith inform the Commission thereof. |

Justification

The amendment is aimed at re-establishing a two year transition period as in the Commission proposal.

VII. EUROPEAN PARLIAMENT LEGISLATIVE RESOLUTION ON THE COUNCIL COMMON POSITION FOR ADOPTING A EUROPEAN PARLIAMENT AND COUNCIL DIRECTIVE ON ESTABLISHING A GENERAL FRAMEWORK FOR IMPROVING INFORMATION AND CONSULTATION RIGHTS OF EMPLOYEES IN THE EUROPEAN COMMUNITY (9919/1/2001 – C5-0388/2001 – 1998/0315(COD)) (23 OCTOBER 2001)

The European Parliament,
- having regard to the Council common position (9919/1/2001 – C5-0388/2001),
- having regard to its position at first reading[34] on the Commission proposal to Parliament and the Council (COM(1998) 612(2))[35]
- having regard to the Commission's amended proposal (COM(2001) 296),[36]
- having regard to Article 251of the EC Treaty,
- having regard to Rule 80 of its Rules of Procedure,
- having regard to the recommendation for second reading of the Committee on Employment and Social Affairs (A5-0325/2001),

   1.   Amends the common position as follows;

---

32.   3 years after the entry into force of this Directive.
33.   2 years after the entry into force of this Directive.
34.   *O.J.*, C 219, 30.7.1999.
35.   *O.J.*, C 2, 5.1.1999.
36.   *O.J.*, C 240 E, 28.8.2001.

2.   Instructs its President to forward its position to the Council and Commission.

Council common position	Amendments by Parliament
Amendment 1 Recital 22a (new)	
	(22a) Member States should take measures to guarantee that employees' representatives are elected by employees or designated by employees' organisations only and have a minimum, renewable term of office.
Amendment 2 Recital 26 a (new)	
	(26a) More stringent, dissuasive penalties and specific judicial procedures applicable in the case of decisions taken in serious breach of the obligations under this Directive should be established.
Amendment 3 Article 2, point (ea) (new)	
	(ea) "social partners" means the competent representative trade union organisation, the employees' representatives, as provided by law, the employers' organisation and/or the employer;
Amendment 4 Article 2, point (f)	
(f) "information" means transmission by the employer to the employees' representatives of data in order to enable them to acquaint themselves with the subject-matter and to examine it;	(f) "information" means transmission by the employer to the employees' representatives and/or employees of all relevant data on the subjects referred to in Article 4, in order to enable them to acquaint themselves with the subject-matter and to examine it, before the decision is taken;
Amendment 5 Article 2, point (g)	
(g) "consultation" means the exchange of views and establishment of dialogue between the employees' representatives and the employer.	(g) "consultation" means the exchange of views and establishment of dialogue between the employees' representatives and the employer during the planning stage of a decision in order to ensure the procedure is effective and to allow influence to be exerted on the decision-making process.

Council common position	Amendments by Parliament

Amendment 6
Article 3, paragraph 3a (new)

| | 3a. Member States, without prejudice to existing national law or practice, shall foster and promote social dialogue also in small and medium-sized enterprises which do not fall under the scope of this Directive. |

Amendment 7
Article 4, paragraph 2, point (a)

(a) information on the recent and probable development of the undertaking's or the establishment's activities and economic situation;

(a) information on the recent and probable development of the activities and economic and financial situation of the undertaking or the establishment, in particular as regards investment, production, sales and structure as well as strategic plans, including changes to organisational structures and market developments;

Amendment 8
Article 4, paragraph 4, point (c)

(c) on the basis of relevant information to be supplied by the employer and of the opinion which the employees' representatives are entitled to formulate;

(c) on the basis of information to be supplied by the employer in accordance with Article 2(f) and the opinion which the employees' representatives are entitled to formulate;

Amendment 9
Article 4, paragraph 4a and 4b (new)

4a. Member States shall ensure that, if the implementation of a decision will have significant adverse consequences for employees, the final decision may be postponed for an appropriate period at the request of the employees' representatives so that consultations may continue with the aim of avoiding or mitigating such adverse consequences.
4b. Member States shall ensure that, if the implementation of a decision will have significant adverse consequences for employees, in particular a decision on transfers, relocations, the closure of an establishment or undertaking or large-scale redundancies, employees' representatives may, in the event of failure to reach agreement and where appropriate, meet the relevant bodies of the undertaking one more time.

Council common position	Amendments by Parliament

Amendment 10
Article 5

Member States may entrust management and labour at the appropriate level, including at undertaking or establishment level, with defining freely and at any time through negotiated agreement the practical arrangements for informing and consulting employees. These agreements, and agreements existing on the date laid down in Article 11, as well as any subsequent renewals of such agreements, may establish, while respecting the principles set out in Article 1 and subject to conditions and limitations laid down by the Member States, provisions which are different from those referred to in Article 4.

Member States may entrust the social partners at the appropriate level, with defining freely and at any time through negotiated agreement the practical arrangements for informing and consulting employees. The social partners may conclude agreements respecting the general objectives laid down by the Directive and subject to generally applicable conditions laid down by the Member States. Where legislative arrangements and/or statutory minimum standards at national level do not exist, such agreements may contain rules and arrangements which provide for fuller rights for information and consultation than those laid down by this Directive.

Amendment 11
Article 7

Member States shall ensure that employees' representatives, when carrying out their functions, enjoy adequate protection and guarantees to enable them to perform properly the duties which have been assigned to them.

Employees' representatives shall, when carrying out their functions, enjoy adequate protection and guarantees to enable them to perform properly the duties which have been assigned to them. In particular, employees' representatives shall be entitled to:
(a) enjoy legal protection against disadvantage in respect of their career, wage and training during their term of office and for six months thereafter, and
(b) receive appropriate and continuing training, including paid leave for training, organise regular meetings among themselves and with all the employees and use the undertaking's internal computer networks.

Amendment 13
Article 9a (new)

Article 9a
Public administration
Member States shall examine in cooperation with the social partners appropriate ways to implement the principles laid down in this Directive in public administrations.

Council common position	Amendments by Parliament
Amendment 15 Article 10	
Article 10 Transitional provisions Notwithstanding Article 3, a Member State in which there is, at the date of entry into force of this Directive, no general, permanent and statutory system of information and consultation of employees, nor a general, permanent and statutory system of employee representation at the workplace allowing employees to be represented for that purpose, may limit the application of the national provisions implementing this Directive to: (a) undertakings employing at least 150 employees or establishments employing at least 100 employees until . . . .,[37] and (b) undertakings employing at least 100 employees or establishments employing at least 50 employees during the two years following the date in point (a).	Deleted

VIII.   DEBATES IN THE EUROPEAN PARLIAMENT

Informing and consulting employees

Ghilardotti (PPE), rapporteur – (IT) Mr President, ladies and gentlemen, the information, consultation and participation of workers has been a key subject of debate in Europe ever since the first social action programme was adopted by the Council in 1974. Since then the Commission has launched several initiatives, but these have often met with resistance. In a context of continuous change, the adaptability of employees is of crucial importance and forms an integral part of the employment strategy adopted by the Luxembourg European Council.

Almost all the EU Member States have a legal framework – be it statutory or contractual – to ensure that employees are informed and consulted. It has to be said, however, that the current state of affairs – with its limitations and flaws – has proved not to give workers sufficient information and opportunities to be consulted on issues that really matter for the decisions of the undertaking. Consequently, the purpose of this initiative is to complete the existing national and Community framework, thereby helping – by improving the legislation – to prepare for change, ensure that restructuring takes place under reasonable circumstances and give employment the priority it now deserves. The proposed framework is therefore aimed at remedying the gaps and countering the shortcomings of the existing national and Community legislation currently in force.

---

37.   5 years after the entry into force of this Directive.

The objectives are: to ensure the existence of the right to regular information and consultation of employees on economic and strategic developments in the undertaking and on the decisions which affect them; to consolidate the social dialogue and relations of trust within the undertaking in order to assist risk anticipation, develop the flexibility of work organisation within a framework of security, enhance employees' awareness of the need to adapt and encourage them to participate in measures and operations designed to boost their employability; to include the situation and anticipated development of employment within the undertaking among the subjects of information and consultation; to ensure that workers are informed and consulted prior to decisions which are likely to lead to substantial changes in work organisation or in contractual relations; and to ensure the effectiveness of these procedures by introducing specific penalties for those who seriously violate their obligations in this field.

I should like to congratulate the Commission on its initiative. There is no doubt that, with a single currency and a large single market, with increasingly interdependent economies and fiscal policies which, albeit belatedly, are starting to be coordinated, social policies are bound to become increasingly supranational in scale, so as to preserve and further promote our social model, which is recognised by a large number of authoritative sources as one of the decisive factors in our competitiveness.

In particular, this proposal will ensure minimum standards for information and consultation to be applied throughout the Community, by harmonising the fundamental rights of employees and helping to strengthen the European social dimension. It is therefore deplorable that the negotiations between the social partners at European level for an agreement in accordance with Article 4(2) of the Social Protocol have failed, in particular because of one side's total unwillingness to negotiate. The Commission was quite right to fully exercise its right of initiative as sanctioned by the Treaty.

The European Parliament, through my report, is proposing certain amendments. Here I wish to thank all those colleagues who have tabled amendments, thereby contributing significantly to the committee's work. Our amendments – on which we must hear the views of the Commission and which I hope the Council, in adopting its position, will regard as the European Parliament's firm wishes – are designed in particular to specify the means of implementing and defining information and consultation, especially as regards the point in time when information must be communicated, in other words planning, so as to enable employees to anticipate change, extending the content of information and consultation to other subjects which directly involve the rights of employees and their future; to extend the scope of this directive, proposing that it should include the public sector, and that the Member States should consider the possibility of including SMEs; and to ensure that minimum requirements are laid down at Community level from which it is not possible to derogate except to the benefit of employees.

In conclusion, I am absolutely convinced that if the period of profound change which we are currently experiencing is to have a positive outcome, both in terms of increased competitiveness on the part of undertakings and of greater civil and social harmony, a major readiness for dialogue is required. This proposal, improved and strengthened by the report now under discussion, is an innovative means of promoting social dialogue, by informing and consulting employees, so as to guarantee stability and respect for the laws of the Europe we are striving to build.

Flynn, Commission – Mr President, I wish to begin by thanking Mrs Ghilardotti and all the other rapporteurs for their work on this particular Commission proposal. I also wish to thank those Members who have taken the time to make valuable contributions to this debate. I should like to express my personal satisfaction and gratitude for your support for this very important initiative of the Commission.

It is, in our view, an important proposal, which, once adopted, could add an indispensable missing element to Community European labour law. Having listened to what has been said here – and I have read the draft opinion – I believe you are willing and ready to play a decisive role in the negotiations leading up to the adoption of this proposed directive. Once adopted, it will complete and make more coherent the acquis communautaire in the field of employee involvement and make a decisive contribution to building the social dimension of the internal market. In a way Ms Oddy is right: it will fill a gap that needs to be filled in European labour law.

Nevertheless, it is a controversial proposal, which is illustrated by the reservations which employers and some Member States have expressed. We are aware of the difficulty of the debate and that is another reason why I am particularly pleased with your position of clear support for the initiative, while having to be prudent about the caretaker Commission at the moment and what it can do with this proposal just at this time. So while the Council has not even started discussions on the text, and taking into account the absolute need to preserve the political viability of the proposal – notably within the Council – it is wiser at this time, and particularly at this stage, to act with some caution.

I fully understand all of your requests at this time. Most, if not all, of the issues they raise were the subject of intense debate within the Commission in the period leading up to the adoption of the proposal. In the end the Commission reached a delicate balance between the different points of view and divergent interests on what is regarded as a very sensitive issue. It would be inappropriate to depart from this balance at this stage, at least as regards the proposed amendments relating to the four main sensitive issues of the proposal: the thresholds, the definitions of information and consultation, the extent to which the social partners may derogate from the directive's provisions and the question of sanctions.

I am sure that all your proposals on these central issues are going to be very much at stake in the discussions between the European Parliament and the Council leading up to the adoption of the proposal. The Commission will play the role attributed to it by the Treaty in the course of the codecision procedure while facilitating the approximation of the positions of both parties and, in the end, ensuring consensus. So you will understand my caution when reacting today to some of your amendments, even if some of them could certainly be envisaged by the Commission in the future, in the light of the developments that will take place in the Council.

In spite of my caution, I should like to be as positive as possible today. Some proposed amendments can clearly be accepted by the Commission immediately, and they certainly improve the text. This is the case for Amendments Nos 1, 17, 8, 10, the first and the third elements of Amendment No 13, and Nos 19 and 35.

A second category of amendments concern more substantial issues. Nevertheless, I believe I can express my support for them as they are reasonable and do not seem to affect the delicate balance of the text. This is the case of Amendments Nos 4 and 15, Nos 6 and 32 – they are related to the non-aggression clause – No 16 on the level of information and consultation, No 22 – the illustrative list of issues subject to information and consultation – and the first part of No 33, concerning the application of the principle of the directive to the public sector, which is referred to, although the proposed formula needs to be reworked somewhat.

While Amendment No 34 is wholly consistent with our approach of involving the social partners, we could not envisage that change to the basic formula used for the implementation of Community legislation. I could, however, accept a recital based on this amendment. As for the other amendments, in the light of the circumstances I have mentioned, the Commission feels it will be difficult to accept them. In any case, as I have mentioned before, they will be very much present in the future institutional debates on this important proposal and so the debate on these central issues is far from being closed.

I must say to Mrs Weiler that it really is about minimum standards. It is very important for the European social model. As Mrs Ghilardotti said, in a way, it is all about mutual confidence between employers and employees. I regard this particular proposal as a key piece of European labour law. Even though I shall be watching it from afar, I will be extremely interested in the adoption of this particular piece of European legislation. It will do an amazing amount of good for employers and employees in the development of the European social model. I thank you for your support.

Index

The numbers refer to pages